Democratic Designs

DEMOCRATIC DESIGNS

International Intervention and

Electoral Practices in

Postwar Bosnia-Herzegovina

Kimberley Coles

The University of Michigan Press   Ann Arbor

Copyright © by the University of Michigan 2007
All rights reserved
Published in the United States of America by
The University of Michigan Press
Manufactured in the United States of America
⊗ Printed on acid-free paper

2010   2009   2008   2007   4   3   2   1

A CIP catalog record for this book is available from the British Library.

Library of Congress Cataloging-in-Publication Data

Coles, Kimberley.
    Democratic designs : international intervention and electoral
practices in postwar Bosnia-Herzegovina / Kimberley Coles.
        p. cm.
    Includes bibliographical references and index.
    ISBN-13: 978-0-472-09985-6 (cloth : alk. paper)
    ISBN-10: 0-472-09985-X (cloth : alk. paper)
    ISBN-13: 978-0-472-06985-9 (pbk. : alk. paper)
    ISBN-10: 0-472-06985-3 (pbk. : alk. paper)
    1. Elections—Bosnia and Hercegovina.   2. Democracy—Bosnia and
Hercegovina.   3. Bosnia and Hercegovina—Politics and government—
1992–   4. Intervention (International law)—Political aspects—Case
studies.   I. Title.

JN2203.A95C65   2007
324.94974'03—dc22
                                                   2007008825

To Popocatépetl and Waverley

CONTENTS

ILLUSTRATIONS

TABLES

ABBREVIATIONS

ICTY	International Criminal Tribunal for the Former Yugoslavia
IFOR	Implementation Force, the NATO-led military forces (Dec. 1995–Dec. 1996)
IGO	Intergovernmental Organization
INGO	International Nongovernmental Organization
KM	Bosnian Convertible Mark
MEC	Municipal Election Commission
NATO	North Atlantic Treaty Organization
NGO	Nongovernmental Organization
ODIHR	Office of Democratic Institutions and Human Rights
OHR	Office of the High Representative
OSCE	Organization for Security and Co-operation in Europe
SFOR	Stabilisation Force, the NATO-led military forces (Dec. 1996–Dec. 2004)
UN	United Nations
UNPROFOR	United Nations Protection Force

ACKNOWLEDGMENTS

I owe a great debt to the many colleagues, friends, and strangers who, in their actions and comments, gave rise to this text. Their good humor, permission, and willingness to be scrutinized were as crucial to this analysis as my synthesis and interpretation. Even when they did not comprehend what I was doing or understand my data-collection strategies, I was welcomed. I hope I have remained true to my claim that I was not writing an exposé or an evaluation of democratization efforts in Bosnia-Herzegovina. I apologize to those who asked me to put the juicy stuff in the footnotes. While this text represents a critical stance, it is less a commentary on the successes or failures of international aid or of democracy promotion and more a dissection of the overarching logics of democracy and humanitarianism and of the practices that arise out of those logics.

The research was financially supported through a dissertation fellowship from the Institute for Global Cooperation and Conflict; summer grants from the University of California, Irvine School of Social Science and Department of Anthropology; a University of California Regents Writing Fellowship; a travel grant from the National Council for Eurasian and East European Research; travel monies from the University of Redlands; and multiple secondments and volunteer missions through the U.S. State Department and the Organization for Security and Cooperation in Europe, (OSCE's) Mission to Bosnia-Herzegovina. The School of Social and Political Studies at the University of Edinburgh graciously bought me some time as I was completing production of the manuscript.

The OSCE Mission to Bosnia-Herzegovina gave me wonderful care, employment, and affiliation, providing me with a home for many months between May 1997 and December 2000. Within my home, I found a ready family of colleagues and friends. The personal, the professional, and the ethnographic blurred as we played at work and worked while playing. I dearly thank them all for their companionship: Ben, Susan and David, Peter, Liz, Badger, Stef the Fireman, Michael, Hasim, Igor, Adnan, Jana, Jesper, Henrik, Thomas, Lex, Simon, Kate, Tanya, Martin, Andrew, Craig, Manfred, Iain, Tony, Tony, Matt, Michael, Helen, Claudia, Judith, Idoia, Alberto, Orflaith, Matt, Esko, Ernst, Marc, Caroline and Jason, and Tasha and Sean.

Above all, John Ging supported social science research and my project. His backing opened many doors in the head office, in regional centers, in field and election offices, and in the departments. Susan Carnduff and Jasna Malkoč allowed me access to the Departments of Elections and Democratisation during my fieldwork in 2000. The drivers and guards of the Bank Building played a fierce game of indoor football and laughingly allowed the California chick to play as well. I will be forever grateful to the doctors and nurses stationed during the summer of 1997 at Swiss Camp, the German Field Hospital at Rajlovac, and Landstuhl Regional Medical Center at Ramstein Air Base in Germany. My life would truly not be the same without their skill and care. Venad Osmanović and Anne Grandvoinnet Serafini were all I could have asked for in colleagues. The Hotel Intercontinental in Zagreb provided outstanding cordiality and service; I remain in awe of anyone's ability to host a thousand people at once.

In addition to all the people in Bosnia-Herzegovina, many colleagues contributed important commentary, advice, and critiques: Mukulika Banerjee, Victoria Bernal, Tom Boellstorff, Keith Brown, Susan Coutin, Megan Crowley, Tom Douglas, Drew Gilbert, Susan Greenhalgh, Elissa Helms, Jennifer Heung, Rhonda Higdon, Karen Leonard, Robert McLaughlin, Liisa Malkki, Tobias Kelly, Marty Otañez, Julia Paley, Kyriaki Papageorgiou, Annelise Riles, Christina Schwenkel, and Alex Smith. Bill Maurer, Jim Ferguson, and Teresa Caldeira crucially supported and guided this project; their scholarship continues to inspire me. "Doing Nothing: The Practices of Passivity" was improved through the comments of the anonymous reviewers at the Society for the Anthropology of Europe, the Association of Political and Legal Anthropology, and *PoLAR: Political and Legal Anthropology Review*. "Election Day" benefited from the comments of Ann Anagnost and anonymous reviewers for *Cultural Anthropology*. At a late stage in the final revisions, a small conference, Politics and Society Ten Years after Dayton, held in Sarajevo through the Human Rights Centre at the University of Sarajevo, was inspirational and was crucial to my refinement of some of the text's arguments; the participants deserve my special gratitude. The final work was substantially improved through the insights and provocative questioning of Caroline Brown, Bianet Castellanos, Ellen Moodie, and Hinda Seif. During the manuscript's final editing, I enjoyed conversations with Janet Carsten, Stefan Ecks, Ian Harper, Laura Jeffery, Jonathan Spencer, and Richard Whitecross; Teo provided—indeed, demanded–a change of pace. Steve Wuhs's close reading of all versions of this work has made me a better scholar. I thank him for his constant encouragement. My family has always been there, wherever I am—who could ask for more?

Substantial portions of "Election Day" appeared as "Election Day: The Construction of Democracy through Technique" *Cultural Anthropology* 19 (4) (2004): 551–80. A slightly different version of "Doing Nothing: The Practices of Passivity" appears in "Ambivalent Builders: Europeanization, the Production of Difference, and Internationals in Bosnia-Herzegovina." *PoLAR: Political and Legal Anthropology Review* 25 (1) (2002): 1–18, and as a chapter in *The New Bosnian Mosaic: Identities, Memories, and Moral Claims in Post-War Society,* edited by Xavier Bougarel, Elissa Helms, and Ger Duijzings (Burlington, VT: Ashgate, 2006).

PROLOGUE

On February 16, 1886, the Anthropological Society of Washington heard James H. Blodgett read his report, "Suffrage and Its Mechanism in Great Britain and the United States." Published in the newly established journal, *American Anthropologist,* three years later, the report detailed an extensive range of practices, rationales, and legal statuses in relation to electoral elements such as voters, registration, ballots, ballot boxes, financing, and representation in more than 40 legislative bodies in the United States and Great Britain (Blodgett 1889). He framed his descriptions of suffrage with a serious question for democracy: What are "the best modes of securing a true representation of the community?" For example, while the British Ballot Act of 1872 replaced public declaration with a secret ballot, Blodgett noted that in the United States, "ballots are only incidentally recognized in the laws of a few States." Were ballots a better mechanism for democratic representation than public declaration, especially given the size of modern societies? But how should the ballots work? His data demonstrated that no single answer existed. Marking on the back of ballots was generally prohibited; some states prescribed the size of ballots; two states (California and Louisiana) provided paper to secure uniformity; errors in the spelling of candidate or party names invalidated the vote in some states, while other states specified that unless the spelling introduced doubt about the voter's intent, the ballot should be counted (1889:70). In the late nineteenth century, therefore, variance characterized the administration of elections.

A discussion of proof of residency followed Blodgett's talk. While states and territories limited franchise by a variety of factors, including gender, age, literacy, property ownership, and tax payment, almost all had residency requirements, which ranged from three months to two years. Three members of the Anthropological Society picked up the interesting but unexamined question of how potential voters demonstrated residency. According to the *American Anthropologist,*

DR. ROBERT FLETCHER stated that when offering a vote at Nashville, Tenn., he was asked where he had his washing done, and found, when about to resent the inquiry as impertinent, that it was the legal test of residence.

COL. F. A. SEELEY gave instance in which the residence of canal boatmen, whose place of occupation was movable, was sometimes determined by the question where their washing was done.

COL. GARRICK MALLERY instanced an important suit in which the plaintiff, suing as a citizen of New Jersey, was non-suited because the jury determined that as his washing was done on the west bank of the Delaware, or in Pennsylvania, his residence was in the latter State. (Blodgett 1889:73–74)

These comments demonstrate how residency interacts with class, occupation, gender, and location and thus also with political representation. It is also possible to imagine the policy brainstorming that might have gone into deciding how to prove residency for the highly mobile or the poorly housed. How did laundry become the proxy indicator? Would laundry also have been a test of residence for women if they had achieved suffrage?[1] Why did Dr. Fletcher consider the question impertinent? Under what circumstances was the question asked, and to whom?

Debates about how best to represent the people and count their will took place at philosophical and pragmatic levels as well as in the general public. Phenomena such as ballots (and secret ballots) were contentious throughout the nineteenth century. Objections toward ballots revolved around the increased possibility of fraud (e.g., people impersonating other voters, voting more than once); the supposed unmanliness of voting by ballot rather than by voice; whether ballots preserved aristocracy, given the necessity of literacy; whether secrecy diluted democracy (i.e., truly free men proudly voted in public) (Brent 2006; Markoff 1999). Discussion of how representation could be technically manifest was loud, and experimentation was active. In Australia, for example, ballots and ballot marking schemes had already gone through several developments by 1886. The Victoria ballot, introduced in 1856, is often described as the first secret ballot. Other "secret" ballot systems were in use around the world prior to the Victoria, but they involved voters supplying their own paper or taking them from political parties and candidates (Brent 2006). The Victoria system was revolutionary because the government printed the ballot, it bore the names of all the candidates, and voters were required to prepare their ballots in private (Brent 2006). Thus, no one could any longer distinguish between ballots. Observers could not determine a voter's will by the color of his ballot or by watching from which pile he chose his ballot, and voters could not wave their ballots grandly in full view of passersby. Two years later, in 1858, legislation changed the marking scheme from an "obliteration" system to a "mark-in-square" system, in part to save ink. Rather than striking out the names of candidates for whom they did not intend to vote, voters were required to make a cross opposite the name of the candidate or party being voted for. However, the new system confused electors and was consequently highly unpopular; even its inventor, William Boothby, considered it a mistake. Most Australian jurisdictions reverted back to or retained the strike-out method until federation (in 1902), while most countries adopting the Australian ballot (as the Victoria system came to be known) shifted to the mark-square method.

When read against voting in contemporary democracies, washing as a proof of residency, ballots as written and self-furnished, and crossing out unwanted candidates might appear bizarre or old-fashioned or even quaint. The incredible historicity of electoral objects and democratic practice is immediately striking. Now, government-issued identification documents, standardized and preprinted ballots, and marking with a tick, check, or cross next to the name (or sometimes the picture) of the person or party desired is universally standard. Democratic practice has become narrower and narrower with the passage of time; there are fewer and fewer ways of being democratic.

When read against postwar elections in Bosnia-Herzegovina (1996–2000), the strangeness of early election administration does not seem so strange. Rather, these two phenomena together highlight the contingency, pragmatics, arbitrariness, and experimentation of election-eering, pinpointing the mental, technical, and logistical work under-taken by publics and administrators seeking to achieve democratic rep-resentation, participation, and trust. Almost contemporary with Blodgett, an 1892 *Los Angeles Times* article (fig. 1) can be read as one instance of this work. Informing readers about the new layout and modus operandi of California voting, the article attempted to make a novel system simple and clear, walking voters through the polling place

Cut No. 2 shows the position of the ballot clerks, voters in the stalls, and the officers of election checking the voters as they deposit the ballots in the box near the exit. Enter with the man to the right of the cut, and get a ballot from the gentleman standing at the end of the table, provided the young man at the desk finds your name properly registered in the Great Register open before him.

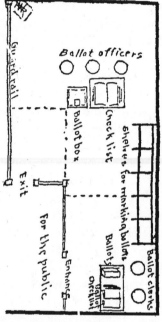

Then walk over to one of the open stalls and mark your ballot in accordance with your wishes, and pass in front of the group at the left and announce your name to the judges of election. When the young man sitting at the desk finds your name properly registered you are permitted to deposit the ballot in the box and pass out. That is all there is to it.

Fig. 1. Excerpt from an August 21, 1892, *Los Angeles Times* article explaining how to vote under the newly adopted Australian system. The polling station layout is remarkably similar to layouts in Bosnia-Herzegovina (see fig. 11).

and procedures step by step. The article also detailed how the new electoral system—a variant of the Australian ballot system—prevented fraud and trickery:

A correspondent of the [San Francisco] Examiner warned the California electors of the method by which the Australian ballot system was beaten in Montana. . . . The voter is forbidden to leave the booth until he has delivered up the ballot he has received on entering. He must give it to the inspector if he wishes to vote it, or return it to the ballot clerks in case he does not. (*Los Angeles Times* 1892)

In this regard, the 1892 text resonates with information pamphlets from Bosnia-Herzegovina that explain polling procedures, how to mark ballots correctly, voter registration procedures and criteria, the electoral system, and the fraud prevention checks built into it. All of these factors are material articulations of making democracy work. A handout (fig. 2) given to people waiting to vote during Bosnia-Herzegovina's 2000 general election specified,[2]

> From the moment you arrive at the polling station to the moment you leave the polling station, you must pass the following procedure:
>
>> In every voting screen, you will find a pen that you can use to vote, but you can use your own pen if you prefer.
>>
>> If you spoil your ballot paper, you can exchange it for another if you give the spoiled ballot back to a member of the polling station committee.
>>
>> Read carefully the instructions of the poster "Description of the Ballot" or the explanation on the ballot itself to be sure that you vote correctly.

Graphics with captions gave form to the six steps of voting: (1) having fingers checked for invisible ink, (2) presenting appropriate identification, (3) signing the voter register, (4) having fingers marked with invisible ink, (5) taking a ballot, and (6) going to the voting booth and voting. The back of the handout provided more detailed information about what a voter should do if his or her name did not appear on the voter register or if he or she needed assistance. Without these informational messages given to voters—whether in 1892 or 2002—democracy could not work properly: voters need to know what to expect and how to act properly, and they need to trust in the integrity of the system.

This is not to suggest that no changes have occurred over the past century, of course, or there would be no reason for this book. Rather, it shows that democracy is neither natural nor intuitive. It is not the mode of government toward which humans inherently gravitate. The introduction of democracy does not always have the same effects or out-

Процес гласања на бирачком мјесту

1. Провјера трага невидљиве тинте на прсту

Од Вашег доласка на бирачко мјесто па до тренутка напуштања бирачког мјеста проћи ћете кроз сљедећу процедуру:

У свакој гласачкој кабини биће завезана оловка која ће бити коришћена за гласање, али такође можете користити и своју оловку.

Ако упропастите свој гласачки листић, може Вам бити издат други гласачки листић ако члану бирачког одбора вратите упропашћени гласачки листић.

2, 3

4. Означавање прста невидљивом тинтом

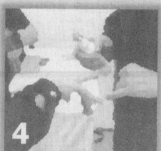

4

2. Идентификација бирача
3. Потписивање бирача на бирачки списак

5

5. Добијање гласачког листића

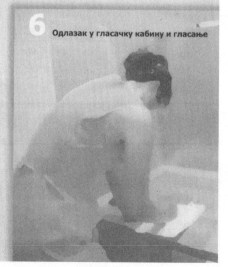

6 Одлазак у гласачку кабину и гласање

2000
ОПШТИНСКИ ИЗБОРИ

Да бисте правилно гласали пажљиво прочитајте упутства на постеру "ИЗГЛЕД ГЛАСАЧКОГ ЛИСТИЋА ЗА ВАШУ ОПШТИНУ" или упутства на предњој страни гласачког листића.

Fig. 2. "The Voting Process in the Polling Station," 2000. This informational sheet was to be handed to voters while they waited in line to vote so that they were prepared for what was to come. (*Courtesy of the Organization for Security and Co-Operation in Europe, Mission to Bosnia and Herzegovina.*)

comes. Peter Pels et al. (2007) highlight the reshuffling, recombining, and reinventing that occur when technologies travel to other sets of social, political, and economic circumstances. The secret ballot, for example, did not always liberate individual choice, as is usually presumed, but could instead limit access, articulate the alienation of state authority, or act as a means to continue traditional decision making in a new form (Pels et al. 2007). Technological change does not always map onto or fit into a neat narrative of progress. We should be wary of evolutionary tales in new guises as well as assumptions of universality. Indeed, the term *democratization* suggests an evolutionary linearity, with democracy as the end point. This book analyzes the democratization effort in Bosnia-Herzegovina not from the point of view of democratization strategies or their efficacy but as a lens through which to view the cultural and political practice of democracy making. I am concerned with how the democratic process makes meaning rather than with teasing out an evaluation of democracy or of efforts to promote it. Reading democracy and democratization within a progress narrative is dangerous as it often hides and displaces the work that goes into legitimating and actualizing democracy at any particular point in history. For example, democracy historically carried negative connotations as a result of its associations with anarchy and mob rule. Furthermore, cultural analysis suggests that we should never assume that anything will remain fixed; cultural forms are dynamic and constantly in flux via innovation and contestation. Too often, evolutionary arguments assume an end point—often a single end point. Reading democratization in a progress narrative suggests that a possible end point exists and that different states lie at different points on a democracy scale. This uniscalar valuation of democracy is unhelpful. It is also not helpful to construct straw men, of course, and many scholars would point to the wealth of literature on the electoral fallacy (i.e., democracy and elections are not synonyms) and the plurality of democratic forms and regimes (see Dahl 1971; Lijphart 1977, 1984, 1999; Lijphart and Aitkin 1994; see also Collier and Levitsky 1996; Schmitter and Karl 1991 on reconceptualizing democracy). However, at the same time that we take seriously comparative political science and hear cries espousing democratic variance and the need to think of democracy on a matrix rather than on a continuum, we see international democratization efforts engaging in what some have called cookie-cutter approaches (see Call and Cook 2003; Ottaway 2002). What then is the same, and what is different? The evolutionary progress line assists in the codification of certain features and the erasure or delegitimation of others.

This work seeks to understand which features and meanings are becoming normalized and naturalized and how this process is occurring. As a result, there is a danger of neglecting democracy's emancipatory qualities and the very real struggles for recognition taking place around the world. This book does not ignore events such as the 1994 South African elections, described as miraculous by many participants who never even dreamed of voting and who had viewed the elimination of apartheid as unthinkable (Thorold 1995).[3] Rather, like Nicolas Guilhot, I seek to understand democracy as one of the organizing principles of the new international order (2005:1). In *The Democracy Makers,* he lucidly documents how the form and function of emancipatory activism has changed with the professionalization and specialization of democratization as a field of study and as a business industry. As he says, "State institutions, international bureaucracies, and professional networks have colonized the turf of social movements" (2005:3). Democracy has become a vehicle with many other passengers (e.g., neoliberal, legal, and moral norms).

In the new millennium, work is still occurring around the globe to make democracy and elections desired and actual end points, as in California in 1892 or Australia in 1886. Substantial cultural, political, social, and economic effort goes toward explaining how democracy works, making it work, and convincing people to want it. This volume, then, studies how this process occurred in Bosnia-Herzegovina in the years immediately after the dissolution of Yugoslavia, when socialism "lost" the cold war and Francis Fukuyama (1992) famously commented on liberal democracy as the final form of government (as the end of History).

INTRODUCTION

Is democracy working? People learning about my research on elections in postwar Bosnia-Herzegovina tended to ask me this question. Depending on who was asking, I responded with one of what became a standard stock of appropriate answers. Sometimes I sighed and said that it was difficult to tell but that it appeared that the nationalist parties had less of a grip than they did during the war and its immediate aftermath. I would caution that it was a slow and jagged process—three steps forward, two steps back. For other conversation partners, I would laugh awkwardly and say that because it was an extremely complicated and contentious question, I was fortunate that it was not my research question. For yet others, I responded that the elections were going very well: electoral fraud was down and confidence in the results was up. All of these answers were problematic, flawed, and evasive. Yet each answer also responded to a democratic assumption, be it the existence of institutions such as competitive elections or the putative values and attitudes of democracy. I recently hit on a new answer that comes closer to doing justice to both the question and my research's ability to answer: it depends on what you think democracy is supposed to do. My problem in answering this question all these years is in part that it was hard to tell, that it was not my research question, and that electoral trust did seem to be rising; in addition, however, democracy and elections were overworked in Bosnia-Herzegovina. They were being asked to transform too many things.

Who was asking democracy to work so hard? Building democracy in postwar Bosnia-Herzegovina was the purview of the "international community." Bosnians did not independently create or demand democratic institutions; rather, the international community implemented and reg-

9

ulated postwar elections and other democratic institutions on behalf of Bosnians through the legal authority of the 1995 peace treaty brokered at Wright-Patterson Air Force Base in Dayton, Ohio. Elections were agreed upon in Annex III of the peace treaty, with the Organization for Security and Co-operation in Europe (OSCE) receiving responsibility for the implementation, supervision, and certification of an election to take place six to nine months after the peace treaty's signing. The mandate was repeatedly renewed, and the OSCE ultimately organized six elections between 1996 and 2000. The *Is democracy working?* question framed the existence for election and democratization personnel working for the OSCE as part of the international community—their jobs were rationalized by the hope that the eventual answer would be yes.

In the pages that follow, I turn on its head the *Is democracy working?* question asked by political scientists, election personnel, and my various dinner companions. Instead of asking whether democracy has been implemented and what impediments to implementation remain, I ask *How do democracy and elections work? What work do they do? What allows the question, and others like it, to be asked at all? What allows it to be answered?* Turning the question around allows democracy to be treated as a cultural and political practice and as a form of social knowledge rather than as a dry set of institutions or a universal ideology solely affected by culture, politics, and knowledge. Many scholars now acknowledge the role that culture plays in democracy and democratization (see Dahl 1997; Diamond 1996; Huntington 1997; Putnam 1993).[1] Yet by treating "culture" as a variable that hinders or promotes the successful development of "democracy," these authors essentialize culture, isolate it from other domains of social existence, and imply that other domains—such as the "technical" or "bureaucratic"—are somehow noncultural. This research draws from literature that suggests that culture is crucial in the definition and practice of democracy itself (see, e.g., Holston and Caldeira 1998). Democracy depends on cultural norms and practices not because they obstruct or limit it but because they create democracy and articulate its possibilities.

Thus, this work reconceptualizes democratization as a project concerned with the production of social knowledge rather than as a process of removing obstacles or promoting democratic characteristics and conditions. Taking that social knowledge as its object, the book ethnographically investigates the making and meaning of democracy in postwar Bosnia-Herzegovina through careful attention to the technical and bureaucratic tools through which democracy came into being—ballots, electoral rolls, voter preparation guides, and international electoral supervision. Through a documentation of the production of elections on the one hand and the phenomena that elections produced and normalized on the other, I argue that international intervention and apolitical technologies combine to introduce, establish, and normalize particular practices and epistemologies of democracy. Through its examination of elections and the practices of implementing elections in postwar Bosnia-Herzegovina, this work analyzes contemporary meanings, mentalities, and mechanisms of democracy and global governance and exposes the epistemological and legitimation work of democratic practice and power.

Something called the international community deploys itself all over the world. Representative of a post–cold war international order, this conglomeration of actors—often discursively treated as unitary—increasingly attempts to resolve conflicts, reconstruct societies, and transform, incubate, and act as governments in places as diverse as Afghanistan, Kosovo, Mozambique, Haiti, and East Timor. In Bosnia-Herzegovina, one of the first postwar reconstruction cases taken on in the aftermath of the cold war, the international community became deeply involved in the new country's physical, economic, social, and political transformations. Indeed, international organizations have been so influential and powerful in Bosnia-Herzegovina that many observers insist that Bosnia-Herzegovina was simply an international protectorate in disguise (e.g., Chandler 1999a, 1999b), given international agencies' hubris, lack of accountability, and unilateralism (e.g., Divjak 2001; Hayden 1998; Knaus and Martin 2003). However, the situation was pragmatically ambiguous and normatively confusing, as other commentators called for this conglomeration to act more like a protectorate (e.g., International Crisis Group 1999).[2] Bisecting the evaluation of the role of international intervention into a neat dichotomy, however, simply helps occlude the on-the-ground intricacies of power and governance and problematically continues its erroneous representation as unitary, stable, and singularly purposeful. While almost all international reconstruction activities were framed by the logics of transformation, liberalism, and neoliberalism, their coordination and complementarity were not necessarily givens despite organizational charts, established hierarchies of power and prestige, and the deployment of inter-agency "coordinating bodies." There were simply too many actors and agendas on the ground.

International personnel and projects called for major changes in

Bosnian infrastructure, institutions, and behavior; however, they simultaneously demanded that Bosnians implement and take responsibility for those changes. International agencies formally and informally championed the concept of Bosnian ownership, which included ownership of phenomena as abstract as destiny and as concrete as property, as well as control over government and rebellious citizens. The tension between the power of international agencies and personnel—and the dominant discourse of ownership led to a perverse situation some commentators labeled "enlightened absolutism" and "enlightened colonialism" (P. Moore 2002; Rieff 1999). Both these terms have historical precedent. Hearkening back to seventeenth-century monarchs such as Frederick II of Prussia and Catherine the Great of Russia, "enlightened absolutists justified their absolute authority by proclaiming themselves servants of the state or the people. The enlightened served the state by pushing for reform in the government in order to stamp out unequal treatment before the law and preserve rights and property" (Hooker 1996). Similarly, "enlightened colonialism" melded the exploitation of resources for colonial interests with a "civilizing mission," an appreciation for native culture, and support for new local governing elites (Chatterjee 1986; Merry 1991, 2000; cf. Kipling 1899). The existence of enlightened absolutism and enlightened colonialism in postwar Bosnia-Herzegovina references current notions of progress and modernity within a larger system of authority and exploitation, all via the idea of stewardship. The still emerging system of global liberal governance, of which the international community in postwar Bosnia-Herzegovina constituted just one instance, takes as its object both the transformation of institutions and of the conduct of a population (Duffield 2001; see also Ferguson and Gupta 2002; Foucault 1991). The international community attempts to reach these two goals through complex political machinery—tools and techniques that act explicitly and implicitly through coercion and desire—and through specific logics and rationales of being and truth.

Croatia and Slovenia, two republics of the now defunct Yugoslavia, declared themselves independent in June 1991 after a decade of economic deterioration and political paralysis (following Josip Tito's death in 1980). Their secession effectively sealed Yugoslavia's demise (see Malcolm 1994; Ramet 1985; Silber and Little 1995; Woodward 1995a for historical accounts of Yugoslavia and its precursors). War officially began in Bosnia-Herzegovina on April 6, 1992, when armed soldiers fired on Sarajevo from the mountainsides that overlook the city. More than three years later, in November 1995, the presidents of Serbia, Croatia, and Bosnia-Herzegovina signed a peace treaty, stopping the carnage and setting the stage for the reconstruction of Bosnia-Herzegovina. The signing of the General Framework for Peace, otherwise known as the Dayton Peace Accords or simply Dayton, marked the end of the 44-month-long war, the arrival of masses of international workers, and a corresponding shift in their goals from humanitarian aid and peace brokering to (re)building and reconciliation processes. The peace treaty did not merely end the bloodshed; it also provided a liberal and neoliberal prescription for Bosnia's ills and a model for and legitimation of intensive interventions by international institutions.

> The peace agreement signed at Dayton was unlike any other peace treaty of modern times, not merely because it was imposed by powers external to the conflict, but because of the far-reaching powers given to the international community which extended well beyond military matters to cover the most basic aspects of government and society. The majority of annexes to the Dayton Agreement were not related to the ending of hostilities, traditionally the role of a peace agreement, but the political project of democratizing Bosnia, of "reconstructing a society." (Chandler 1999a:43)

Chandler continues by arguing that Bosnians and Bosnian institutions, despite the rhetoric of self-government and international withdrawal, had little space to make or implement policy. Dayton marked a new mode of international intervention.[3]

Employees and volunteers with international organizations were the "experts" who designed and implemented these state-building and society-molding strategies—that is, the actual bodies of this powerful, discursive international community. In this book, I highlight the members of the community—"internationals," as they called themselves—in their own right, examining the institutions, practices, myths, and rituals that patterned their lives and work. The international community exists not in its essence of reality but through these bodies and their languages, texts, schemes, and other material-making practices. Refusing to treat these diverse international entities as a given allows a detailed, microlevel examination of the workings of what James Ferguson and Akhil Gupta (2002) call the emerging system of transnational governmentality—that is, the modes of government that are being set up on a global scale. This government of conduct is characterized by "the outsourcing of the functions of the state to NGOs and other ostensibly non-state actors" (Ferguson and Gupta 2002:990). Internationals in postwar Bosnia-Herzegovina, working for IGOs such as the World Bank, the European Community Monitoring Mission, or the UN Development Programme; NGOs such as the International Committee of the Red Cross, Catholic Charities, or Save the Children; or corporations such as Coca Cola and Volkswagen (to name just a few of the most well known), were the persons taking on these roles and functions.

I take as a point of departure the need to understand the quotidian within international and global forms of governance, knowledge, and transformations in the same way that scholars of colonialism seek to understand the workings of colonial power and state agents. In this way, this book complements scholarship focused on the effects and impacts of global processes on states and societies, often through the existence of international organizations or institutions. However, this literature runs the risk of leaving unmarked the cultural practices of those organizations and their foreign experts. Assumptions of neat hegemonic or unitary operations by international forces or institutions should not be made; like colonialism, globalization and global governance are neither monolithic nor omnipotent (Cooper and Stoler 1997; Hannerz 1987). Any reification of the international community or internationalism conceals the fact that its power, authority, and ability to impose systems of order are put into place by people—by men and women of different classes and nations who may conceptualize their participation in distinct ways. After all, an international has to come from somewhere. The task, then, is (at least) twofold: to question how and why experts and their interventions become so familiar, expected, and natural and to examine their efforts at (and tensions involving) power, authority, and imposition.

Elections are considered the centerpiece of democracy. However, as scholars have pointed out, an election is not sufficient for democracy; there must be more, such as respect for the rule of law, a thriving civil society, and a free media (Carothers 1997a; Schmitter and Karl 1991). Efforts to expand democracy past the dominant minimalist definition championed by Joseph A. Schumpeter–"that institutional arrangement for arriving at political decisions in which individuals acquire the power to decide by means of a competitive struggle for the people's vote" (1947:269)—have resulted in expansive definitions that acknowledge social and economic conditions and processes. Yet little attention has consequently been paid to cultural, instrumental, or technical aspects of democratic government. I contribute an anthropological perspective to scholarship on the place of elections in democracy and processes of democratization; the development of electoral institutions, rules, and systems; and the development of electoral management bodies. This research, based primarily in the disciplines of political science and international relations, tends to be highly pragmatic and utilitarian, focusing on effective and efficient determinants, systematic or sociohistorical obstacles, and prescriptions for the future. My research widens the unit of analysis, analyzing the knowledge system in which both elections and election scholarship reside (cf. Barry and Slater 2002a, 2002b on how the discipline of economics acts as a technology, as something that attempts to frame economic processes and shape material economic arrangements). I do so here through an ethnographic study of electoral materials such as ballots, electoral rolls, voter preparation guides, and international electoral supervisors.

Focusing on the agents of elections—the human and nonhuman actors that give elections form—demonstrates that technique (or techne) creates democratic facts, knowledge, and order (see Barry 2002; Callon 1998; Latour 1988, 1999; Latour and Woolgar 1979; Law and Hassard 1999). Technical practices disguise interests by rendering them apolitical and mundane (Barry 2002; Riles 2002; Rose 1999). However, the technical and the instrumental (such as bureaucratic practice) are not apolitical, acultural, or simply functional. Recent work (e.g., Ferguson 1994; Jain 2004; Mitchell 1989, 2002; Riles 1998, 2000, 2006) has aptly demonstrated that they form an epistemological base for modern rationality and authority. Through what could be called the government of democracy, international assistance efforts and apolitical technologies contribute to the introduction, establishment, management, and ordering of modern social relations and forms of authority. That is, the techne of democracy produces social knowledge, which in turn specifies and naturalizes "how conduct should be conducted" (M. Dean 1999; Foucault 1991; Gordon 1991). As democracy promotion and exportation become more entrenched as foreign policy goals—including at the UN and European Union—it is important to understand the facets that go into making it work.

Elections, though no longer solely equated with democracy, remain the top-funded and -promoted democratization project. Many critics have charged that there is an overemphasis on elections (e.g., International Crisis Group 2000b on Bosnian elections), but the emphasis is not fading. As Marina Ottaway (2002) points out, the "cookie-cutter approach" appears to demand elections about two years after a peace treaty. The gap between analysis and practice suggests that elections, as technical exercises, are at the forefront of transformation models.

At this point, it is necessary to stress the particularity of current meanings of democracy. The cold war "triumph" of neoliberalism led to a global circulation of democratic discourse (Verdery 1996) and new circulations of professional elite who advise, manage, teach, promote, demonstrate, and advertise liberal and neoliberal solutions and practices, including "democracy" and "democratic" forms of governance and power. As one international remarked during an interview, "Democratization is a new form of missionary work—elections simply replace the Bible." But what messages are embedded within the evangelical sermon? Since the cold war, democracy and democratization efforts have moved away from strictly procedural criteria and toward an alignment with cultural components such as vibrant civil society, tolerance, and willingness to compromise (Chandler 1999a). Democratization projects are increasingly incorporated into international humanitarian and development packages given to aid-receiving areas. Indeed, in some areas, governments must prove that they are taking concrete steps toward democracy (and market reform) to receive aid packages from donor governments and international agencies. However, this primacy as a policy strategy by Americans, Europeans, and the UN, among others, is relatively new. During the cold war, democracy may have been communism's foil, but combating the Red Tide did not necessarily translate into efforts to promote democracy. Right-wing dictators were preferable to democratically elected leftist leaders, and proxy wars were not uncommon. The internationalization of democracy in the 1990s was made possible in part through the mapping of emancipatory values and human rights onto democracy; however, Guilhot argues that the newest push for democratic political systems was tightly connected and entirely subordinated to the imposition of neoliberal economic orthodoxy (2005:192–93).

Shifts in democratic meaning, the problems of categorizing democracy, and the qualification of hundreds of types of democracy suggest that democracy is fluid. In their discussion of the tension between analytical differentiation and conceptual validity, David Collier and Steven Levitsky (1996) list some of the many adjectives used to qualify democracy, including *praetorian, plebiscitarian, procedural, electoral, semicompetitive, full, illiberal, one-party, hybrid, mature, incomplete, neopatrimonial, consol-*

idated, parliamentary, postauthoritarian, fragile, uncertain, neocolonial, bank-rupt, low-income, unruly, elitist, dual, blocked, overinstitutionalized, and *tarnished.* They call for greater consistency and clarity of meaning in scholars' usage of the concept as a way of avoiding conceptual stretching yet retaining an ability to differentiate. These goals, of course, cannot be wholly accomplished simultaneously—or they at least imply a trade-off. Of course, scholarship in political science and sociology has developed useful distinctions that bridge some of the debates on what democracy is and what it should be (e.g., Huber, Rueschemeyer, and Stephens 1997 on formal, social, and participatory democracy). However, I suggest that the constant and endless contestation in scholarship and in the public realm over meanings and definitions also points to an ever more important need to understand democracy in and through its localities and particularities—for example, as a political form, in the diversity of values associated (or conflated) with it, in the constitutive nature of its practices, as well as in its relationships with power. The on-the-ground variance of democracy suggests that cannot be defined a priori (Paley 2002).

Imposing Democracy?

Even on my first visit to Bosnia-Herzegovina, in December 1996, one year after the signing of Dayton, I was struck by the nature of the international interventions in Bosnia-Herzegovina. The intensity and scope of the interventions were mind-boggling. Out of this concentrated chaos, a paradox emerged: the idea of imposing democracy. If a dominant signifier of democracy is rule by the people and thus embodies a spirit of group decision making (whatever form that takes), then how are we to reconcile the enforced adoption of this form of rule? The imposition of democracy by a foreign minority appeared contradictory. This paradox led me into an examination of two linked spheres: Who was imposing, and what was being imposed? That is, what were the practices of internationals, and what were the practices of "democracy"?

The spheres of internationality and democracy are not separate, of course, but extensively mediate each other. For example, an excerpt from my fieldwork journal written during the 1997 voter registration period unsurprisingly demonstrates that the context of election registration was firmly embedded in international social and political power relations. More surprisingly, it shows that the content was as well.

Work is a zoo, or rather a circus. If you get past the tedium of processing 70–90,000 forms a day, then it is quite amusing. We spent
all day opening envelopes from Croatia and Serbia today (refugee
voter applications). No problem; except the supervisors at the
Registration Centers like to attach little notes to the forms (which
are scanned by high speed machines that DON'T like little notes).
The little notes (taped, stapled, and paper clipped to the forms)
say things like: "Dear Sir or Madam, this elderly refugee lady cannot remember her birthday. However, she should be allowed to
vote, I certify it is okay." Or: "This gentleman walked out without
his stamped receipt. However, we noticed that he left his name
blank as well as his identification number blank on the forms.
However, he is a valid voter and should be allowed to vote." And
how are we to know who this gentleman is? At any rate, we throw
these cute notes away, and get increasingly upset when we open
envelopes with notes since we can't do anything about any of
them.

The relationships between content and context are important yet are
under-studied within the realms of purportedly acultural technical and
bureaucratic processes. International supervisors, representatives of
democracy and enforcers of electoral rules, negotiated the rules and procedures from particular social locations: as professionals and as technical
specialists (and as members of their individual nation-states). These
social locations informed the way technique was practiced, for example,
giving some supervisors (in their minds) the authority to bypass the procedures. The registration form required a birth date and an identification
number; the supervisors felt fine "certifying" that some voters did not
need to record that information. The technique, meant to be standard
and universal, was not so, either in its design or in its implementation.

The mediations between democracy and internationals were further
apparent at one post–Election Day congratulatory meeting for the international electoral staff, a group that included me. The speaker made two
statements that hinted at some of the underlying logics of the international intervention and the project of democratization in Bosnia-Herzegovina. After applauding us for our work, she told us that we should be
proud since "this has been an exercise in demonstrating democracy."
She continued on a more solemn note, with a gesture toward the political outcome of the election, "You don't always get what you've paid for."

The election results had strongly backed the nationalist political parties that the international powers desperately wanted out of office. According to internationals, their presence in Bosnia-Herzegovina constituted an expensive pedagogical exercise with few results to justify the expense. I, as a participant in this meeting and in the exercise of "demonstrating democracy," wondered exactly what I had demonstrated and how I had demonstrated it.

Democratic Dreaming

During the November 2000 election period, the voter information branch of the Election Department of the OSCE released an election song as part of a voter turnout campaign attempting to counter increasing signs of apathy and the growing belief that voting did not change anything.[4] Like the political parties, the OSCE was angling for votes; that is, OSCE election officials hoped for high voter turnout (and the consequent increased legitimacy of the election as form and as result). A catchy pop tune, "Zgrabi svoju sreću" (Grab Your Luck) highlighted the connotations and dreams associated with elections and by extension democracy. The song repeatedly emphasizes the ability to choose one's own future:

> I know the times are hard
> Scratch, look under the sand
> Maybe you'll find luck
> Smaller or bigger
> Why does the same song always play
> When you can choose
>
> Life goes sideways
> Because it has no tracks
> Dig under the surface
> You may just dig out luck
> Smaller or bigger
> Why does the same song always play
> When you can choose
>
> Life sails without sails
> Put your hand in your chest
> You may touch clear luck

Smaller or bigger
Why does the same song always play
When you can choose

Nothing will fall from the sky
Somewhere somebody needs you
And finds you in his luck
Smaller or bigger
Why does the same song always play
When you can choose

Grab your luck
It's somewhere near you
Grab your luck
You hesitate without need
And may everyone choose their own luck

The song refutes the popular complaint that nothing ever changes and reminds listeners that they have the ability to change the song of the future; life is hard, life sails along uncontrollably, life is scary, but it does not have to be. The lyrics question why listeners always choose the same song and implore them instead to make an active choice in determining the future—to grab their luck. Rejecting the connotation of fate, luck is lyrically associated with the ability to choose, having an opinion or voice, and the potential for a better future. Luck, they sing, is of one's own making. Created in an attempt to promote the election and put focus on "issues" rather than ethnonational rhetoric, the song pinpointed Election Day as the moment of choice. Election Day and the voting process constituted the way toward easier times, a forward-moving, on-track life, and smooth sailing.

This song was just one of the electoral propaganda items that appeared during the registration and campaign periods. Aimed at reaching a broad audience, electoral messages—passed to the public in everyday situations via magazine ads, radio jingles, drink coasters, grocery bags, sugar packets, billboards, and television commercials—informed the public that an election was imminent and attempted to attach particular meanings to elections and democracy.[5]

Ads and public announcements also often urged voters to favor politicians who campaigned on concrete improvement issues and who offered pragmatic action. As late as September 2002, after the elections had already been "handed over" to Bosnians, the High Representative called on voters to "give their vote to politicians and political parties who are prepared to implement necessary reforms" (OHR 2002b). Issue topics were implanted into the swirl of electoral messages, such as "stamping out corruption" and "improving the economy," but elections themselves were always also offered as solutions. Slogans developed for the various elections expanded on the basic definition of election as choice by linking choice to agency, decision making, change, and the future. For example, during the election period for the 1997 municipal elections, beer mats proclaimed, "The Decision Is in Your Hands!" (fig. 3). The election's official slogan was "Elections Are the Way for Your Future." Later elections similarly proclaimed themselves mechanisms for change: "With Change to a Better Life" and "Vote for Changes." Even "how to vote" informational posters plastered around towns and outside polling stations carried those phrases—in larger font than any other phrase or even the explanatory content of the poster. Not surprisingly, the widely touted "change" slogans upset the larger political parties in power, which saw the tactic as the international powers' not-so-subtle suggestion that voters oust incumbents.

Typical rhetoric expounded around the world paints democracy as holding the promise of salvation and progress but as being too often encumbered by "politics" and politicians; Bosnia was no different. Elections were touted as an avenue for citizen (rather than politician) participation in decisions about the future. During the 1999 registration period, another beer mat scolded Bosnians, "Don't Let Other People Decide for You. It Is Too Late When You Make Decisions about Your Registration on Election Day." The coaster conveyed the message that voting (via registering) was a way to give input on important decisions and suggested that all Bosnians should participate in the election so as to not allow decisions to be made without them. Media campaigns emphasized Election Day (through voting) as the means through which citizens could influence politics, change their living situations, and express choice. Within the propaganda, the political nature of elections (and democracy) (as compared to elections as merely an instrumental means of organizing and structuring politics) was completely absent, replaced by omnipresent associations between progress and agency. Downplaying and deemphasizing the limitations of elections and the reality of democratic negotiations and debate while marketing a decontextualized, technical event as transformative and progressive demonstrates that the

Fig. 3. Beer mats (coasters) were common sites for electoral messages suggesting how much time Bosnians (and internationals) spent in café-bars. The slogan in the lower right corner reads, "Elections are the way to your future." *(Courtesy of the Organization for Security and Co-Operation in Europe, Mission to Bosnia and Herzegovina.)*

democratic model is predicated on an ideology of improvement and change. However, its practices are neither necessarily progressive nor intrinsically transformative.

Despite active voter turnout campaigns, Bosnia-Herzegovina never faced low voter turnout. The first postwar elections had an original estimation of 109 percent turnout (International Crisis Group 1996a:54) with high charges of double voting and voting by dead persons. The five elections held during my fieldwork had turnout rates between 60 percent and 88 percent. This compares favorably with an estimated average global turnout rate during the 1990s of 64 percent (Institute for Democracy and Electoral Assistance 2002). Although voter turnout decreased in each postwar election, especially among younger adults discouraged by the lack of change and poor economic outlook, slogans and logos were not strictly necessary vis-à-vis voter participation. Rather, they were necessary to reach certain voters, to implant particular connotations in voters, and to articulate the functionality and importance of voters and their decision making to democracy: to make democracy work. Juxtaposing these electoral imaginations and promises against electoral practices demonstrates that elections and democracy are not simply means by which citizens choose their governments but also mechanisms through which particular conceptualizations—in this case, of participation, agency, democracy, progress, choice, and Europe—are naturalized and normalized, to the detriment of other possibilities.

Inquiries

Can you be here Tuesday? This question was posed to me over the phone, long distance from Bosnia-Herzegovina. It was Thursday morning in California. Thus began a peculiar blend of fieldwork into international efforts to bring or build democracy in Bosnia-Herzegovina and participation in the efforts themselves. When I arrived in Sarajevo on Tuesday, June 3, 1997, I had no idea that I was embarking on a long-term field project into electoral practices. In fact, by mid-July, a mere six weeks later, I had quit my electoral job as a registration supervisor, opting instead for a research position with a well-regarded international NGO that was rebuilding 200 homes for returning refugees and displaced people in northwest Bosnia and wanted the process documented and evaluated.[6] The project manager knew that housing was crucial—and potentially inadequate—for successful reintroduction and socioeconomic survival. He wanted to know what returnees' real and perceived conditions were and would be. This project would have led me into interesting anthropological terrain, analyzing postwar conditions and adaptations in Bosnia-Herzegovina as well as new transnational networks between returning refugees and their host country, in this case, Germany.[7] Because of a health emergency, I was ultimately unable to conduct the research, instead returning to California to recuperate for the rest of the summer. But I had not seen the last of elections. The election was scheduled for mid-September, and much remained to be done. E-mails trickled into my California inbox, asking if I would be able to return to Bosnia-Herzegovina. I replied cautiously yet affirmatively, fearing for my health and fearing the wrath and anguish of my doctor and my family. The situation remained vague and undetermined (at least in my eyes) when an express mail envelope arrived from a travel agent with a round trip ticket to Split, Croatia, the arrival and departure location for international election supervisors. With guarantees from the OSCE that I would be in Sarajevo (and thus near medical facilities) and guarantees from me that the illness had resolved itself, I spent two weeks in front of a computer screen hammering out a database program to determine the validity of tendered ballots.[8] In retrospect, my last-minute, opportunistic, and serendipitous arrivals were typical of other international arrival narratives I heard during my research. My favorite conversations often began with, "So, how did you get here?" It seemed that everyone had a story with a seemingly random twist, an unexpected turn, or a frantic decision.

The harried and uncertain nature of these international positions led many people to ask, "What type of person can take up these positions?" Who can, on one or two weeks' notice, pack up their lives and move to Bosnia (or Cambodia or East Timor or Côte d'Ivoire) for between six weeks and six months? The tempo of the job recruitment process affects the tenor and dynamics of international life.[9] Among other things, the tempo and short-term nature of hiring and contracts in Bosnia combined with postwar living conditions created a lively social scene as internationals sought companionship, entertainment, and sustenance. Reflecting on the changes in international daily life over almost a decade of intervention, a human resource administrator stated that the situation had really settled down since "the early days."

> I think the international community has normalized—[now,] it's like living anywhere else. People spend more time in their houses now because they have nice creature comforts. I live in a nice house with a lovely yard. I have satellite TV with more [channels] than before. Now we get film channels [too]. My life could be the same in Atlanta. I get up, shower, go to work, maybe see friends, come home for dinner, watch television, sleep, get up and do it again. On the weekends, I garden and go grocery shopping—the same things I'd do in Georgia. Normally in expat world, people are looking for a life different than the suburb they could have in France or the U.S. So there are fewer mission junkies now; we tend to have more specialists, more senior professionals. It's still difficult to get skilled people sometimes, given the diplomatic pressures we face, but neither are we taking fresh people like before.

"Mission junkies" is a term that many people use to refer to those who simply go from crisis to crisis, drawn to the adrenalin, the pay, the danger, the morality, and the freedom allowed under such start-up, emergency conditions. According to the same administrator, mission junkies are a type of "lifer" or "hanger-on":

> I think that the lifers are a certain type of person—one who is trying to escape. There are mission junkies going from crisis to crisis, but there are also some who can't manage to do anything else.

They're here from a fluke. Economically, they could get at home maybe half of what they earn here. And there are others, which I have no respect for, who just reinvent themselves so they can stay. Sometimes that's because they can't have their life with power, a nanny, a cleaner, and a driver, back at home. Sometimes its because there isn't the same action back where they're from. They don't want to go back, and that rejection of their norms and homeplace is unhealthy.

Over the course of a decade's involvement with internationals and international organizations in Bosnia-Herzegovina, I learned from others how hard it was to leave given the ordinariness of life "at home" and the uncertainty of what might come next. Friends and colleagues told me how reassuring it must be for me (and I always agreed) that I always returned to the same place (i.e., the university and my department).

I ultimately held five positions within the Election Department over the course of five elections and four years (1997–2000): registration supervisor, polling supervisor, chief of administration for the election supervision branch, and (twice) election trainer. Most of these positions were similarly uncertain or unplanned in their origination. I was often extremely lucky—in the right place at the right time and meeting the right people. I also earned a reputation as a serious and competent employee, which apparently assisted in my repeated assignments. Along with the flexibility needed to match the last-minute, anxiety-filled, and rushed nature of the international organizations, these factors helped me to obtain my jobs and later to receive permission to conduct research within the OSCE. The jobs facilitated my in-depth understanding of the election bureaucracy in a way not possible through more traditional participant observation. "Becoming a native" may be one of the best ways to understand and examine modernity's forms, especially bureaucratic ones. Many ethnographers now take this tack through, for example, obtaining internships, volunteering time and/or expertise, or becoming an employee, consultant, or "expert," as few organizations are willing to set up a chair in the corner for an ethnographic interloper. Becoming a bureaucrat allows a type of intimate access not accessible through observing, listening, and asking.

Given my background as an OSCE employee, I was surprised at the access and gatekeeping issues I later encountered while conducting independent ethnographic fieldwork. As I bitterly joked to a neighbor after being thrown out of a meeting because the organizer felt that it was not relevant to my research, "He needs to worry about what I already know, not what I still want to find out." However, one colleague equally bitterly remarked that my access issues were the same issues that everyone dealt with on a daily basis—fighting for information, justifying one's existence, trying to impress the "right" people and to avoid making enemies. He claimed that my struggles were participant observation par excellence. Just as issues of "studying up" are tinged with power plays and fears of exposure (Nader 1972), so are many relations between staff members and their supervisors. I truthfully told leery electoral administrators that I was not interested in a journalistic exposé; I was not evaluating their practices, I constantly reiterated, but was conducting a cultural and sociological analysis of the democratization projects in Bosnia-Herzegovina. However, electoral officials had difficulty seeing how attending logistics meetings or training events would help me. Barraged by media and political criticisms, my note taking made some officials nervous and reluctant to be open. Although I had received high-level permission, access had to be repeatedly negotiated at lower levels of the regional and departmental chain of command and with individual colleagues. Issues of access, fear, and exposure constantly mixed with popular ideas regarding what anthropologists study and how they collect data.

Similarly, my encounter with the managerial, logistic, and other technical practices of international bureaucracies and electoral administrations provoked anxieties about my choice of ethnographic methods and sites. My bureaucratic and elite data seemed terribly thin and already known. These practices were not difficult to infiltrate: spreadsheets, memos, note taking, teaching, and organizing files were not necessarily new to me, although I had never thought of myself as an expert (or a professional) in these areas.[10] Annelise Riles (2000, 2002) remarks on the difficulty of researching and analyzing the analytical and organizational devices groups use when they are the same devices social scientists use. In her study of the character and aesthetics of information, she comments that the material she describes may feel achingly familiar because she had an "ethnographic encounter with knowledge practices already familiar to, and indeed in use by, the anthropologist" (2000:5). Anthropology should continue its queries of the practices that are predominantly unmarked in our own lives, such as logistics, pragmatism, research, and bureaucracy, because they are powerful tools of interpretation and understanding and we are not alone in using them. Like scholars of technique and form, including those from within science and technology studies who argue that an effect of scientific practice is the creation of conceivability and possibility, I demonstrate here, through a detailed description and analysis of democracy's inner workings—electoral quotidian life—that democratic practice does not discover facts as much as create them. In this way, it may be productive to think of Bosnia-Herzegovina, at least metaphorically, as a large laboratory. Not only were social engineering experiments occurring through the transformative intentionalities of aid and development projects, but particular epistemologies also were becoming codified and institutionalized, particularly in the realm of "democratization." Conducting ethnographic analysis on the everyday life of internationals and their practices thus represents a commitment to understanding how the world is shaped by the analytical tools of modernity, including social science, statistics, analytical reports, and other shared features of both my ethnographic and my election work.

Power, Privilege, and Unintelligibility

Beyond confronting the methodological and analytical constraints of familiarity and elite access, I faced questions of how to study large, intermittent technobureaucratic events and how to address the high degree of change and uncertainty running through my fieldwork and the international context (cf. Greenhouse, Mertz, and Warren 2002). Not only was I attempting to study a political process—democratization—based on ideals of transformation, but my colleagues were in constant flux. International organizations in Bosnia-Herzegovina had a high turnover rate, and many positions were contract based, ending when the funding dried up. The relatively short-term employment opportunities within election work (generally two weeks to six or eight months) and an average tenure in Bosnia of approximately two years for those in other fields meant that my informants changed from year to year and even month to month. They often knew little about or had little experience in Bosnia-Herzegovina, let alone in their particular job positions—everyone was thrown into the mix and did their best to muddle through work and life. How does ethnographic analysis work when few people know the answers, when people disagree on the answers, or when people do not care that they do not know? Definitive interpretations were not always available. Given this state of ethnographic affairs, Ferguson comments that "miscommunication and partial communication were not simply temporary obstacles in the methodological process of the ethnographer but central features of the 'authentic' cultural experience" (1999:208). In the case of my informants in Bosnia-Herzegovina, this was true inside work as well as outside. Inside their job contexts, informants did not always know why X was X, why Y had been implemented, or why Z had changed. They often left Bosnia-Herzegovina just as they began to gain some semblance of knowledge or experience. Unfamiliar with Bosnian languages yet circulating in Bosnian public life, few international workers could pick up the conversations swirling around them, read newspaper headlines or watch television programming, or talk to Bosnians on the street. In this sense, anthropologists must take seriously unintelligibility and the idea that culture may not be shared or agreed upon. In his analysis of modernity in Zambia, Ferguson (1999) argues that the social significance, effect, and import of Copperbelt cosmopolitanism may be in its "noise." Can we, he asks, read the production of noise itself as a social practice? In Bosnia's international project of elections, unintelligibility acted to give greater authority to fixed objects and practices. The aesthetics and form became more important than the intent. Consequently, I focus extensively on electoral objects—what were the relationships among objects, unintelligibility, and the zeal to bring order to Bosnia-Herzegovina? As a result of the unintelligible noise experienced by many internationals, decisions are represented in this text as agentless. This is because informants often did not know why or how a change had been made or who had made it. Little on-the-ground knowledge existed of whether a change was part of a strategy with a goal, an economic necessity, or a rectification of an oversight. Part of the struggle of this fieldwork was sorting out the ex post facto explanations that informants constructed for themselves as the most logical alternatives despite their gloss or lack of knowledge.

One of the most disturbing features of internationals was their poor language skills, especially in light of their ability to make decisions for and judgments about Bosnia-Herzegovina and Bosnians. The disconnect surely contributed to the structural division and societal separation of internationals and international institutions from Bosnia-Herzegovina. However, it also affected knowledge practices. As an American diplomat confided to me about his previous posting with the U.S. State Department, "Before, where I was stationed, I really understood [what was going on] because I got out there. Here, we don't have any idea. It's all recycled or recirculated information. We're not really talking—just to other internationals." Both Ann Janette Rosga (2005) and Andrew Gilbert (2004, 2005) crucially theorize the effects of international uncertainty and unknowledge (what I call gloss) combined with transformative potential and authority. Rosga, for example, details the assumptions underlying her confusion and annoyance when some members of a training program refused to participate in a pedagogical exercise that she had designed for them. Only afterward did it become apparent that the Serbs in her group were nervous conducting "on-the-street" interviews in Sarajevo, a predominantly Muslim city after the war. As an international, the gaps in her knowledge included areas of linguistic translation, international donor distrust, war anxieties, and intra-Bosnian resentments and affected the project she was implementing (on child trafficking) from design to data collection to writing the final report. However, as Gilbert (2005) points out, knowledge too can be dangerous if it is not predicated on "careful and systematic observations of various kinds of interactions and social action where meanings are negotiated and become effective in the practices of everyday life." This is what I term *gloss:* not all internationals realized that their "knowledge" was only a veneer; however, in all cases, their policy and practical work was based on this "knowledge."

Comments by paraethnographers like the American diplomat—following George E. Marcus's conceptualization of social actors critically conscious of their own situations and often located within centers of power and privilege (Marcus 2000; Holmes, Marcus, and Westbrook 2006)—as well as the circumstances discussed by Rosga and Gilbert suggest that the incredible power and transformational strategies of internationals' interventions were based on knowledge that was at best superficial. My language skills mirrored those of the typical international worker: rudimentary. As an anthropologist, I found my isolation disturbing yet fascinating, since it also gave me incredible insight into the world of most international workers. While some, including some high-level diplomats, among them at least one American ambassador, spoke Serbo-Croatian fluently, some spoke Serbo-Croatian because of their family backgrounds, and a few learned the language to a conversational level or better, internationals on the whole relied on interpreters, translators, English-speaking Bosnians, hubris, and a healthy sense of the functionality of goodwill.[11] I used strangeness and fascination as methodological tools to probe into the internationals' world of partial understandings and limited communication yet privileged authority and aggrandized self-representations.

Methodologically, I also took advantage of the fact that multiple elections occurred during a relatively short amount of time. Within four years, I participated in five internationally implemented elections. In this research, I used data from all five elections, although my data are more thorough, varied, and detailed from the two election periods in 2000 when I was explicitly gathering ethnographic data. The scale of the election project was immense, however. Unable to observe it all, I learned as much as possible via my own positions and roles. I worked or observed at three distinct operational levels—headquarters, regional office, and field office—in teams or suboffices. Thus, I intimately learned about an electoral position and its relationships yet maintained observations of other electoral positions and relationships. I also devised strategies to gather information from other positions that I could not observe as a result of temporal and spatial constraints. For example, I asked municipal election committee supervisors to keep diaries of their experiences during their six-week tenures. Similarly, I gave questionnaires to hundreds of registration and polling supervisors in 1998 and 2000 to help me understand their practices and their interpretations of their role in bringing democracy to Bosnia-Herzegovina. Simultaneous events and tasks made it difficult to grasp a sense of the larger whole; these textual responses were one way to engage with other electoral positions on Election Day and the weeks preceding it. I used these strategies in tandem with fieldnotes, interviews with a wide range of electoral staff, observations, and the collection of administrative, technical, and electoral materials.

Observing and participating in election implementation over the course of several elections broadened the range of possibilities. However, it also highlighted how much change was occurring in Bosnia-Herzegovina and within the community of internationals. Throughout this book, I take advantage of this longitudinal perspective, since significant changes in content, context, and focus occurred during this four-year period. I document processes of production and usage in democratic forms, practices, and knowledge rather than simply providing a snapshot of any single moment in time. While capturing change undoubtedly benefited my study, it poses problems in terms of representation. How does one describe an activity when the details are different each time it was witnessed? I primarily use two strategies: (1) choosing one election's activity as an exemplar, and (2) focusing on the shared components. In most cases, I have chosen to focus on an exemplar but point out shifts in practice or logics as appropriate. I have avoided drawing composite events, since doing so appeared to be counterproductive to analyses of processes. What is interesting is the continuity of logic underneath the change as well as representations of progress within the process. Similarly, as is conventional in ethnographies, I have endeavored to protect my informants' identities. This required changing person's names as well as modifying nationalities, job titles and responsibilities, residence location, and, occasionally, dates of residence in Bosnia. These strategies were used to protect the confidences of, and any unintended or undesirable effects of those confidences on my informants, friends, and colleagues. However, they also serve to discourage spurious connections with identity or temporal and spatial fixity. For this same reason, some narratives and quotes are simply anonymous. However, the book's attention to the deployment of power also required that I make every effort to match pseudonym names, positions, nationalities, and the like to the reality of any given person's location in networks of power relations, hierarchies, and competencies.

Polling Anthropology

This book is divided into two parts. The first section examines the logics of the international community through an analysis of the practices and rationales of the community's members, be they internationals or Bosnians. The second section takes up the logics of democracy through a close examination of the practices that constitute it. Each section is prefaced by an autoethnographic vignette of my introduction to these strange yet oddly familiar worlds. I hope that these vignettes make the familiar a little less so and give some life to the technical and bureaucratic. I begin, however, in "Blueprints and Builders," with a discussion of the "international community" in Bosnia-Herzegovina, suggesting that it is important to examine *it* as a *them*: the international community is a social and political construct, not a singular political entity. I describe the scope and role of the international interventions in postwar, postsocialist Bosnia-Herzegovina after the signing of the Dayton Peace Accords in November 1995. Then the book turns toward "Internationality" through a focus on the relationships between international personnel and mechanisms of government built into a model of international intervention with a transformative mission. Through detailed descriptions of these internationals' work practices and the assumptions embedded within them, the chapters shed light on the practices and epistemologies of government hidden within explicitly and specifically political projects.

Turning toward what was imposed and how, the chapters in "Democratic Governance" examine the processes, norms, materiality, and practices created or set in motion by elections. The usage and deployment of ballots, voters, polling and counting procedures, and the like help to create the neutral, inclusive, and universal representations embedded in democracy. However, each chapter also seeks to problematize the authority on which democracy rested in Bosnia-Herzegovina. I close the book with a consideration of the international circuit of democracy promotion as a foreign policy tool for the consolidation of democratic knowledge. As described and analyzed in this work, an election is not solely or even primarily about participation. Analyzing the techniques of electoral and democratic government demonstrates that much of the work done is epistemological. The seemingly unimportant notes attached to the registration forms matter—a lot. Complex interpretive and technical tasks articulate democratic governance and its possibilities.

BLUEPRINTS AND BUILDERS

The initial four-year recovery and reconstruction program for Bosnia-Herzegovina proposed by the international donor community (e.g., the World Bank, the UN, the European Union, and individual states) was US$5.1 billion (World Bank 1996). This financing goal was meant to provide basic needs and offer critical resources for the recovery process. That same year, the OSCE budgeted 244.9 million Austrian shillings (US$24.4 million) for its Mission to Bosnia-Herzegovina, almost doubling its 1995 budget with one line item (OSCE 1997). Bosnia-Herzegovina was neither the only democratizing nation-state nor the only one recovering from war, of course. However, donor countries and IGOs devoted a lot of money and resources to Bosnia-Herzegovina. Similar types of reconstruction packages are now regularly put together for other needy sites, whether as a result of conflict (e.g., Cambodia, Haiti, Iraq, East Timor, Afghanistan) or of natural disaster (e.g., the 2005 earthquake in northern India/Pakistan, the 2004 Indian Ocean tsunami, or the 1998 Hurricane Mitch damage in Nicaragua). For comparison, contributions to the similar Afghan reconstruction packages between 2002 and 2005 totaled just over US$1 billion (World Bank 2005). For its time, Bosnia's aid package was massive.

Bosnia's package of goods included items related to what is known in policy circles as a triple transition. Bosnia needed to recover from (1) war, (2) authoritarianism, and (3) communism. The prescription, as documented in the Dayton Peace Accords and embodied in the presence of international actors, included programs promoting peace and conflict resolution, democratization, and neoliberalism. The on-the-ground manifestation of this triple transition was Bosnia's saturation with international resources, personnel, and projects. In concert with

33

international military forces, three major international organizations coordinated Bosnia's journey: the Office of the High Representative (OHR), the OSCE, and the UN. Along with hundreds of international nongovernmental organizations (NGOs or INGOs), these three groups penetrated and intervened in practices governing Bosnians through activities such as running elections, lending money through micro-credit programs, rebuilding houses, assisting trauma victims with music and art therapy, demining land, creating state symbols, training nurses and doctors, retraining lawyers and judges, hosting conflict resolution radio talk shows, building playgrounds, supplying hospitals with equipment, and reforming legal and financial institutions.[1] Internationals—the employees of and volunteers with international organizations—designed and implemented these state-building and society-molding strategies.[2] In large part, internationals were professional managers and technicians, although in my research, their training varied remarkably from field to field. The electoral and human rights fields, for example, employed a wide range of professionals, including teachers, lawyers, former military officers, diplomats, bureaucrats, and managers. Many internationals, especially the younger ones (a large portion of the community), were attempting to make international work a career and hoped that their experiences in Bosnia-Herzegovina would propel them into longer-term international employment. Indeed, for some, work in Bosnia catapulted them into international circuits—in the five years after leaving Bosnia, Claude (a native of France) worked elections in Uganda, Haiti, Afghanistan, and East Timor; Rory (from the United Kingdom) had nearly constant work in Iraq, Palestine, Kosovo, and South Africa. Others struggled to get into the network but managed, like Sarine (Portugal), to cobble together medium-term (3–6 week) assignments in Indonesia, Serbia, and Kazakhstan. Those seeking more stability sometimes found semi-permanent international employment in head offices or long-term positions with organizations while remaining highly mobile geographically. Many internationals in Bosnia, however, were unable to launch themselves into new career trajectories, chose to return home, or considered their foreign employment only a onetime or occasional event. Hanne (Sweden), for example, loved the two-month gigs he arranged every few years. Between his wife and family and his work, he could not always get permission, but when he could, he happily signed up for missions wherever Sweden was sending volunteers.

International organizations, with their origins in post–World War II reconstruction and liberal expansion, have had an ever-increasing influence in global and local political, economic, and social arenas.[3] Michael Barnett and Martha Finnemore argue that international organizations offering and delivering humanitarian aid and development or recovery assistance carry tremendous power and authority that is based in their ability to define, create, classify, and fix meanings in the social world and in their ability to diffuse norms and actors around the globe (1999:11; see also Escobar 1997; Ferguson 1994, 1995; Kaufmann 1997; Klotz 1995; Malkki 1994, 1998; Rew 1997). In Bosnia-Herzegovina, for example, David Campbell (1998) carefully documents the myriad of international practices through which Bosnia (or meta-Bosnia) came into being, especially the understanding of "Bosnia" ethnically. These ethnicized problematizations led international institutions to negotiate particular solutions to the Bosnian wars (see also Gilbert 2005). As Campbell argues, if Bosnia-Herzegovina had been understood differently, nonethnic solutions might have been possible:

> Had the question of identity been thought of in terms of a necessary but political production that creates the grounds that are supposedly fixed and natural, then an appreciation of the political effects of particular representations could have been part of the process. (1998:162)

David Chandler (1999a) also documents the epistemological power of international organizations in Bosnia-Herzegovina, focusing on the assumptions and contradictions of international policies of democratization that nonetheless serve as guideposts for international interventions.

Along with states, international organizations have become major purveyors of development and its promises of modernity. Of course, institutions and organizations are embodied and enacted by individuals. Because the international community is constituted through these individual agents, it is important to pay attention to the members of the community and recognize that, as in all communities, the borders of inclusion and exclusion are contested and policed and the representation of harmonious and homogeneous relations and values hides the differences and conflicts. That is, the international community should be analyzed as a social and political construct. Attention to the agents of states and statelike discursive entities such as the international community allows us to see within the conglomeration and note its internal dynamics and makeup rather than further the tendency to unify and reify "it." Disaggregating the international community or even international organizations quickly demonstrates the depth of the political and social relationships, the competing sets of interests, the arbitrariness of some decision making, and the contingencies at play.

This chapter describes the international interventions in Bosnia-Herzegovina, examining their creation, justifications, and relations with Bosnia-Herzegovina primarily through this lens of individual actors and the relations and activities of their daily life, work, and play. Indeed, throughout this book, I refer to members of the international community as they referred to themselves, as "internationals."[4] In so doing, I emphasize the social community made up of real persons. Following Akhil Gupta's (1995) theorization of the state, I argue that Bosnians and internationals alike constructed the "international community" through their everyday experiences and relationships with its fragments—local bureaucracies and bureaucrats, individual members, and imagined representations. A focus on internationals, as in this book, gives depth to understandings of the cultural, social, and political works of international interventions through an emphasis on the practices of the agents of interventions rather than on disembodied ideologies or abstract and agentless effects. The second half of the chapter continues the focus on internationals' postwar relations with Bosnia, specifically in regard to the violence of the Bosnian wars and its destructive effects, which clearly affected and shaped Bosnia-Herzegovina and Bosnians. However, conflict also mediated the experiences of international workers in postwar Bosnia-Herzegovina. The radical difference in Bosnians' and internationals' positions regarding violence led internationals to place different meanings on the term and the possibilities for "recovery" and "justice." Internationals' conceptions tended to temporally and spatially bind and displace violence and destruction, perhaps because, unlike Bosnians, internationals primarily experienced violence's vestiges rather than its fury.

The international interventions in Bosnia-Herzegovina were explicitly positivist and progressivist in nature. That is, the transformations envisioned particular ends (conceived as improvements) leading to a better Bosnia-Herzegovina. The rhetoric of the Dayton Peace Accords as a "blueprint for Bosnia-Herzegovina" amply demonstrates what ends were desired: primarily the development of liberal and neoliberal institutions and subjects (i.e., the creation of a central bank and public corporations, democratic elections, human rights enforcement, and the privatization of property) but also healing the social fabric of Bosnian life. Dayton, as a document, is essentially a series of annexes. The main text of the peace agreement proclaimed the equal territorial sovereignty and mutual recognition of the warring parties; subjected them to the international principles of the UN, the Helsinki Final Act, and the OSCE; and referenced their accordance with the items in the annexes. The annexes, in order, regulated, created, or determined: the military aspects of the cease-fire, the military stabilization of the region, internal boundary lines, elections, the state's structure and institutions, dispute settlement as arbitration, human rights, refugees and displaced persons, national monuments, public corporations, a coordinator and facilitator for the civilian aspects of the peace agreement, and an international police task force.

The OHR, an agency created in Annex 10 of Dayton, led the institutional international community in Bosnia-Herzegovina. The High Representative and his office were responsible for the civilian implementation of Dayton. Thus, the office worked on issue areas such as the return of refugees and displaced persons, state institutions (e.g., legal reform, educational policy, national symbols, and pension provisions), and human rights protections. Its responsibilities as well as the roles of other major organizations were clarified and codified during the Peace Implementation Conference held in London in December 1995, one month after the agreement at Dayton was concluded. The conference created the 55-member Peace Implementation Council to sponsor and direct the peace implementation process. Demonstrating the deep ties that bind together international organizations, the Peace Implementation Council's steering board nominates the High Representative, and the UN Security Council, which approved Dayton and the deployment of international troops in Bosnia-Herzegovina, endorses him.[5] (As of February 2006, there have been five High Representatives, all male and all European politician/diplomats.)

These international organizations wielded extraordinary power over the fledgling Bosnian state and its nascent institutions. Annex 10 tasked the OHR with the establishment of political and constitutional institutions. The office clearly would make its mark. However, its power was also felt through more directed decisions and action. For example, the High Representative ousted mayors and presidents, sanctioned municipalities and cantons, and chose the new Bosnian flag (just in time for the 1998 Winter Olympics in Nagano, Japan).

> [The High Representative] is the final authority in theatre regard-
> ing its [the Dayton Peace Accords'] interpretation, authorised to
> impose legislation and dismiss obstructive officials and tasked with
> co-ordinating the activities of other international civilian organi-
> zations. (OHR 2002a)

These actions attested to the power of international organizations and their unusual relation to the sovereign Bosnian state. At the same time, however, they always remained in dialogue with Bosnia-Herzegovina's political, economic, and social climate. Bosnians' actions affected, lim-ited, and framed the possibilities for international transformation strate-gies. The larger international system also shaped and framed the possi-bilities for international action. Interventions were legitimated and made possible through a global discourse of democracy and develop-ment that emphasized both the necessity and the morality of such involvement (see also Chandler 1999b). As Mark R. Duffield (2002) argues, development has become a tool of conflict resolution and social reconstruction and humanitarian aid a tool of global liberal governance (see also Mosse and Lewis 2005). The OSCE's various mandates in Bosnia-Herzegovina reflected the new resolution/reconstruction and governance roles for development and aid: disarmament and regional (military) stabilization, elections and democratization, and human rights.

International military forces were also in Bosnia-Herzegovina under the authority of Dayton, particularly Annex 1A.

> The United Nations Security Council is invited to adopt a resolu-
> tion by which it will authorize Member States or regional organi-
> zations and arrangements to establish a multinational military
> Implementation Force (hereinafter "IFOR"). The Parties under-
> stand and agree that this Implementation Force may be composed
> of ground, air and maritime units from NATO and non-NATO
> nations, deployed to Bosnia and Herzegovina to help ensure com-
> pliance with the provisions of this Agreement (hereinafter
> "Annex"). The Parties understand and agree that the IFOR will
> begin the implementation of the military aspects of this Annex
> upon the transfer of authority from the UNPROFOR Commander

to the IFOR Commander (hereinafter "Transfer of Authority"), and that until the Transfer of Authority, UNPROFOR will continue to exercise its mandate.

These military forces were led by NATO, although non-NATO forces also participated.[6] A Stabilization Force (SFOR) succeeded the IFOR, which held a one-year mandate beginning immediately after the signing of the peace treaty. Similarly, IFOR followed the UN Protection Force (UNPROFOR), which attempted to monitor the 1992–95 wars and protect civilians. Although the military is not always discursively included in the "international community," it was a key cog in the Bosnian international infrastructure, providing security, logistics, and material goods to internationals as well as muscle for their authority and legitimacy.

The institutional frame for international interventions in Bosnia-Herzegovina presents a picture of international institutional cooperation and diplomatic power sharing. The nested relations and linked lines of communication and action give credence to the conceptualization of the international community as a coherent and unified entity. However, the term *international community* is simply too neat to capture the unwieldy myriad of forces and practices that are subsumed within this conceptually diffuse term. Where can we reconcile all of the different modalities of the international community, from activist networks to the World Trade Organization, including diplomats, experts, student interns, and mercenaries as well as missionaries? This international entity actually constitutes a heterogeneous composite of organizations and people from various countries and backgrounds. Far from a monolith, tensions, hierarchies, and contradictions exist within and between international agencies, organizations, and individuals. Nor is the international community just a political or institutional entity; while much was made on the ground in Bosnia-Herzegovina of the turf wars and disagreements between international agencies (sometimes resulting in the creation of coordinating councils and point persons), relations of power also mapped onto those individuals that constituted the community. For example, several white Western European colleagues expressed amusement, tinged with a sense of confusion and worry, that international election supervisors from Tajikistan could properly promote democracy since they did not live in a democracy. Internationals from Western democracies were not immune to criticism, although it rarely came from within the international community itself; I overheard a Bosnian question British supervisors' ability to promote peace and democracy in light of the troubles in Northern Ireland. Similarly, many Bosnians delighted in pointing out Americans' misplaced trust in their election system during the 2000 U.S. election fiasco in Florida. Americans and (Western) Europeans constituted the demographic majority within the foreign community in Bosnia-Herzegovina during my fieldwork, but they were not the only members and did not themselves constitute a monolith.

Despite the divisions and oft-stereotypical hierarchies within and between internationals, these distinctions were not formalized. Rather, the key division in Bosnia-Herzegovina's aid and development organizations was local-national/international, not governmental/nongovernmental, as scholars might expect based on the attention given to the recent proliferation of NGOs.[7] This differentiation marks interesting new divisions and territories in governance in a globalized world since it is not arranged around state involvement but territorialization. This particular dichotomous split suggests a new hierarchization of interventions in that the nonterritorialized are blessed and equipped with resources, power, and the ever-present exit option also well known to anthropologists. States fade from the limelight in this configuration, suggesting perhaps the reach of their tentacles (i.e., many NGOs are funded with state money) or alternatively their displacement as governing bodies. Is the state less of a demarcated foil because it is everywhere or because it is nowhere? But the international community is not a state or even a superstate; it has no territory, for example, and using Max Weber's (1918) classic definition of a modern state, it has no monopoly on the legitimate use of physical force. Furthermore, the division of interventions into national/international rather than governmental/nongovernmental marks the subject position of the intervention rather than its orientation. However, this subject position of international interpolates a rather nebulous entity with claims and practices of authority and legitimacy, even while the grounding for that authority and legitimacy is neither stable nor tangible. As James Ferguson and Akhil Gupta (2002:996) suggest, the task "is to understand the spatiality of all forms of government, some of which may be embedded in the daily practices of nation-states while others may crosscut or superimpose themselves on the territorial jurisdiction of nation-states." The international community in Bosnia-Herzegovina defies analytical and empirical classification using existing categories and distinctions. As such, it must appear as a new governmental configuration, not as something already known in a new guise.

The subject position of the international was juxtaposed against that of the people being helped—the Bosnians. Again, I use an international emic reference to describe Bosnia-Herzegovina's residents and citizens. The designation has certain limitations in that it can be rightfully criticized as problematically assimilating Herzegovinians, excluding ethnic Serbs from any national labeling, and ignoring citizenship laws. It also conflates political and social identities and entities. The peace accords politically divided the country into two parts: Republika Srpska (Serb Republic) and Federation of Bosnia and Herzogovina. These two territories are separated by the IEBL, the Inter-Entity Boundary Line (the content of Annex II of Dayton), and were accepted as ethnically-defined and -controlled territories by most Bosnians and internationals alike, especially in the immediate years after the war (the IEBL runs, for the most part, along the military front lines as they stood in late 1995). The designation *Bosnian* thus also speaks to a dominant tension in the life of internationals: acknowledging yet rejecting the tendency to balkanize Bosnia-Herzegovina into smaller and smaller ethnic components. For example, Manuela, an Italian international with whom I often spoke, said her work entailed promoting a nonethnic Herzegovinian identity, one which had historical precedents. Herzegovina, a geographic region of Bosnia-Herzegovina, incorporates the western and southern lands and runs along the length of the Dalmatian Mountains. Herzegovina had always included ethnic Serbs, Croats, and Bosniacs, and she believed that it could logically do so again. She wanted nothing to do with institutional ethnic codifications. The term *Bosnian* should not be confused or conflated with *Bosniac,* which references the ethnonational group of Bosnians who are historically Muslim. Bosniac was an ethnic rather than religious category under Tito's regime.[8] Many Bosnian Muslims—Bosniacs—were not actively faithful. The issues of religion in Bosnia-Herzegovina, Europe, and among internationals are fascinating in themselves. Here, I place them in the background, simply noting that the tendency for secular Christianity to remain unmarked within the international community (and its liberal and neoliberal prescriptions) is rampant (cf. Bornstein 1999, 2005).

A sociological portrait of internationals residing in postwar Bosnia-Herzegovina demonstrates changing and perhaps contradictory rationales about what skills were desired and who had them. Evidence suggests that the international projects in Bosnia-Herzegovina also served as job markets for unemployed or otherwise wayward yet educated Europeans. I found that many jobs were relatively interchangeable in that a wide range of persons could fill them, including some positions that seemed to require specialized skills. For example, Jon (from Canada) had a degree in management. He came to Bosnia-Herzegovina to visit a girlfriend and decided to stay. His skills in large-scale logistics served him well, and he quickly achieved a high-level administrative position. Hannah (a native of France) began in electoral education, moved into budget and administration, and when I left Bosnia-Herzegovina was a human rights officer although she had little if any formal training in human rights work. Martin (United Kingdom), who had a legal background, first came to Bosnia-Herzegovina as an administrator within the Election Department (hired by a university acquaintance) and eventually became an important legal adviser to bankers working on economic reforms before he left for another international position in the UN administration of Cambodia. To the dismay of the election personnel office, internationals commonly used jobs in the election field as stepping-stones to bigger and better positions. The office faced constant recruitment problems as other departments and agencies repeatedly stole staffers. For example, one election trainer left to become a political analyst one week before election training began—at that late date, it was not possible to find a replacement trainer. Very few international workers that I met were Slavic or Balkan specialists; rather, they were either newcomers or old hands (i.e., they had aid experience in other countries rather than any long or enduring ties to the Balkans). In conjunction with prejudices about the competency of potential Eastern European colleagues, the high rate of position mobility and flexibility suggests that a primary skill for these jobs was simply being modern, educated, and democratic. As aid becomes a career choice and an industry, it is important to investigate its interactions, strategies, visions, and employees. International interventions were legitimated through a discursive regime of morality and security, but the on-the-ground implementers shared only partly in this hegemonic myth—as a Norwegian colleague, Lars, said about taking up international aid work, "It's one-third for the excitement, one-third the money, and one-third the morality."

Many commentators have compared colonialism with the interventions in Bosnia. Most noticeably, Gerald Knaus and Felix Martin's (2003) article, "Travails of the European Raj," equating the High Representative with British colonial administrators in India, unleashed a flurry of debate about whether the High Representative was like the British Raj and whether any similarities were good or bad. Responses also critiqued the tendency for aid practitioners and scholars to fall into good/bad, success/failure dichotomies before launching into alternative prescriptions for Bosnia's progress into democracy, neoliberalism, and Europe and countering Knaus and Martin's suggestion of more international involvement and cooperation with Bosnians.

Colonial comparisons merely lead down a well-traveled path of moralized and politicized judgments. More interesting perhaps, is the frame of colonialism that pervaded international life. When an author of a response to Knaus and Martin asked for my input, I replied that they did not seem to be saying anything particularly new; for ten years, internationals and Bosnians had already made political purchase of parallels between international interventions in Bosnia and colonialism. Long before the publication of the Raj article, reflective internationals sometimes pondered whether they and their work were more "missionary" or more "colonial." Of course, scholars have shown that these two projects were often two peas in a pod although their interests and strategies often diverged or conflicted (see Burke 1996; Comaroff and Comaroff 1997; Merry 2000). Colonialism and missionaries went hand in hand, sometimes traveling abreast of each other, sometimes with one leading the other, but overall depending on and legitimating each other and their respective and complementary "civilizing" processes. Because many internationals in Bosnia-Herzegovina were college educated and some held postgraduate degrees, they could reflect critically on their experiences in comparison to those of their historical comrades.

Steve, a particularly thoughtful American working for an INGO focused on promoting reconciliation and cooperation among Bosnia-Herzegovina's religious bodies, said after some contemplation, that he thought the international community was more like a missionary operation than a colonial project because "we do not intend to rule the country or extract resources from it." In his view, the aims of the international community ran more toward changing the people's minds, toward convincing them that the new, introduced ways were better. Then, after Bosnians had been convinced, he surmised, they would change their behavior. The international community was also involved in transforming political and economic institutions (to house the newly changed or soon-to-be converts), but again, he said, the international community had no desire to control these new governmental structures but rather desperately wanted to give up control and have Bosnians take the reins.[9] In contrast, internationals had direct and straightforward links to missionaries: "We want to change" the Bosnians, Steve continued, "We believe in the goodness and morality of what we are doing." Some internationals recognized the ills and devastation wrought by these modern-day, well-meaning, but sometimes mean-spirited or conflicted missionaries, but they were, in general, just as confident in their goodness and the necessity of their transformative projects as the colonial-era missionaries were of Christianization.

Violence and Justice in Postwar Bosnia-Herzegovina

On April 6, 1992, armed soldiers fired into Sarajevo, signaling the start of the three-and-a-half-year war, although as Campbell (1998:57–60) points out, a significant build-up of forces and separatist behavior had occurred during the two years preceding the official start of the war. Brawls, the establishment of paramilitaries, shootings, and secessionist political behavior occurred between Yugoslavia's collapse around 1990 and the international recognition of Bosnia-Herzegovina in the first days of April 1992. The inclusion or exclusion of various events drastically influences interpretations of the violence and affected the policy choices and arrangements that international actors took in relation to the war. Scholarship also had a tremedous impact on political practice, international diplomacy, and narrative explanations for the outbreak of war.

Much post–World War II academic scholarship on the Balkans focused on the "problem(s) of co-existence" among nationalities (or ethnicities or religions) (see Alexander 1979; Banac 1984; Bertsch 1976; Donia 1981; Lockwood 1979; Ramet 1985). Assumptions based in ethnic essentialism also clearly framed many political and social analyses of the latest Balkan war and the "dissolution of Yugoslavia" (Bowen 1996; Campbell 1998; Ceh and Harder 1996; Maass 1996; Woodward 1995a; cf. Kaplan 1993) despite the wealth of scholarship that has shown that ethnic identities are not primordial or natural but historically constructed (see among many others Anderson 1983; Bowen 1996; Eley and Suny 1996; Hobsbawm and Ranger 1983; Malkki 1994, 1995; Renan 1996). As has been widely reported, U.S. President Bill Clinton relied on the "age-old ethnic hatred" descriptions in Robert Kaplan's (1993) political travelogue, *Balkan Ghosts,* in framing a noninterventionist foreign policy toward the wars in Bosnia-Herzegovina, Croatia, and Serbia. As the volume's back cover explains, the author "deciphers the Balkans' ancient passions and intractable hatreds for outsiders." This made it easier for American and European policymakers to view intervention as futile and unproductive (Malcolm 1993).[10]

Furthermore, ethnic assumptions make it easier to think of violence as characteristic of a people rather than as a product of political acts. It paints people as less rational and less modern than those doing the judging. These narratives do not naturally or necessarily cause ethnic tensions and violence (Bowen 1996; Ceh and Harder 1996; Maass 1996). Rather, they justify or create atmospheres that permit certain practices. For example, Hayden (1996, 1999a) demonstrates that the constitutional logic implemented in the former Yugoslavia at dissolution set the stage for the terrible ferocity of the wars. Mart Bax (2000) argues that the course of ethnic homogenization can largely be traced back to local vendettas and a long-standing conflict between Franciscan friars and diocesan priests. Reducing the complexity of the conflict to the banalities of ethnic essentialism is depoliticizing and obscures its historical production (Campbell 1998; see also more political-economic explanations of the outbreak of war, including Silber and Little 1995; Woodward 1995a).

Among my international informants, the historically and ideologically constructed nature of ethnicity and identity was clear; many had heard, for example, testimonies from local colleagues who had not realized their Serbness or Muslimness until after the war began. As a neighbor told me, "I never felt Muslim before. But now I feel Muslim. I am Muslim. They made me realize it when they wanted to kill me for being Muslim." With this in mind, internationals often attempted to nullify ethnicity as a salient category. Some purposely avoided learning the ethnicity of Bosnian colleagues; others referred to the now distinct languages as the "local language" or ridiculed (along with many Bosnians) the cultural politics that distinguished coffee into three ethnicized drinks—Serb *kafa*, Croat *kava*, and Bosniac *kahva*. Internationals' negotiations with Bosnian identity politics were complex, varied, and a large enough topic for another book.[11] The conscious avoidance of ethnic marking or labeling did not liberate Bosnian peoples from dangerously reductionist representations, however. Rather, the conviction that Bosnia-Herzegovina should be a single nation-state may have furthered the solidification and maintenance of singular representations. Here, though, I do not seek to provide an accounting or an explanation for the origins or even the events of the 1992–95 war in Bosnia-Herzegovina, although I do wish to remain vigilant to the ways particular narratives shape understandings of and responses to the war because these narratives also shaped people's understandings of postwar Bosnia-Herzegovina, including the internationals working in and on relief and development projects.

Knowledge produced by intellectuals about the war informed Western and Balkan political practice and policy in relation to the war and consequently affected how the war was waged (Allcock 2000; Campbell 1998; Cushman 1997; Hayden 1996; Woodward 1997). It is impossible to analyze the war without also taking into account the understandings and knowledges of the larger system within which the war was conducted. Narratives affect actors outside of the direct conflict. Nick Ceh and Jeff Harder (1996), for example, discuss some other nonnationalist external ideological interpretations of the Bosnian conflict. First, a "colonial ideology theme" constructed the conflict as pitting civilized Westerners against non-Western barbarians inclined to violence and irrationality. The authors argue that this view lent credence to arguments supporting nonintervention and added to racist constructions of the Other. An alternative, the "cold war theme" of totalitarianism, linked socialism to terror and a false ethnic peace. Thus, its collapse brought on the war. In contrast, scholars and activists agree that many actors and many groups perpetrated the violence, although these observers disagree even among themselves about the distribution of blame and culpability and on the judgments of aggressiveness, victim, and criminality.

For convenience, I will characterize the two main strands of thought as "relativist" and "specifist." The relativists generally argue that all sides did horrible things and are equally at fault. Proponents of this view do not pinpoint one group as bearing the blame (see Denich 1994; Hayden 1996). Thomas Cushman (1997) argues that these relativist styles of thought were responsible for the West's ambivalence toward military intervention to stop the war and the refusal to assign responsibility. Paul Hockenos (2003) documents how diasporic Serbs hired public relations firms to spread disinformation and emphasize the relativist argument. Specifists, conversely, tend to accuse one side of being the primary instigators and the most violent and inhumane (see Bennett 2000; Cushman 1997; Cushman and Mestrovic 1996). Labeling or categorizing violence and its instigators is a key determinant in responding to violence and creating punishment. Hence, human rights lawyers gathered documentation regarding strategic and specific planning by militias and armies (see Hagan 2003). Like the detailed planning of death and destruction by the Guatemalan military described by Jennifer G. Schirmer (1998), the rapes, the bombs, and the destruction of historical and religious structures were deliberate demoralization strategies on the part of militarized forces. Documents show, for example, that Croatian President Franjo Tudjman and Serbian President

Slobodan Milošević met to carve up the territory of Bosnia-Herzegovina. Evidence also supports the deliberate construction of "rape camps" (Hagan 2003; Stiglmayer 1994).

On the ground, internationals rarely discussed the war or placed war blame. With few exceptions, internationals came to Bosnia with the impression that the leaders bore primary blame for the war, the atrocities, and the manipulation of the population. One of the more pragmatic effects of this logic was relatively fluid personnel placement in field offices. Internationals who kicked up a fuss about being sent to Croat or Serb areas were few and far between, and many of them shifted regularly among field offices located around the country and thus into contact with different ethnic groups. The one time I encountered such a situation, I saw a teary short-term polling supervisor adamant about not wanting to go to the Serb area where she had been assigned. The personnel officer hearing her complaint firmly told her, "We are here to help all Bosnians. If you do not want to help the country as a whole, then I am going to send you home on the next flight." "Politics" (defined ethnically) was deemphasized, while achieving justice and "moving forward" were heavily promoted.

Violence continued to shape Bosnia-Herzegovina even after the war technically ended. With the risk of trivializing the carnage through brevity, Bosnia-Herzegovina was rebuilding from the consequences of a war that included 258,000 missing or dead inhabitants, 1,370,000 displaced people, 1.2 million refugees, economic losses of US\$60 billion, the destruction of the governance system, a substantial and sustained brain drain, a drop in gross domestic product from 13.05 billion DM in 1991 to 2.87 billion in 1995, an 80 percent drop in industrial production, and the laying of 750,000 land mines (International Committee of the Red Cross 1997; UN Development Programme 1998). These stark figures cannot account for the destruction of social ties, relationships, and trust or suffering, although they begin to show the extent of the devastation. Of course, knowledge in this context may not have to be measured as social science and governmental data would have it. Substantial visual clues spoke directly of the enormous number of dead, missing, displaced, maimed, raped, unemployed, impoverished, and uneducated Bosnians.

During my research trips, violence was an all-pervading background for life in Bosnia-Herzegovina. For internationals, violence not only constituted their professional raison d'être but also marked their mundane lives. Besides working to reconstruct government, rid land of mines, piece together bodies from mass graves, and manage home reconstruction projects, international workers lived in an environment marked by the consequences of war—homes with bullet holes, inadequate and inconsistent water supplies, damaged buildings and roads, and social tension, poverty, and misery. I found the physical scars on Bosnia-Herzegovina the most disturbing—the houses with no or partial walls, roofs, and windows—because they whispered the horror. Elaine Scarry (1985) reminds us that invisible suffering and pain are difficult to communicate. It was hard to understand Bosnians' bodily and emotional trauma, but the landscape hinted at it. Driving along a road, staring at kilometers and kilometers of destruction and land mine tape, was a sobering experience for every international with whom I discussed violence and war damage. Election supervisors were not surprised by my asking, for example, which road in Bosnia-Herzegovina they found the most depressing—the answers I got suggested either the roads just north and south of Mostar or the road between Doboj and the Croatian border, where for more than an hour's drive, it was difficult to see anything but ruined shells of houses. However, the scenes were repeated everywhere. For miles along many roads, not a house would be standing. It was worse when only one or two houses were standing, because it opened up the question of why and who escaped. Concurrent with mine awareness training, these scenes reminded internationals that the country was heavily mined and that such normal activities as parking on the shoulder of a road or strolling in the countryside were dangerous. The omnipresent rubble made the violence real for most internationals.

The reminders of war were memorialized in postcards (fig. 4) available for purchase at the international military exchanges. By far the majority of the postcards available, like travel postcards available for Bali, New York City, or Paris, showed postwar Bosnia's "scenic sights." That is, Bosnia's real scenic sites—the historic buildings, bridges, and neighborhoods or the deep river gorges—were displaced in favor of scenes of destroyed office buildings, apartment blocks, and military guards. These postcards and other commoditized war objects constitute a form of war tourism. Without condoning war-as-spectacle but before chastising this phenomenon as repugnant and morally suspect, war tourism made sense within the logic of tourism. At the time, Bosnia-Herzegovina was known for its war, which constituted the reason international workers arrived in Bosnia-Herzegovina. Few foreigners were visiting Bosnia solely as tourists (in 2004, the OHR began a concerted

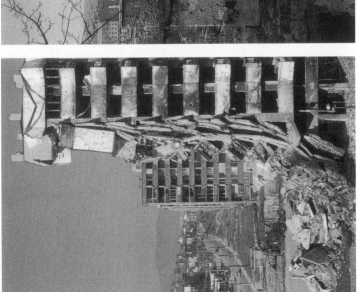

Fig. 4. Postcards of Sarajevo bought at a military PX. With labels such as "a humble citizen taking care of his property," "view of the capital's center from the east," and "war damaged buildings in the eastern area," these postcards documented the social and physical landscape that soldiers and other internationals lived and worked within. Sending them to loved ones also served to legitimize their presence in Bosnia and away from home.

effort to push, reform, and revive Bosnia as a tourist destination). So, while the Eiffel Tower depicts Paris, beaches and the Hollywood sign symbolize Los Angeles, and charismatic animals represent Kenya, shell-pocked and half-destroyed apartment buildings represented Sarajevo. International visitors to Mostar were likely to visit the relatively preserved Old Town (but with its central historical masterpiece, the stunning 16th-century Stari Most [Old Bridge] destroyed by artillery shells on November 9, 1993) as well as the front line a mere five blocks away.[12] The metallurgy shops in the Bascarsija (Old Town) of Sarajevo all sold elaborately engraved mortar casings as well as coffee grinders and vases made out of the empty cartridge cases of the small armaments used to shell the city. Maps of the snipers' trenches overlooking Sarajevo were sold alongside woolen rugs and filigree necklaces. For many towns, war damage was the only remaining site. With more historical distance, war sites can become well-documented tourist attractions, such as Gettysburg National Military Park, the D-Day beaches, and more recently the Vietnamese National Liberation Front's tunnels. But in Bosnia-Herzegovina, as of 2002 these sites (except for a new war memorial at Srebrenica) were not institutionally memorialized by the state—rather war sites were everywhere.[13] Of course, while postcards documented damage and trinkets recalled violence for international workers and visitors, Bosnians remembered the war in more personal and political ways (i.e., personal remembrances and trauma, political movements to find missing persons or honor veterans) (see Wagner 2006; see also Schwenkel 2006).

Even casual conversation with Bosnians demonstrated that although I shared with them the experience of living in a postwar zone, our cultural conceptions and the meanings we attached to social institutions differed starkly. In the earliest stages of my research, I twice had pause to contemplate varying interpretations of the beautiful Bosnian countryside, which I admired from afar due to the potential risk of land mines. While looking at an apartment for rent high on the fifteenth floor, I mentioned the wonderful view to the landlady. She responded by pointing out the sniper lines and encampments from which Sarajevo suffered its thousand-day siege. She told me how long it took to carry two pails of water up fifteen flights of darkened stairs when the electricity failed. Our views were informed by our experiences (or lack thereof). This is not a novel argument, although I take it one step further: not just the view differs, but the understandings of what can and cannot be done based on that view. Like the lives of Mayan widows described by Linda Green

(1999), the lives of Bosnians are now constituted in tandem with violence and fear. Green argues that "violence is not simply the historical background . . . it is implicated in the ways in which women refashion social memory and cultural practices" (1999:6). Political violence operates locally, and structures of violence become embedded within social institutions and cultural conceptions. Green documents how Mayan widows live in a "chronic condition" of fear that penetrates social memory and is factored into the choices and decisions that men and women make. The violence implicates itself into daily life. This was the case when Sarina, my Bosniac landlady, and I disagreed about whether the town of Pale was beautiful. Nestled in a mountain valley, the town, a main stronghold for Bosnian Serbs, has postcard potential. The hamlet's buildings dot the hillsides, and in the summer the land is lush with grass and wildflowers. Sarina could not agree with my aesthetic as a result of her strong associations of repression, violence, and fear as a consequence of the actions of people who lived in Pale. She could not imagine why I wanted to visit the town, or fathom why I would eat at the well-known trout farm-restaurant nearby. At one time, it had been a favorite destination for Sarajevans (a mere 20-minute drive away) taking day trips; now it was bathed in blood, misery, and fear. There is a disjuncture between the suffering and the comprehension of the suffering based on incommunicability (Scarry 1985). Internationals, most of whom arrived after the cessation of armed hostilities, knew and saw the physical damage but could not comprehend it in the same way as those who had suffered and experienced it. Internationals and Bosnians inhabited different landscapes.

Internationals were not immune to the weight of destruction, hopelessness, and poverty. The scale of destruction overwhelmed them, and the constant visual markings of death, destruction, and war affected many internationals' mental health. Many were outwardly and openly unhappy, and they had a sometimes obsessive desire to get out of town as often as possible. However, the lack of memory attachments to destruction also gave some internationals the ability to look past the destruction; although it was a part of everyday life, it also became "just" the context for everyday life. The damaged buildings were "normal" and part of the background. As Ciara, an Irish neighbor told me, "To dwell on it would make life unbearable. . . . You have to go on." This sentiment held as true for internationals as many internationals felt it should for Bosnians. These internationals, however, failed to recognize the meanings—fear and suffering—that were attached to the destruction ingrained in

Bosnia-Herzegovina and that penetrated Bosnian daily life, social institutions, cultural conceptions, and decision-making processes (e.g., voting behavior). This is perhaps one reason why Bosnia-Herzegovina did not "recover" as quickly as many internationals had hoped and expected.

Internationals' frustration with the "slow recovery" (and indeed, their labeling of the processes of rehabilitation and recovery "slow") might have resulted from a lack of understanding of how finely ingrained and deeply embedded violence, fear, and suffering had become in Bosnian life. Here, I will examine more thoroughly this idea of recovery. What did it mean when someone talked about the ways in which Bosnians could or should move on? What practices counted as steps toward moving on? Like all practices and processes in a modernist system, reform and recovery projects were framed by a progress narrative—that is, a forward- and future-oriented perspective informed the internationally promoted state, societal, and individual reforms in Bosnia-Herzegovina. This progress narrative used the past, memory, and remembrance in particular ways. In Bosnia-Herzegovina, international rhetoric conceptually categorized the past as bad, backward, immoral, criminal, and destructive. Thus, progress was defined less as improving on the past—a more typical narrative in capitalist story lines—and more as something that should be erased or stricken from the present. Rather than a stepping-stone, the past constituted an obstacle. Not all reform and recovery strategies attempted to ignore, avoid, silence, or forget the past, although some did; instead, strategies located the past as a hurdle to overcome. But bounding the past and making it an object removed it from its place in the present. The past was treated as a thing—as a narrow strip of time—that could (or should) be put into the background. However, the past is clearly a set of memories and effects that guide and structure the present. It cannot be easily displaced.

International projects—such as refugee returns, restoration of property rights, and crimes tribunals—negotiated the past in a variety of ways. Whether confronting, ignoring, or only alluding to the past, projects were primarily future centered and prescriptive. What should government look like? What ought to be done to solve the problems? While still based in the language of moving on, projects acknowledged and/or grappled with the past. They did so, however, in ways that attempted to purge the violent past of its gains and successes, returning to how things were in 1991, conveniently just one year before the start of the war and the time of the last census. A re-created 1991 then became the desired jumping-off point for many postsocialist and war-recovery transformation projects.

In the summer of 1999, I traveled with an American democratization officer, Cyndi, into the hills behind the town of Bijela Planina. She wanted to visit an elderly couple who had recently "returned" to their village. Bijela Planina was small—all of the townspeople knew one another, including those who stayed, those who fled, and those who arrived during the war years. The village had been "cleansed" during the war, and the elderly couple were the first of the "cleansed" ethnicity to return for this village. Cyndi spoke of the couple as having great courage to think of returning, let alone doing it. As an encouragement for their tentative step, her office and other international donors had offered funding and physical assistance to rebuild the couple's home and orchard. They had moved back a few months earlier. We were visiting, however, because some neighbors had recently beaten up the old man, inflicting a variety of injuries, including a broken nose. The fight nominally involved a cow. As I heard the story, he found one of his neighbors' cows in his yard and took it upon himself to return the cow to the proper field. A group of men came upon him with the cow, began to harass him, and, believing that the old man was stealing the cow, beat him up.

From the beginning of postwar international intervention, returns of people of the now non-dominant ethnicity in a particular municipality (i.e., "minority returns") constituted a priority for organizations like the OHR. Minority returns became a means of erasing the effects of the war, of returning Bosnia-Herzegovina to the way it had been in 1991. In that regard, statistics of returns were used as a measure of evaluating the success (and failure) of international intervention. The year 1998 was even declared the Year of Return. It was a dismal year for refugee and displaced person returns, however, and soon thereafter, the main international organizations formed specific working groups and task forces that would socially, politically, logistically, and economically encourage returns. But the years between 1991 and 1999 had left a legacy of fear, destruction, and hate, and as this incident demonstrates, people are not willing to parenthesize the past.

Cyndi sympathized with the elderly returnees and encouraged them to be civil to their neighbors yet careful, and we left to visit the family that owned the cow. Drinking coffee with the matriarch, Cyndi rejected her suggestion that the beating had been either a mistake or the elderly man's fault. She asked the matriarch, "When is it ever okay to beat up someone?" More interestingly, at least for this analysis, Cyndi incessantly invoked and emphasized the future in getting the village to cooperate as a whole. That way, she said, they could—together—ask the municipality for services such as electricity, running water, and paved streets. "Don't you want these things?" she asked. "Is cooperation too much to ask? Without cooperation, you will get nothing." Although the village had returned to the past circa 1991—or was in the process of doing so, since more returns were planned—the villagers were not being asked to stay in the past but to move forward directly into 1999, skipping over the intervening eight years. As this case demonstrates, the past cannot be easily classified as a single, unified object. It is not "the past." Rather, the past has multiple phases and layers. Thus, while return projects harnessed the past, searching for and creating a prewar halcyon, they simultaneously wanted to cut out and deemphasize the more immediate past. And people or projects that prioritized the more immediate past were chastised and distrusted.

Projects based on the restoration of property rights also attempted to turn back the clock by giving property lost during the war back to its original residents (i.e., property was not always owned before the war as Yugoslavia had been a socialist state).[14] Property could not be simply reoccupied by returning residents because, through a series of wartime logistical and legislative actions, most "empty" properties had been occupied by or reallocated to arriving displaced persons as well as to some members of the political elite. War-time laws had allowed for the transfer of ownership or occupancy rights of private and socially owned property that local authorities declared abandoned. Consequently, from a legal point of view, most potential returnees no longer held or had a right to property. Estimates hold that more than 50 percent of the country's population—some 2.2 million people—fled or were expelled between 1992 and 1996, including some 80,000 people after the signing of the peace accords as land changed political hands (UN Development Programme 1998). The peace accords provided the right to have property restored to original owners or occupants. Thus, property laws passed during the war were nullified, and a claims process was established. As of May 2000, 210,054 claims had been filed, but only 26.6 percent had been decided through the claims process (OHR 2000). A paltry 10.6 percent of claims had actually resulted in property being repossessed (OHR 2000).[15]

This process also attempted to return Bosnia-Herzegovina to its 1991 world. As rights-bearing newly liberal subjects, Bosnians had the right to their property, even if they chose not to return to it. However, property (and return) projects generally assumed that Bosnians wanted to regain their property and return home. Such did not appear to be the case for all displaced people. Some were content with their new arrangements as a result of economic opportunities or a sense of ethnic solidarity. Furthermore, the people and places to which Bosnians were returning had been altered. Residential property returns were considered part of the reconciliation process because the victims were given back some of what had been taken from them by the war. This reconciliation erased the immediate past physically and residentially but did little to reconcile people socially or psychologically. In these latter modes, residents were encouraged to cooperate and focus on their future, especially their "common future," as seen in Cyndi's desire for the community to band together to push for water and other municipal service. This focus on the future did not fully engage with the violence of the past but rather urged a compartmentalization of the war, allowing it to be blocked off and set aside.

Much of the culpability for the war and the mass destruction fell to the leaders and military commanders or soldiers. They were called on to appear in The Hague at the International Criminal Tribunal for the former Yugoslavia (ICTY).[16] The establishment of the ICTY and the prosecution of war criminals were perceived as an important step in the reconciliation process. As stated in a report written by Bosnian intellectuals for the UN Development Programme,

> An important dimension to reconciliation remains, however, the pursuit of justice. At a practical level, the continuing freedom of alleged war criminals, particularly those in positions of authority, is a significant deterrent to normalisation of life and to creating a climate conducive to return. At a more abstract level, impunity for serious crimes permeates the fabric of the rule of law creating an underlying sense of insecurity. (UN Development Programme 1998:86)

The war past was being confronted most visibly and directly at The Hague, a place removed from Bosnia-Herzegovina yet saturated in its tragedies. As of spring 2002, 73 persons had been indicted, although 23 remained at large. According to many international commentators, including Human Rights Watch and the UN, the continued freedom of these alleged criminals hindered the ability of Bosnia-Herzegovina and

Bosnians to move forward. SFOR, for example, faced particular criticism for its failure to arrest Radovan Karadzić, thus preventing his trial at The Hague. The tribunal became the sole mechanism for addressing the tragedy of and culpability for the war. It was also treated, through an appropriation of the term *justice,* as the main means of achieving a return to normalcy.

The placement of the ICTY—the major institutional mechanism addressing the war past—outside of Bosnia-Herzegovina left the country with few reconciliation projects that actually grappled with the war. Two of the primary foci of international assistance—returns and property rights—attempted to nullify the displacement and ethnic homogeneity caused by the war. These projects inadvertently promoted the displacement of the war and implicitly attempted to cast it out of the past. International intervention projects framed and used "the past"; however, the past was considered an obstacle. Given this construction, projects had little option but to try to slip by the past in their future-building strategies. The past was simply not considered an appropriate stepping-stone or launching point for reform. It was acknowledged quickly but set aside in favor of a focus on the future. This strategy might have been possible because the ICTY had been designated as the institutional mechanism for prosecuting the war. In that case, the establishment of war criminal courts erroneously displaced the ability and necessity of coming to terms with societal and individual war experiences. It is more difficult to establish political or legal culpability (as well as victimhood) when violence results from a set of relationships or a process rather than an event (Das 1995). Bosnians were still dealing with their war past, as seen by "slow" returns, the harassment of returnees, and the low number of property claims and slow rate of property decisions. Internationals, conversely, displaced the war to The Hague and thus had more trouble figuring out why it continued to live on in daily life.

INTERNATIONALITY

ARRIVAL STORIES

The Swiss flight left Vienna each Tuesday afternoon, arriving in Sarajevo about two hours later. In later years, commercial flights became regular—from Vienna, Zurich, Istanbul, Ljubljana, Budapest, Zagreb, and Frankfurt—but in the beginning, many foreign aid workers took the Tuesday afternoon flight offered by the Swiss military as part of its contribution to peacekeeping in Bosnia-Herzegovina. In June 1997, when I first took it, the baggage flew with the passengers in the cabin rather than in the underbelly storage compartments. Crammed into a large heap, the baggage filled the last four or five rows of seats. The stewardesses wore blue worker-style coveralls, jazzed up with cheery neck scarves and tightly cinched belts. It was not a typical flight, and these were not typical flight attendants. The passengers were all internationals, perhaps about twenty of us in all, winging our way into Sarajevo, first over the Austrian Alps, then across the plains of Hungary and Croatia, and finally over the valleys of Bosnia. As we descended into the Sarajevo area, buildings and houses came into clear view. Quickly, at hundreds of miles per hour, houses transformed from cute, minuscule dots in a romantic rural panorama to brick skeletons without roofs or window glass. What looked like rural bliss from a distance had clearly been a nightmare for its onetime inhabitants.

I sat next to two Americans about my age, Paul and Alex. Both were returning to Bosnia-Herzegovina after short breaks at home. Alex and I had met the day before over dinner in Vienna. The U.S. State Department had informed me by fax that another American was staying at my hotel and would also be on the Tuesday flight, so we had arranged to meet for dinner. We traded stories over bratwurst and sauerkraut at a café/restaurant that Alex's *Lonely Planet Guide* for Austria had recommended as "off the tourist path." Alex, who was newly contracted into a long-term position, had gone home because the extension of his contract allowed him paid home leave. However, he confessed, he really had gone home to pick up some proper clothing for his work environment. He found that his "field gear" had not been appropriate for his job in Sarajevo among diplomats, politicians, and electoral policymakers. Thus, he was replacing the heavy boots and other casual work clothes now back in Houston with business suits and other office attire. He gave me the lowdown on the OSCE and the international community in Bosnia-Herzegovina—in his view, a sinking ship. He was very critical of the international community—or, better put, of the internationals as a community—and of their hierarchical attitudes toward the "locals," as internationals called Bosnians at the time. He said that he felt that *locals* was a derogatory term, loaded with connotations of inferiority. His attitude resonated with a phone conversation I later overheard, where a UN grant coordinator said to the person who answered the phone, "Oh, hi," then paused and asked, "Is an international there?" Apparently, any international would have done; the anonymous local was dismissed as incapable or unworthy of discussion or decision. In perhaps the most scary or ominous part of our conversation, which had continued into an Irish pub located firmly on the tourist path, was when he called my expected work location the "Heart of Darkness" and the "Dungeon." Although the name made me nervous, he assured me that "everything goes through there. I'll be glad to know someone there who can give me information." The thing with Alex, as I came to know over the years, was that despite his criticism, he never left the community of internationals. Like many others, he became entrenched in it, loving the power, the hectic work, and the lifestyle even while being repelled and frustrated by it. He was neither the first nor the last to find it very difficult to leave, even when unhappy.

Paul was dressed for Alex's mythic field, wearing heavy boots, jeans, a flannel plaid long-sleeved shirt, and a cap. On his belt he carried one of those multiuse Leatherman tools that holds within it knives, screwdrivers, miniature saws, corkscrews, pliers, and wire cutters. At the time, he had been in Bosnia-Herzegovina on and off for four years, which meant that he had been there during the war. This gave him a cachet and knowledge possessed by few other internationals. Like Alex, Paul criticized the international community and the internationals that formed it. An extremely gregarious and forthcoming jack-of-all-trades, Paul was going to be employed as a crisis manager for the elections—a glorified gopher, he called it. However, the job suited him and kept him where he was most skilled, in the "field," solving problems as they reared up. In later years, he would be chastised for being too friendly with locals, which according to the international who reprimanded him, threatened Paul's ability to be neutral and certainly the perception of his neutrality.

As we landed abruptly at the airport, I saw the remnants of a plane that had not been as successful. The Ilyushin 76 aircraft crashed on New Year's Eve 1994 after failing to make the sharp descent required by pilots to limit exposure to antiaircraft fire. The crew missed some of the runway, ending up in a bunker set up at the end of the airport's space. They walked away unhurt, but the airplane remained there for years, serving arriving and departing guests as an impromptu memorial to the war. According to the rumor, the outskirts of the airfield were heavily mined, making removal of the aircraft extremely dangerous. This rumor made sense, given that the airfield had been fought over, that the neighboring community had been decimated, and that an escape tunnel used by fleeing Sarajevans and supply smugglers had been dug from this community, under the runways, to the foot of Mount Igman.

After we landed, a French soldier led us across the tarmac, and we lined up in a makeshift outdoor hallway where our passports were cursorily examined and checked against the flight manifest. People retrieved their bags and made off in a beeline for a spot behind a military barricade. I followed blindly, dragging my bags awkwardly toward what I hoped was a taxi stand. It turned out that shuttles were waiting for the OSCE staff and would take us to the organization's headquarters in town. A shuttle met every Tuesday Swiss flight; however, as the years progressed, friends or colleagues often greeted me and took me into town or the office in a separate OSCE vehicle rather than the shuttle.

Shelly, the woman who had hired me, had taken the shuttle to the airport to meet me. She welcomed me and quickly let me know we had to hurry because as soon as I was settled, she was leaving for a three-day vacation. In this case, getting settled meant signing a one-month contract, receiving an ID card and a cash advance on my per diem (US$90/day, paid out in deutschmarks), getting keys to and the address of my temporary accommodations, and taking a tour of my new workplace. Everything was hectic that day, and everything remained hectic for the next four years, regardless of whether a hectic state of mind was warranted.

These arrivals mark the international as a subject. It was strange to immediately embody an identity that I little understood. The identity is relational, always marking the foreigner against Bosnians who were known first as "locals" and then as "nationals." It was, to make use of a basic anthropological and sociological term, an ascribed rather than achieved status. The term was given and embodied; it was not something to which one needed to aspire. The immediateness of the identity, even though I had done nothing but arrive, was striking, as was the fact that the "international community" to which the media referred was far more than a discursive entity of country representatives in the UN's buildings in New York and Geneva or the supposed collective opinion of foreign ministries around the world. The international community in Bosnia-Herzegovina may have had institutional and organizational entities that pronounced policies and judgments in its name, but individuals created and lived it. Internationals' attitudes, behaviors, and myths shed light onto the forms of international intervention that are increasingly common in the post–cold war order. The chapters that follow analyze exactly how these interventions take shape, not in public policy discussions or parliaments but through the daily practices of the people who intervene.

HYPER-BOSNIA

International Privilege, State-Building,
and Differentiation

A colleague of mine, new to America but familiar with Bosnia-Herzegovina and the other Yugoslav successor states, confessed that he had mistaken one of the maps of Bosnia-Herzegovina on my office wall as being of "somewhere in America because of all the [English] road names." What he had seen was in fact an international mapping of the road system, an overlaid organizational system used by some if not most international agencies and created and maintained by the international military forces (fig. 5). For example, Bosnia-Herzegovina's road maps show the main Sarajevo-Mostar road as Route 17, but the road was internationally known and mapped as PacMan, the name bestowed by SFOR. All major thoroughfares as well as some secondary roads and dirt roads had SFOR names, such as Sparrow, Corbieres, Gull, Aurore, Hornblower, and Arizona. The road names were linked to the nationality of the military division in charge of the area: names of routes in the French sector were more likely to be French in origin, many routes in the U.S. sector were named after American states, and bird and animal names were common in the British sector. PacMan, a popular 1980s video game that had a character survive by eating pellets and avoiding killer ghosts, was also a main supply route for the military forces, providing nourishment and the means to avoid its own form of troublesome ghosts. The SFOR system was generally well marked throughout the country. Small yellow signs (affixed to traffic sign poles, telephone poles, and the like) noted the road name and direction every 500 to 1,000 meters. Civilian internationals kept to these roads and often referred to them by name

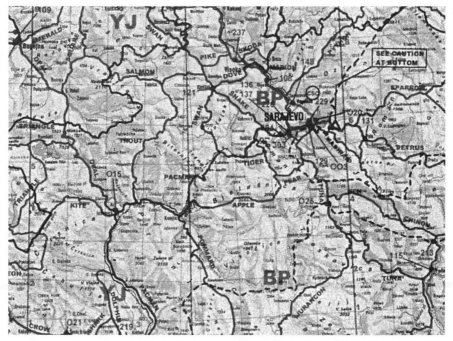

Fig. 5. International map overlays. Source: SFOR Election Map, 1998.

when giving directions or relating a story. Thus, while a Bosnian might have given directions to central Bosnia by telling a person to take the road up to the town of Jablanica, then toward Prozor and Gornji Vakuf, an international was more likely to get to central Bosnia—on the same road—by relying on the small yellow signs marking routes PacMan, Opal, and Gull. This organizational system and its referent map took a Bosnian actuality and created a separate and parallel reality for internationals from that used by Bosnians: a hyper-Bosnia.

Hyper-Bosnia, a parallel world of statelike practices and institutions laid out on top of Bosnia proper, is a hyperstate. Following Jean Baudrillard's (1994) general formulations of hyperreality, simulacra, and mimicry as conditions of postmodernity, hyper-Bosnia has the appearance of a state and of living in a state and has the trappings of a state. However, it is based on an idealized version of the state and is a reality only by proxy. The simulacra seeks to be more like the original than the original or to replace the original. Hyper-Bosnia in this manner simulates state practices and institutions such as physical, regulatory, and administrative control over roads, borders, currency and banking, security, health care, and material consumption (i.e., shopping). For some citizens in the world, the nation-state remains a primary regulator of daily life and existence, but for privileged others it has been relegated to a secondary status in the wake of globalization (see also Ong 1999). For the international elite, it is fast becoming a relic—a precious relic with which they must at times negotiate, but a relic just the same.

The rest of this chapter develops the analytical device of hyper-Bosnia, first by describing international supra- and hyperstate practices and then by analyzing Europe's place in the reconstruction of Bosnia-Herzegovina (and Bosnia's place in Europe) via consideration of the postwar projects of European (re)integration and the practices of differentiation and exclusion characteristic of internationals in Bosnia-Herzegovina. These internationals, negotiating the tricky world of state-building in a context saturated with challenges to sovereign state control, lived in a hyper-Bosnia of and for their own use. Hyper-Bosnia demonstrates current relations with state institutions, which are characterized by privatization and displacement. That the persons engaged professionally (and residentially) with creating one of the world's newest nation-states were those most disengaged with the normal or typical services and regulations of nation-states (without much attention to the efficacy of those services) emphasized social gaps between internationals and Bosnians.

Hyper-Bosnia is thus also indicative of the processes of integration and differentiation embedded in the daily life of internationals—in this case, the mostly European members of the international organizations charged with the task of building a democratic Bosnia-Herzegovina.[1] Set within a political and social framework of Europeanization, mechanisms of differentiation undermined the goal of integrating Bosnia-Herzegovina into what was an idealized, imagined, and mythic Europe. Through their aid projects and programs, internationals consciously attempted to integrate Bosnia-Herzegovina and Bosnians into their "rightful" place in a newly unified Europe. However, I found that the internationals were highly ambivalent about the European enlargement project on which they worked, simultaneously drawn to and repelled by the process and the idea. They viewed Bosnia-Herzegovina as geographically part of Europe and explicitly worked toward the goal of the country's political, social, and economic inclusion into a common and unified post–cold war Europe yet constructed boundaries that maintained difference. Boundary shifts kept Bosnians categorically separate, as non-European (or as not yet fully European) and as lacking, in some cases inherently, certain requisite features of a supposed cosmopolitan pan-European mentality. While the aid projects I researched focused mostly on the institutions Bosnia-Herzegovina lacked but needed to join a "modern" and unified Europe and to become a "functional" sovereign state, internationals' complaints and frustrations highlighted Bosnians' different worldviews and capabilities.[2] As an electoral logistician told me, "Well, they aren't really European, are they? They have a completely different attitude." The problematic differentiation and judgment of purportedly Bosnian skills, attitudes, and ethics set up a moral hierarchy for internationals that legitimated international interventions and governance structures as well as existing power relations. Hyper-Bosnia, created in part by internationals as a response to the nonfunctioning of Bosnian state institutions, contributed to a categorization and differentiation process between internationals (mostly Europeans) and Bosnians that interacted with and complicated those same internationals' professional projects of integrating Bosnia back into Europe.

Supranationality and Hyper-Bosnia

Internationals, on the whole, were marked by shallow integration into Bosnian society. As in other expatriate communities, such as diplomatic or developmental circles, most internationals felt alienated from their Bosnian hosts. Even in Sarajevo, which came the closest to welcoming the international guests (rather than openly despising them or complaining about their presence), many internationals agreed with one of my colleagues when she said, "I'd never feel at home here." Cris Shore notes that this style of tight-knit community, isolated from its larger residential context, exists among expatriate European Union civil servants in Brussels, and it is well documented among people who are displaced or uprooted (2000:161–64). He also comments that this alienation forges stronger senses of common identity and, specifically in the Brussels case, of Europeanness. How, then, does this well-documented societal separation play out in everyday experience, and what can it tell us about the larger relationship between internationals and Bosnia-Herzegovina as well as the changing role of governmental regulation? Globally, the increasing expatriate residential patterns of elite foreigners suggest profound changes in governance, particularly within the realm of sovereignty and sovereign authority. In the case of Bosnia-Herzegovina, internationals existed above and beyond the Bosnian state and outside of Bosnian society.

Although my interviews included internationals married to Bosnians, entrepreneurs with no thoughts of leaving, and several people who declared an affinity for Bosnia-Herzegovina and Bosnian society, statements such as, "Sarajevo is my all-time favorite European city," and "We love it here; life is so fulfilling," were in the minority and did not necessarily suggest any conscious attempt at integration or involvement. Even in these interviews, Bosnian "culture" was often consumed but not incorporated. Most internationals showed little evidence of willingness to become involved with the Other. Those willing to search beyond the international community for genuine friendship were few and far between and popularly viewed as brave, unusual, and often biased. Bias and the preservation of neutrality were key concerns in the international community, as in the case of Paul, whose superiors reprimanded him for being "too friendly" with local Croats. He vigorously denied the allegation, saying that he was friendly with local Serbs and Bosnian Muslims as well. Neutrality and unbiasedness were associated with lack of involvement. Other alternatives, such as unqualified friendship or engaged professionalism, were less a part of the international construction of neutrality.

Similarly, internationals were rarely heavily engaged or involved with the Bosnian-Herzegovinian state, despite their professional work in creating and reforming state institutions through such practices as running democratic elections, privatizing state-owned businesses, or training police officers. That is, internationals generally did not partake or participate in Bosnian state services or Bosnian society, nor, in many cases, were they subject to its regulatory mechanisms. Their activities and presence transcended national boundaries, authority, and interests, even as their presence and activities articulated Bosnian nation-state boundaries, authority, and interests. This disjuncture between building the Bosnian state and not participating in it has serious side effects. If the persons building and reforming the political and civil structure do not engage with state institutions, what message is transmitted to Bosnians about the state's place in modern society?

Many internationals, particularly IGO employees, also legally and financially existed outside their own nation-states; they worked for organizations that were either supra- or international in scope. They often signed statements pledging loyalty to an organization rather than to their nation and its national interests, as in this excerpt from a 1997 letter of appointment one international shared with me:

> You shall serve in your personal capacity and not as a representative of a Government or any other authority external to the [organization]. . . . You shall neither seek nor accept instructions regarding the services to be performed for the [organization] from any Government or from any authority external to the [organization].

An international's legal relationship with his or her national state begins to fade, even if the nation provides a salary, which is not always the case. For example, many internationals in Bosnia-Herzegovina were not subject to national taxation as a result of long-term foreign residency, tax treaties, foreign employment, offshore accounting strategies, and/or the politics of payment (i.e., stipends rather than salaries). They may have also been cut off from national health plans, such as French colleagues without enough residence time in France to qualify. This, of course, did not stop people from close collaboration, networking, and information dissemination with their foreign ministries or embassies, nor did it stop rumors of spying or complaints about overly influential foreign offices. At the same time, some internationals felt socially isolated from their nations. Several interviewees told me that they wished never to return to their "homelands." They were cut off from their own societies even while representing them to the rest of the world. Others commented on continuing feelings of alienation when they did return home (culture shock). An American married to a Bosnian and living in Bosnia said that she and her husband had returned only after a "failed attempt to live in Florida." Many of her American acquaintances had also had trouble returning home, with problems ranging from finding adequate or interesting jobs to "fitting in."

The internationals were supranational. On one hand, their relationship to their home nation-states were fractured and disjointed. Although their foreign ministries often had selected them for IGO work in Bosnia-Herzegovina, they were removed from their states' regulatory apparatuses. On the other hand, while they explicitly worked to construct Bosnia-Herzegovina, they were not of it, neither using its services nor being subject to its regulatory mechanisms. Internationals were involved at most only minimally in the services of public and private Bosnian institutions (e.g., banking, identification services, health care and hospitals, transportation), and they were not always subject to Bosnian governmental regulations (e.g., taxes, traffic laws, border regulations).[3] Instead, international organizations, either individually or in consortium, often provided their internationals with services that took the place of state and private services. These acts of replacement signal growing comfort with the privatization or other displacements of state control and regulation. Increasingly, governance contests sovereignty through shifts into private or corporate and suprastate regulation. Common international relationships with just two of the most central domains of the modern state—currency and border access—demonstrate the practices that formed part of the hyper-Bosnia in which internationals lived. Hyper-Bosnia also existed in other domains such as shopping, where internationals could skirt prices and taxation on items such as tobacco, electrical goods, beer, and spirits through acquisition of a PX ration card (or by piggybacking on a friend who had a ration card), and health care, where few internationals used the Bosnian system, either flying out of the country for private care in, for example, Austria, or using an IGO's health care offerings (e.g., through the international military hospitals).

The June 1998 introduction of the Bosnian convertible mark (KM) was one of the first institutions and symbols of Bosnia-Herzegovina to be accepted across the entire country. Pegged first to the German mark (deutschmark) and then to the Euro, the KM is extremely stable.[4] Unique national currencies became a part of state-building and unifying projects starting in the mid–nineteenth century. According to Eric Helleiner (2003, 1999) homogeneous and exclusive territorial currencies were seen as a means of strengthening as well as, for example, reducing currency transaction costs and controlling the money supply for macroeconomic purposes. Following this logic and despite the growing official use of foreign currencies inside domestic territories (e.g., "dollarization"), the OHR and the Central Bank of Bosnia-Herzegovina created a territorial Bosnian currency. This single currency was expected to replace the multiple currencies in use during and immediately after the war, thus helping to consolidate a single and shared Bosnian identity through common usage, and to assist in Bosnia's economic recovery. The KM's design attempted to avoid overtly political overtones. The fronts of the notes depict artists and writers, while the backs show artistic or architectural elements; however, notes issued in the Republika Srpska feature Serb writers and artists, and those issued in the Bosniac-Croat federation feature Muslim and Croat figures. Only the five KM bill shows the same author in both locales, Meša Selimović, a novelist both Serbs and Bosniacs consider to belong to "their" literature. The notes use both Latin and Cyrillic scripts and are signed by the governor of the Central Bank (at the time of my fieldwork, a New Zealander, Peter Nicholls).

Despite international backing and leadership, international organizations were slow to fully participate in the Bosnian currency regime. Several large organizations did not begin using the KM in their financial transactions (such as salary payments) until mid-2000, two years after the currency's debut. The delay resulted in part from discontent among both national and international staff about being paid in KM. Two months after the KM's introduction in 1998, a prospective international from Toronto wrote to me in my role as chief of administration for election supervision about her concerns with per diem payments in KM instead of the "normal" deutschmark. She complained that "having to exchange KM in Canada will mean a financial loss that would, for me, make this mission to Bosnia totally senseless." Concerns revolved around stability, convertibility, and convenience: the KM was not easily convertible to other currencies, and commissions would be charged.[5] However, this money (a per diem) was intended primarily for use while internationals were in Bosnia-Herzegovina. Furthermore, except for Germans, internationals had to convert their savings out of deutschmarks when leaving Bosnia-Herzegovina anyway. My faxed response back to her was not sympathetic; although our office realized that international supervisors could save money even when on very short contracts, we felt it should not be their primary rationale for coming.

Although the KM—introduced, designed, and controlled by internationally led organizations—is the official currency of sovereign Bosnia-Herzegovina, at the time I conducted my research, three of the four residential groups (Serbs, Croats, and internationals) used separate money. The Yugoslav dinar remained in widespread use until 1999, and the Croatian kuna was still popular in majority Croat areas such as western Herzegovina through at least 2000. During the tenure of the Bosnian dinar (1992–98), Bosnian merchants and landlords accepted—indeed, perhaps preferred—the deutschmark as legal tender. The Bosnian dinar was neither stable nor accepted across the entire region. International authorities, however, considered the use of the kuna and the Yugoslav dinar by Bosnians a mark of noncooperation with Bosnian state structures. What, then, can be said about internationals' resistance to the KM despite their organizations' commitment to this currency? The lack of interest in supporting these new Bosnian-Herzegovinian institutions in daily life jeopardized state-building projects and should call into question internationals' commitment to state creation. Internationals continued to work professionally to build Bosnian institutions and civil society and to assist in the country's mental, physical, and social recovery while not living or wanting to live within those structures. Like the governing elite's disinterest in national currencies in the eighteenth and early nineteenth centuries described by Eric Helleiner (1999), internationals' increasing preference for convenient and easily transferable currency rather than sovereign currency demonstrates displacements in sovereign authority and salience.

Borders are the delimiting lines of sovereignty, and all countries control or attempt to control the movement of objects and persons in and out of their marked territory. Internationals, depending on their affiliations (e.g., UN, UN partner agency, OHR, OSCE, SFOR), were not subject to the same border protocols as other persons passing into or out of Bosnian territory. These internationals had to show border agents only their organizational ID cards rather than passports. The ID card, an organizational artifact, replaced the passport as a marker of foreign and legal identity. This phenomenon was not merely accepted and taken as part of the natural order of things. Rather, stories abounded about the thrill of being able to use an ID card rather than a passport and of refusing to produce a passport when asked. Internationals I spoke with carried their passports with them when traveling to the Croatian coast, but many said they explicitly only offered their ID cards when asked for their passports just to prove that they could. ID cards were also used instead of passports when checking into hotels. On one occasion, I used mine as the proof of identity needed to open a bank account (when I was not receiving a salary from my organization and was not eligible for its banking regime).

The organizational ID card not only replaced state-issued and state-accepted (foreign or local) legal identification but also granted privilege. On a practical level, the ability to pass through borders with non-state-sanctioned identification meant that there was no need to sit in the omnipresent line of cars waiting for the border guard. Here, suprastate identity became a form of privilege. It is true, however, that the vehicle also had to carry international identification (i.e., license plate). I interviewed only two internationals who declined to register their private vehicles with diplomatic or foreign plates. One woman specifically registered her car with the appropriate Bosnian service as a political and social statement against international privilege and segregation. Another couple simply kept the valid Bosnian registration in place when they bought the car, subsequently renewing it because they "didn't like to stand out" and had strong feelings about what they called the abuse of international status:

> It doesn't make the Bosnians like you better when you cut the queue at the border. [They think,] "Who the hell do they think they are?" Why are we so special that we deserve to get to our vacations before Bosnians?

Two years later, still in Bosnia, they had bought another car and had put diplomatic plates on it, although they said they always waited in the border queue. Another colleague who agreed that cutting in front of the border line was rude nevertheless admitted to doing so from time to time. Internationals' interactions and experiences with sovereign control (e.g., borders and identification), like that of currency, suggest a blurring of governance mechanisms. Living above the real Bosnia-Herzegovina, with its regulatory policemen, borders, taxes, currency, road systems, hospitals, banks, and public transportation, internationals had an ambivalent relationship to state institutions. They became increasingly comfortable with governance from supra- or nonstate institutions, suggesting a reconfiguration of the place of governance in internationals' lives and minds. Because people have relations with the state through representatives and objects of state power (Gupta 1995), it is noteworthy that internationals may be sabotaging their own attempts at state creation through state displacement. How important is the state if the purveyors of the idea of the importance of viable state institutions act in ways that minimize or displace its authority? Furthermore, as I have suggested, having two sets of governing ideas and institutions created an order that separated and distinguished internationals, primarily European, from their Bosnian-European counterparts.

Imagining Europe and Europeans

Bosnia-Herzegovina has a history of being both part of and separate from Europe. Through its occupation by the Austro-Hungarian Empire in 1878 and annexation in 1908, Bosnia-Herzegovina became increasingly socially, economically, and politically attached to Europe (Sugar 1963). Austro-Hungarian infrastructure investment in the province included roads, a new railroad network, industrial plants, and factory buildings (Sugar 1963). Societal changes accompanied industrialization and the change in government (Donia 1981; Lockwood 1975; Malcolm 1994). Later, Yugoslavia (1918–92), of which Bosnia-Herzegovina became a part, had associations with the European Community and was much more open to markets and assistance, global trade and financial institutions, and labor migration than other socialist states (Woodward 1995b). A 1998 election poster referenced these historical connections in its proclamation "We Do Not Want War! We Want to Again Be in Europe. Think about That in September" (fig. 6), but Bosnia's European history remained in the background and sometimes the distant past for most internationals living and working in Bosnia-Herzegovina.

The Balkans have been objectified since at least the beginning of the twentieth century. Noting the Balkans as historically and geographically concrete (as opposed to an intangible Orient), Maria N. Todorova places the Balkans as inextricably linked with rather than opposed to Europe: "Unlike orientalism, which is a discourse about an imputed opposition, balkanism is a discourse about an imputed ambiguity" (1997; 17; although c.f. Bakić-Hayden 1995, Bakić-Hayden and Hayden 1992). This ambiguity was produced through continually reinvented legacies and perceptions of the Ottoman Empire, processes of modernization or Westernization in the nineteenth and twentieth centuries, and the placement of the Balkans between the West and the Orient. The Balkans, conceived out of contradictions and transitions, are seen as an European alter ego. Following Todorova, the contemporary post-war relationship between "Europe" and "Bosnia-Herzegovina" is not dialectical; exclusion cannot easily be opposed to integration. Rather, processes of integration and differentiation were conjoined through their common source in the practices of international aid workers and a shared reliance on reductionist representations of self and Other.

Otherings based on communism, war, religion, and ethnic Balkanism undoubtedly influenced but were not primary to internationals' representations of Bosnians.[6] Instead, Bosnians, already different under these various conceptualizations, more readily fit into new or modified oppositions. Internationals produced essentialist representations through daily experiences and relationships, including crass stereotyping, misunderstandings of postwar trauma and the legacies of socialism, and the practices and privileges of hyper-Bosnia and the imaginings of what it meant to be European. The production of difference was rooted in those daily activities and in internationals' residence in Bosnia-Herzegovina,

Fig. 6. Election Poster, 1998. The slogan on this poster references Bosnia's historicity as part of Europe. *(Courtesy of the Organization for Security and Co-Operation in Europe, Mission to Bosnia and Herzegovina.)*

which, in turn, constituted explicit attempts to bring Bosnia-Herzegovina into Europe politically and socially. The coupling of integration projects with practices of exclusion indicates the complexity of integration as well as the myriad ways difference is produced and located, even under and through formalized and universalized statements of equality (or integration) (see Foucault 1977). In this case, difference was not located only in identity politics but also in relationships with governing and regulating institutions such as the nation-state.

Europe—what it is and what it should be—has been a focus of debate for centuries, although the latest dominant discourses trace it to the formation of post–World War II institutions, decolonization, and immigration (see also Shore 2000). The formation of the European Union and its various precursors (i.e., European Community, Economic European Community, Common Market, European Coal and Steel Community) has merely comprised one part of the debate about who and what constitutes Europe. Other debates have centered on immigration from Eastern Europe, Africa, and the Middle East, while still others have focused on East-West distinctions, common ideologies, and religious trajectories. During the 20th century, Europe increasingly became a master symbol (Turner 1970), "an icon that embraces a whole spectrum of different referents and meanings" (Goddard, Llobera, and Shore 1994:26). It is by no means a stable object. Rather, the edges of Europe change when particular historical, political, social, or institutional interactions and processes are considered (Goddard, Llobera, and Shore 1994; Lewis and Wigen 1997). Thus, Europe is best viewed as a "configuration of knowledge," debated, disputed, and experienced differentially through space and time. While recognizing diverse, heterogeneous, and dynamic Europes, it would be foolhardy to discount the competitions for conceptual hegemony in the political and social arena; some narratives are more dominant than others (Goddard, Llobera, and Shore 1994). "Europe" is increasingly a political ideal and a mobilizing metaphor associated with European Union neoliberal institutions, multiculturalism, and civil liberties. In Bosnia-Herzegovina, the narrative was deployed as a strategy calling Europeans to identify with a particular definition of Europe. The call—a promise of future benefits and prosperity—reached out to both Bosnians and internationals. Internationals related to this narrative through self-representation; they were promise benefactors as well as promise holders. Bosnians, by contrast, were entreated to accept the call, to sign up for tutorials in modern self- and state-governance.

Press releases from international organizations in Bosnia-Herzegovina such as the OHR and the UN vividly demonstrate Bosnia-Herzegovina's relationship to the idea of a political and institutional Europe. The narrative woven through press releases describes an ideal Europe ready to include Bosnia-Herzegovina into its fold. European institutions were willing to integrate Bosnian-Herzegovinian institutions after they adopted standardized bureaucratic and legal norms. The European Broadcasting Union's 2000 decision to accept the Public Broadcasting Service (PBS) of Bosnia-Herzegovina as a member was but one example, as an OHR press release demonstrates.

> The High Representative informed the Presidency that the PBS of [Bosnia-Herzegovina] has been accepted as a member of the European Broadcasting Union (EBU). This is an extremely encouraging step that will bring sports and other attractive programming to all the citizens of [Bosnia-Herzegovina], including the Olympic games in Sydney. The EBU's decision marks the beginning of a new era for broadcasting in this country. Describing the work of the Transfer Agent, the High Representative said the scale of the problems inherited from the former broadcasting system should not be underestimated. A comprehensive financial and technical review has revealed that sweeping changes are necessary to bring public broadcasting in line with current European standards and practice (OHR 2000a).

In this case, membership was given prior to reform, likely because of the High Representative's strong involvement in establishing the service, issuing legally binding decisions, and naming board members. According to the OHR, membership would bring about the reforms necessary for Bosnian-Herzegovinian institutions to come "in line with current European standards and practices" as well as to allow greater outside influence on media programming and implicitly, by extension, on Bosnian society (OHR 2000a).

More often, membership in European clubs was conditional. For example, Bosnia-Herzegovina's ascension to the Council of Europe depended on the passage of an election law.[7] Likewise, European Union accession required certain, tangible steps. Joining more discursively abstract structures such as the "European family" relied on broad and unspoken measures, such as educational and tax reform, without any definitive statements about what that reform entailed. Invocations of "Europe" called for Bosnia-Herzegovina to conform, reform, and introduce particular standards, unmarked but surely neoliberal in character. For example, according to another press release, Bosnia-Herzegovina's youth needed different "education and expertise" to succeed as Europeans. The unmarked, unlabeled, and thus unquestioned deployment of European traits acted to depoliticize and naturalize powerful definitions of "appropriate" fiscal policy or "expertise" rather than to leave them open to debate and contestation. Further, "Europe" took on a superlative essence and symbolism. European internationals used this dominant representation of Europe as a form of identification for themselves and as a bribe for wary Bosnians.

One of the most visible projects explicitly linked with Europeanness and Europeanization during this research was the election law campaign (ELIC). All of the postwar elections had occurred under the authority of Rules and Regulations written by the Provisional Election Commission, which derived its authority from the OSCE's mandate to organize elections under Dayton. Starting in 1999 and lasting over a year, the ELIC project incorporated legal drafting, public opinion surveys and focus groups, lobbying, and marketing. The drafting officially included international lawyers, Bosnian lawyers from each ethnic group/political party, and various technical and legal consultant experts. During the drafting process, public opinion was solicited via local roundtables, discussion sessions, web questionnaires and chats, voter attitude and election reform polls, and media discussions. The Tell Clearly What You Want campaign concluded that citizens wanted more accountability from elected officials, more women's participation, and more effective representation. High levels of citizen disenchantment with and skepticism about Bosnian politics and capabilities were noted. Public awareness and advocacy of the election law focused on reform in six areas: accountability, fairness and equity, multiethnicity and reconciliation, representative government, transparency, and upholding the peace treaty.

Discussion of Europe and European standards was largely absent during the drafting period, instead surfacing during the subsequent public advertising campaign and lobbying efforts. Ambassadors and the High Representative urged Bosnians to support the proposed election law and to ask their politicians to adopt the measure. International leaders repeatedly stated that the country would not be fully sovereign, functional, or European until it had an election law. Further, membership in the European institutional clubs and councils was made contingent on the passage of an election law. The advertising campaign for the law relied heavily on European symbolism, counting on the draw of Europe to garner popular and political support for the draft law. Despite heavy international pressure, both cajoling and coercive, the election law was not passed when it was first brought before Parliament in October 1999, nor did it pass in multiple introductions. Despite concessions and changes to the law and continuing appeals and invocations of Europe, nearly two years passed before the houses of Parliament passed the law in August 2001. Advertisements urging the law's passage textually and symbolically evoked the possibility of connection to Europe. One linked signing the election law with entrance into the ring of Europe, symbolized by the twelve stars of the European Union. Another, more evocative, depicts Europe the savior, symbolized this time by a halo of European Union stars, holding the election law as a book (or tablet of commandments?) and showing it to a dapperly dressed Bosnia-Herzegovina (fig. 7). The ads also place responsibility and accountability on Bosnians— "The way into **Europe** depends on **You.**" This slogan neatly condenses the ideas of ownership and nationalization that the international community tried to bring to state-building and reconstruction projects. That is, Bosnians should participate in and control their social, economic, and political affairs. They could, after all, write their destinies themselves with the new writing instruments that the election law provided.

Europe's appeal was not strong enough to overcome opposition by political parties and members of Parliament. Did Bosnia-Herzegovina reject its place in Europe? Not entirely. Some of the opposition rested on perceived discrepancies between the draft law and existing European human rights standards. Much of the remaining reluctance centered on how centrally ethnicity should figure in the selection of House of Peoples (the upper house) delegates and the presidency, currently a tripartite rotating council (see also fig. 21). However, an international who had worked in the Tell What You Want campaign and the subsequent lobbying effort for the law told me, "I don't think any law would have passed; [Bosnian politicians'] unwillingness to cooperate supersedes all other factors and desires." International campaigning clearly overestimated the power of European symbolism and perhaps misunderstood the stakes for Bosnian politicians who were not eager to pass the law.

Internationals' self-understanding of the international role in Bosnia-Herzegovina relied on two concepts: assisting Bosnia-Herzegovina to take a place in a unified Europe (i.e., development) and war recovery (i.e., humanitarian aid). As a raison d'être, the international community necessarily relied on the idea of Europe as a goal, a benefit, and a marketing strategy for Bosnia-Herzegovina; even when it failed to deliver, it remained in use. The European Union star circle was frequently called into action, as, for example on a voter registration poster that spatially merged the European Union's yellow stars with the white stars of Bosnia-Herzegovina's flag. Other instances of bringing Europe symbolically into

Fig. 7. This 1999 billboard proclaimed, "The way into Europe depends on you." The figure on the left represents Bosnia-Herzegovina, and the book is labeled "Draft Election Law." The text in the lower left corner reads, "Tell clearly what you want in your election system." *(Courtesy of the Organization for Security and Co-Operation in Europe, Mission to Bosnia and Herzegovina.)*

public debate and consciousness used, for example, the European map (cut into puzzle pieces with Bosnia-Herzegovina being placed into the almost complete puzzle). These invocations of Europe represented one strategy for constituting a new inclusive, imagined community (see Anderson 1983; Shore 2000).

The Borders of Belonging: Exclusions

Interacting with the Europeanization efforts were various on-the-ground interpretations, representations, and actions vis-à-vis Bosnia-Herzegovina as a state and Bosnians as a people that suggest that internationals had highly ambivalent and complex attitudes toward Bosnian inclusion in the idea of Europe. First, as discussed, Bosnia-Herzegovina did not fit into the new world order as experienced by a highly mobile and cosmopolitan professional elite. Increasing globalization, privatization, and the displacement of state governance and public space were at odds with the emphasis placed on building Bosnia-Herzegovina's nation-state and its services. Second, many internationals viewed Bosnians as lacking the proper discipline or self-governance techniques that successful "Europeans" were thought to hold. That is, concurrent with hyper-Bosnia were mechanisms of exclusion that acted to keep Bosnians out of an imagined common Europeanness. These boundaries of exclusion relied less on previous East-West distinctions of the cold war—socialist governance versus liberalism and capitalism—and more on decontextualized differences in attitude and behavior. Frustration appeared to be rooted in Bosnians' perceived inability (or lack of willingness) to put the war in the past and to do what was necessary to join Europe and be European. The dominant narrative was that Bosnians simply did not have the "proper attitude."[8] This narrative was most visible in the work interactions between Bosnian and international employees at international organizations and within the greater context surrounding the implementation of ownership and nationalization programs. Emerging from the idea that Bosnians should take ownership of their social, economic, and political affairs, these efforts sought to transfer responsibility and authority to Bosnians in state-building activities such as elections, human rights monitoring, and law drafting.

Formal international statements promoting Bosnian ownership and nationalization of state-building processes countered individual international complaints of Bosnians' inability to engage in forward thinking and problem solving. "Good workers" of course existed as well and were highly valued and sought after by international staffing personnel as assistants and sometimes colleagues. Indeed, a British woman who had eight years' work experience in Bosnia (1996–2004) told me,

> I adore my staff and colleagues. I don't want you to take this the wrong way, but the national workers for international agencies behave differently because they have worked for us. They are more proactive and less lazy. And they're loyal. They have also taught me a lot, a lot about listening to people or taking time over coffee, for example. It doesn't have to be a hectic go go go.

These nationals were considered something of an anomaly, to have exceptional, non-Bosnian character (whether they possessed these qualities naturally or through training by internationals). Although internationals, when pressed, sometimes acknowledged that most jobs open to Bosnians were low skilled and low responsibility and that many Bosnians had been trained in other professions but needed the money provided by jobs for which they lacked the appropriate backgrounds, in general this knowledge faded in the face of daily struggles to accomplish tasks. In addition, the "obstructionist" (i.e., anti-Dayton) politics of leading and powerful political parties continued to taint the representation of all

Bosnians. At both the institutional and personal levels, internationals devoted surprisingly little attention to socialist legacies. Although internationals blamed the prior socialist government and mentality for a variety of ills, such as dependency, low tolerance of risk, and market obstacles, this rationale was deemphasized in daily life. Rather, Bosnians' negative qualities, which were perceived as hampering their progress into the modern capitalist arena, were often naturalized and taken out of their historical context.

Programs of nationalization and their implementation on the ground demonstrate internationals' and the international bureaucratic structure's ambivalence toward Bosnian ownership of governance structures. As a colleague confided to me in mid-2000, "For Bosnia-Herzegovina to take control, the international community must be willing to cede some." His comments came two years into a nationalization effort he was caught up in, both in terms of trying to stay employed himself and the hierarchical tensions of postwar relations between the purported helpers and the purported helped. In 1998, the OSCE began a nationalization program with the goal of having each department be at least 50 percent national staff. This effort succeeded in many departments, at least on the surface. For example, by the end of 1999, most Election Officers were nationals who without exception had attended an intensive electoral course based at Essex University in England. These institutional changes toward more national responsibility, expertise, and authority led to on-the-ground resistance however. A three-time election worker defiantly asked, "How can there be free and fair elections if the nationals are in charge?" This remark, in response to seeing a chain-of-command chart that showed her position under a national officer, pinpoints the agony and frustration felt in the spring of 2000 by internationals and nationals alike as short-term electoral internationals for the first time found themselves reporting to national staff. The changes in the scope of international participation—from active to more passive oversight—also produced a fair amount of frustration. The losses in internationals' authority and responsibility (as well as privilege) brought to light judgments of Bosnians' capabilities: they were considered incapable of professional neutrality and lacking in the skills needed independently to organize, manage, and implement polling and counting procedures.

During the next election period—in response to the difficulties many national staff encountered with international subordinates—short-term internationals were warned that they were going to report to a "national" and that under no circumstances were they to think of themselves as above this national Election Officer. Training for international supervisors now specifically mentioned the chain of command, labeling who was international and who national and reassuring the internationals, used to feelings of authority, that the national officers were indeed competent. Similarly, time during a staff meeting of national Election Officers was reserved for discussion of how national staff could prepare and manage internationals' egos and condescension. Long-term internationals explained that they knew their Bosnian colleagues could do the work satisfactorily but that the short-term supervisors who lacked the benefits of working with Bosnians for extended periods, were ignorant about Bosnian workers' capabilities. A senior Election Officer from Canada told his (national) staff that short-termers tend to come into the country with particular expectations and assumptions and to act accordingly. Nothing, of course, was this clear-cut. The decision to hire these short-term internationals had been made by other, unknown internationals who perhaps appreciated individual Bosnian colleagues but whose decisions continued to help construct Bosnians as inadequate for the tasks at hand.

For example, officials decided to switch from full to partial supervision for the spring 2000 municipal elections. Under full supervision (used during the previous three elections), each polling station had an international supervisor watching and sometimes participating in the polling and counting processes. In this election, however, one supervisor was assigned to five or six polling stations. Informants explained to me that polling station committees, with two or three previous democratic elections under their belts, were now knowledgeable about the general polling procedures and that fraud, inconsistencies, and irregularities had substantially decreased.[9] Full supervision was thus no longer necessary.[10] Counteracting this newfound confidence in the professionalism of Bosnian electoral officials was a late-stage request for additional advisers and supervisors to be in country four to six weeks ahead of the election. Although not large in number (around 100) compared to the approximately 800 polling supervisors, the added supervisors constituted a way of soothing international fears of an impending disaster. According to a midlevel international election official, the main task of the new additions was to be there "just in case" and to assist the (national) Election Officers as needed. However, because of the existing power dynamic, the new observers did not constitute "added help" but rather added assurance and insurance for the internationals who questioned Bosnians' competency and professionalism. Thus, it came as no surprise that many of these last-minute advisers tried to take control and exert their power as internationals and electoral experts. A few national Election Officers later confided in me that the month had been a nightmare of power struggles and frustration over proving their competence. Some supervisors knew and criticized their roles. As one wrote in his diary,

> It bothers me that it seems that the focal point of my role is to ensure smooth elections—not for the sake of future democracy in Bosnia-Herzegovina and Republika Srpska, but for the sake of being able to say that the elections we organised were successful!

Bosnians were constructed in opposition to internationals and excluded from any identity associated with desirable or modern traits. Internationals' negative perception of Bosnians, valid or not, maintained a categorical exclusion from Europe based on their vaguely defined "non-European" attitudes and capabilities.

What Does a State Look Like? State-Building and Transnational Governmentality

Counterexamples attest to the complexity of integration politics in an era of transnational governmentality. Some of these examples are as mundane as a refugee lawyer who consciously cut back on his legal cases so that he could pass them to his national assistant, whom he self-consciously treated as and considered an equal colleague, or a logistician who socialized with Bosnians because he liked them better than his international colleagues. The story of Maja, a Bosniac woman living in Sarajevo and working for an international organization, may be particularly salient. After her apartment was robbed, Maja called the police, and they came to investigate. The next day at work, Susanna, an international working in the agency's security department, learned of the burglary and became upset that Maja had not informed the department of the incident. I did not think it unusual that Maja had called the police—as could be expected by a Bosnian citizen or, really, any citizen or foreigner in any country. But Susanna argued that the security department should also have been called—and in fact should have been called first so that department employees could have been present at the crime scene to assist the police (who were already assisted by UN police officers). She repeatedly said, "We serve all agency personnel, not just the international ones." This sentiment was uncommon among internationals and within international organizations; most generally acknowledged that Bosnian institutions served Bosnian citizens and international or foreign institutions served internationals. This small story, then, constitutes a statement both on the possibility of inclusion and equality for Bosnians and on the depth of international exclusion from (and intrusion into) sovereign state institutions.

The practices of hyper-Bosnia reflect contemporary modes of state and self-governance at work in the world and especially in the world's "trouble spots." The hyperstate state-building circuit—in places such as East Timor, Haiti, Palestine, and Kosovo—demonstrates an emerging mode of transnational governmentality rooted in differentiation, privilege, and state displacement.

DOING NOTHING

The Practices of Passivity

The modes of international intervention in Bosnia-Herzegovina during the first years of postwar reconstruction were, on the surface, action centered. Internationally funded and administered projects actively intervened in Bosnians' lives and institutions. Interventionist projects such as managing food distribution networks, protecting returning refugees, holding conflict mediation forums, and training farmers in agricultural techniques affected both the physical and social landscapes of Bosnia-Herzegovina, erasing the visual and mechanical reminders of war as well as repairing and creating (and destroying) social, political, and economic relations. However, another, outwardly more passive phenomenon was also occurring. Beyond the bustle of project activity—the signature of the international community—lay another important aspect of international intervention: just being there. This mode of intervention is marked simply by the existence of international bodies. Arguing that the passive presence of internationals is also a social practice of the transformative ideology of international intervention, this chapter details what internationals do when they are doing nothing.

Amid responsibility-packed jobs and a dominant sense of urgency and project importance while on the job, international workers often expressed a sense of helplessness or jadedness about the utility of much of their work-related action. Instead, some internationals emphasized certain functionalities to their mere existence and the power of their presence in Bosnia-Herzegovina. The utility of presence was not always openly acknowledged but can be analytically teased out of the actions and rationale of personal, technical, and bureaucratic decisions and processes. References to international presence were ubiquitous during my fieldwork. Official statements and publications within governmental and nongovernmental international organizations and internationals' speech were peppered with references to "my presence" and "our presence." The meanings of presence for international workers were diverse, ranging from symbolic compassion to rule enforcement to pedagogy. Regardless, no explicit action was required on their part, only existence. Presence—an emic category and a fact on the ground—was a project and an intervention in itself, not just a logistical means of carrying out other projects.

I distinguish a conceptual usage of Presence from the descriptive (i.e., presence) with a capitalized *Presence*. While textually awkward, this usage suggests particularity and specificity; I also mean to infer through this usage that Presence might be analytically treated as a conglomeration of practices. Importantly, Presence is not necessarily functional; it did not necessarily do what internationals thought it did, claimed it did, or wanted it to do. Nonetheless, it made up part of the tool kit of international intervention strategies. My purpose here is not to comment on the successes or failures of Presence or its material effects but rather to trace the contours of internationals' practices of Presence.[1] Understanding the practices of international Presence requires a broadening of conceptions of Presence past a limited understanding of it as simply a necessary condition for the design and implementation of humanitarian and transformative projects. International Presence, which allowed aid projects to move forward, transforming Bosnia-Herzegovina's physical and social landscape, also constitutes a practice of transformation.

Driven by an ideology of transformation similar to missionization or colonization, Presence intersects with issues of modern governance, both self-government and government of subjects. Presence was centrally incorporated into a system of governance (of control, of conduct) brought to Bosnia-Herzegovina by international organizations. For example, democratization projects, largely imagined and then actualized by internationals, attempted to inculcate the Bosnian-Herzegovinian population with "new," "proper" values and behaviors based on specific, value-laden understandings of a liberal order.[2] Transformations undoubtedly have occurred and will continue to occur as a consequence of the processes and practices proselytized and set in motion. However, they will equally undoubtedly not occur as planned, for those targeted for reform respond multiply with complicity, resistance, and accommodation (as seen in past colonial, missionary, and development encounters as well as within postsocialist transitions) (see Burke 1996; Cohn 1996; Comaroff and Comaroff 1991; Merry 2000; Scott 1998; Verdery 2003). Side effects and unintended outcomes may take on inadvertent importance (Ferguson 1999). Understanding transformation schemes clearly requires understanding how they are conducted, not just their effects.

Media reports, politicians, and public policy pundits frequently bandy about the term *international presence,* deeming it necessary to protect against attacks on persons, material assets, and/or territorial integrity. Consequently, a presence of a military nature is often assumed. The U.S. military presence in West Germany or Berlin during the cold war offers one example of this type of international presence. In political and popular discourse, the military presence guarded the West (with weapons) from potential offensive attacks by the Soviet Union and provided the West with a sense of security. Similarly, the mandate of the UN Blue Helmets in Bosnia-Herzegovina (UNPROFOR) during the 1992–95 war was primarily to provide protection and a sense of security for the inhabitants of declared safe areas (UN 1996).[3] While much journalistic commentary and academic analysis exists regarding the Blue Helmets' successes and failures in protecting civilians and the shortcomings of unarmed and/or nonaggressive peacekeeping forces, especially in regard to the massacre at Srebrenica (see Corwin 1999; Hodge 1995; Human Rights Watch 1995; Netherlands Institute for War Documentation 2002; Post et al. 1994; Rieff 1995), here I simply intend to emphasize the intent behind the international presence and its salience in global politics in general and in Bosnia-Herzegovina in particular. Military and civilian international interventions—Presence—are considered security solutions (see also Duffield 2001).

It is no surprise that war and military imagery are linked to Bosnia-Herzegovina and to the idea of Presence more generally. However, the force of military Presence overshadows a broader international Presence, figuratively and physically. The transformations of Bosnia-Herzegovina occurred through a civilian Presence, its projects, and the power within those projects. Civilian organizations took up most of the burden of reconstruction and recovery after the signing of the peace treaty in late 1995. Accordingly, the emphasis of Presence shifted from military to civilian in nature.[4] Civilian organizations played crucial roles during the war as well, but attention centered on military endeavors. After the conflict, the military Presence, though still important, faded from the media and political limelight as armed hostilities eased and stopped.

The boundaries between civilian and military Presence are not rigid or distinct but fluid. Civilian institutions depended on the continued military Presence for security (just like the Bosnian residents) as well as infrastructural support and project assistance.[5] For example, military troops often accompanied returning refugees, especially those with UN High Commission for Refugees logistical and financial support, during visits to their villages, during rebuilding efforts, and when they returned. Similarly, most international workers relied on SFOR, using military medical facilities for personal health care and military maps during personal and professional travels. Further complicating the civilian-military relationship, the civilian Presence may have also served to provide security and feelings of security, in part because threats on foreign civilians would likely have brought in military forces.

Asking what meanings the people involved gave to their Presence, I show that Presence is a key aspect of international intervention and of Bosnian democracy. Indeed, as a set of social practices and in its passivity, Presence acts as a form of governance—a mechanism of international and democratic power. I have separated Presence in Bosnia-Herzegovina into three conceptual modes: sheer, mere, and peer. Each worked individually and in conjunction with the others as mechanisms of international intervention and governance. These three modes are part of a model of transformation that international agencies claimed as the proper course for postwar, postsocialist Bosnia-Herzegovina. Furthermore, they formed an integral part of a strategy of governance based on the body. The international body had an assumed skill set identified as democratic, neutral, authoritative, and knowledgeable. Sheer Presence refers to the quantity of international personnel resident in Bosnia-Herzegovina. It represents the force and the reach of the "international community" through its multiple bodies. Mere Presence, also with its source in the body of the international, contrasts with his or her explicitly professional tasks. Concurrent with their other job duties, international workers played an important role by passively "just being there." Finally, international Presence had implicit and explicit pedagogical implications. Here, I do not mean specific training programs for Bosnians on such subjects as advocacy or fiscal responsibility; rather, certain international workers consciously and unconsciously attempted to demonstrate proper behavior and professionalism in their interactions with Bosnian colleagues and society in the hopes that Bosnians would learn from the example. Internationals hoped that through their Presence, Bosnians would become peers.

To trace the three manifestations of this transformative ideology in Bosnia-Herzegovina—sheer, mere, and peer Presence—I analyze the presence of international supervisors in electoral activities such as voter registration, polling, counting, and campaign monitoring. International supervisors were meant to ensure that the Bosnian elections were conducted in a free and fair manner and that established election rules and regulations were followed. In many cases, supervisors were responsible for electoral integrity, as seen by their sole handling of "sensitive material" and having to sign or cosign electoral documents, such as ballot delivery receipts and accounting forms. In three of the five postwar elections between 1997 and 2000, Polling Supervisors signed the final result forms, thus carrying formal responsibility for the conduct of the election in their specific polling stations. During these three elections (in 1997 and 1998), each polling station was supervised by a Polling Supervisor. For the other two elections (in 2000), supervision moved from full to partial, with each Polling Supervisor responsible for between four and six polling stations. However, the supervisors were no longer required to certify the results with their signatures or to carry the forms, ballots, and other materials back to the local or municipal electoral commission's storage centers. They were no longer solely, bureaucratically responsible for upholding electoral integrity.

Thomas Carothers (1997b) details the growing trend of international election observation, arguing that although it benefits elections by detecting/preventing fraud and strengthening standards, it is plagued by the problems of unqualified observers, an overemphasis on the election day, and poor application of standards. If we add the idea of Presence to his line of thought, a new conclusion might be reached and incorporated into his important critique: it may not matter much what observers do or do not do. In the following pages, I analyze the work done (or thought to be done) by just being there. The transformative potential of passivity can be seen in supervisors' self-perceptions, their perceptions by other electoral staff, and technical and bureaucratic decisions and processes. Their existential presence, beyond actively ensuring free and fair elections, was itself a governance strategy, aimed at controlling and transforming the conduct of Bosnia-Herzegovina, Bosnians, and Bosnian democracy.

Sheer Presence

You can't spit in Bosnia without hitting an international.
—An international, 1998

Sheer Presence refers to the overwhelming number and scope of internationals, international organizations, and international funding in Bosnia-Herzegovina: the magnitude of it all. International personnel in Bosnia-Herzegovina probably numbered between 28,000 and 70,000 in the five years after the war, decreasing over time. At its high mark, the international population equaled approximately 2 percent of the postwar Bosnian populace of 3.5 million residents (UN Development Programme 1998).[6] Military forces accounted for the bulk of personnel, with between 20,000 and 64,000 soldiers, with the figure again decreasing over time, and thus constituted a significant portion (roughly 70–90 percent) of the international Presence.[7] However, the civilian international population was never insignificant. In 2001, the three main organizations alone—the UN, OHR, and OSCE—employed almost 3,000 internationals.[8] During my fieldwork, international staff at those three agencies alongside the approximately 180 INGOs, 28 diplomatic missions or embassies, governmental agencies such as the U.S. Agency for International Development and the European Community Monitoring Mission, and numerous business consultants probably ranged between 5,000 and 8,000.[9] Other estimates held that in Sarajevo alone, 15,000 foreign citizens were present every day (Papić 2001:10).

The sheer number of internationals served as a constant, visible reminder of the international community's might. Internationals were the bodily representation and manifestation of the political, military, and economic power used by international organizations and individuals to force issues, to frame the terms of reconstruction, and to implement policies. This fact was welcomed, tolerated, grudgingly accepted, or actively resented, depending on one's political perspective. Speaking four and a half years after the signing of the peace agreement, Kemal, a Bosniac from Mostar working as an interpreter for an aid agency, worried about the possible reduction or withdrawal of SFOR troops. He said he would not feel safe without them and estimated that the chance of going back into war topped 50 percent if SFOR pulled out. In his mind, SFOR was keeping violent actions at bay, particularly in the Brčko area, where only a very small strip of land separated hostile groups.

> If Brčko starts to fight again, all of Bosnia-Herzegovina will again be drawn into war. This is a certainty without SFOR.

Similarly, one of my neighbors welcomed the international interventions, saying that the "war was simple fascism." For him, international Presence assisted those Bosnians who opposed fascist government and society and helped fight tacit or material support of fascists. Both Kemal and my neighbor felt protected by the large-scale Presence of internationals. These Bosnians were not uncritical or unaware of the force of internationals and international organizations to press particular policies, yet they believed that the benefits outweighed the negatives and in some cases that the policies put forth were best. As Kemal said, the international community constituted "a push in the right direction."

On a more individual level, internationals offered protection through their Presence. Prior to 1998, Bosnians traveling for work purposes to areas where they might be in danger or where they felt nervous commonly received international escorts. As late as 2000, en route to a mountain village, a Bosniac colleague confided to me that he would not have traveled there by himself. He felt safer next to me. This worked both ways: international workers I interviewed assured me that nothing would possibly happen to their (Bosnian) drivers and interpreters when in areas controlled by other ethnic groups. In fact, most looked askance at the question itself. They believed the ethnic hostilities were irrelevant for them and for those in their immediate sphere.

Bosnians and internationals alike also criticized the international community's coercive power. Bosnian critics, often leaders or members of nationalist political parties, referenced the international Presence as an occupying force and as a form of colonialism. Many internationals also readily admitted the colonial or missionary tenor of the international interventions. Indeed, it was hard to miss. As an American election worker, Martha, candidly explained during an interview, "Democracy is my Bible." Internationals candidly criticized the "international community," its hierarchical structure, and its paternalistic behavior, but few felt that intervention itself was problematic. As James Ferguson writes,

> If "development" is today from time to time challenged, it is still almost always challenged in the name of "*real* development"—there are debates on how best to convert the nation-state, but there is not debate on conversion itself. (1994:xiv)

The same could be said for international liberal and neoliberal interventions: criticism is couched in terms of the intervention being flawed in its implementation, not in its essence. Internationals and international projects proselytized the graces that accrue to converts to and adherents of democracy, privatization, the rule of law and transparency. That conversion formed part of intervention's goals was no secret. Internationals who spoke to me specifically regarding the nature of the international interventions attempted to balance what they thought was a necessary change to sociopolitical life, their role in helping bring it about, and (to varying degrees) their discomfort with a system that hierarchically placed them above Bosnians and into separate social, political, economic, and legal existences.

Social Visibility: The Power of Sheer Presence

An important aspect of sheer international Presence, beyond the political and military strength and resources (and perhaps in conjunction with it), is what I term *social visibility,* by which I mean the implicit and explicit show of international concern, resources, actions, and being. To international workers, the magnitude and scale of the international Presence represented the importance placed on Bosnia-Herzegovina (and "fixing" Bosnia-Herzegovina)—as if to say, "After all, look at the dedication of so many resources to it." In internationals' minds, social visibility primarily constituted a positive feature of Presence.[10]

Internationals and international agencies in Bosnia-Herzegovina spent a lot of time and resources making themselves visible. Because of their sheer numbers—the magnitude of their presence—they were by no means invisible, nor was their money. Expenditures by internationals (not their organizations) totaled 2.5 billion deutschmarks per year (Papić 2001:9); by contrast, the Bosnian gross domestic product in 1998 was 6.9 billion deutschmarks.

> This influx is creating a completely artificial virtual picture of Sarajevo, a picture of normal life, a European city, without any basis in the reality of the [Bosnian-Herzegovinian] economy and the city itself. (Papić 2001:10)

Estimates showed that each Sarajevo resident benefited 150 deutschmarks more per month (42 percent of the national average monthly salary) than other Bosnians as a consequence of the overwhelming social and financial Presence of internationals in Sarajevo (Papić 2001:10).

Internationals often remarked on their financial Presence, mostly within a discursive framework of "dangerous dependency." "What will happen to Bosnia-Herzegovina," some internationals and Bosnians asked, "when the internationals pull out? How will Bosnians survive economically?" For example, success for many restaurants depended on the ability to attract international clientele. In one case, a woman's group received aid funds to open a café/restaurant. The restaurant's signature salads, named after world cities, used variety to appeal to internationals bored by the typical Bosnian salad. The menu exclaims, "Not just vegetables!"[11]

NOT JUST VEGETABLES: OUR SALADS!

SALONICCO (tomatoes, cucumbers, onions, feta cheese, black olives) 5 KM

OTTAWA (lettuce, walnuts, gorgonzola, apples, celery) 5 KM

MEXICO CITY (brown beans, white beans, chick peas, corn, spring onion) 4 KM

BOSTON (lettuce, tuna, tomato, gouda, black olives, corn) 5 KM

ROME (mushrooms, parmesan, lettuce) 4,5 KM

SYDNEY (French beans, potatoes, black olives) 4,5 KM

TUNBUKTU (lettuce, tomato, anchovies, black olives) 4 KM

BUENOS AIRES (lettuce, tomato, mozzarella, mushrooms, peppers, ham/chicken/salami) 5,5 KM

SARAJEVO (tomato, lettuce, onion, kajmak, cucumber) 4 KM

MOSCOW (mixed vegetables, mayonnaise) 4 KM

SANTA FE (chicken, lettuce, tomato, corn, celery, mayonnaise) 5,5 KM

The restaurant, Fantasia, which I originally thought was off the beaten track, is not; it is located but a mere 500 meters from the current OHR building. The High Representative visited Fantasia to mark International Women's Day, March 8, 2001, using the restaurant as a success story. However, it was much less clear how the restaurant would sustain itself without its international clientele. Many new enterprises, of course, did not rely on international Presence and the accompanying money. The director of a microcredit organization told me that "by far," the majority of his clients were "opening café/bars and hair salons." He was not confident of the ultimate success or business model of these enterprises, but at least they were theoretically self-sufficient.

Another aspect of social visibility was project advertising. International colleagues sometimes sighed at the glut of project billboards (e.g., located at the beginning of a village or at the entrance of a building). However, they were also considered necessary strategies for positive propaganda. For example, CARE, the Danish Refugee Council, the UN High Commission for Refugees, or any international organization might be funding and implementing the rehabilitation of a water treatment facility, the demining of agricultural fields, or the reconstruction of destroyed homes. Near the site location, a sign would note the project title, beneficiaries, and aid providers. In one case, a large INGO helped negotiate and fund the rehabilitation of a well-traveled city street (i.e., installing streetlights, filling mortar craters) that had come under heavy attack during the war. The NGO let the newly elected city leaders take credit for the improvements with the idea that doing so would lend credibility to these moderately cooperative leaders. However, as an international staff person told me, although the NGO was pleased to support city politicians, the organization's leaders "would have liked to at least have been invited to the opening ceremony." Their significant contributions were simply ignored. Advertisements and publicity such as project billboards attempted to inform the Bosnian public of the activities of internationals and international organizations and to let Bosnians know that the foreigners were not sitting idle even if their work was not readily apparent.

Other types of international advertising beyond project announcements included billboards, radio jingles, television spots, and magazine ads. A press officer told me that he had to negotiate with press officers from other international organizations for billboard space because Bosnia had too few billboards for all the messages the INGOs wanted to get out. Ads sometimes promoted the actions of internationals, such as SFOR's Ovdje za Mir (Here for Peace) public relations campaign. Large billboards featured a peace dove with the caption, "SFOR: Here for peace, here for Bosnia-Herzegovina." Other flyers promoted SFOR's work on, for example, rebuilding bridges: "So [you] can be in contact with your neighbor again." Other times, media advertising implored Bosnians to think in particular ways. OSCE asked them to think about corruption, announced election dates, marketed democracy as progress (see Paley 2000 for similar marketing in post-Pinochet Chile), reminded them about illegal occupancy, and urged tolerance.

The election effort in Bosnia-Herzegovina offers a particularly good example of international social visibility and the symbolism of numbers and resources. It was a large enterprise, both in terms of personnel and resources. The international population peaked during election periods with the arrival of hundreds of medium- and short-term international election staff. On Election Day 1998, with an overall budget of US$39 million, the Election Department had more than 10,000 persons under its domain. This figure included approximately 2,625 polling supervisors, an interpreter for each supervisor, and, on average, one driver for every two supervisors. In most field offices, an extra building had to be rented to house the Election Department. According to one electoral administrator, the department endured jealousy from other departments because of the attention elections demanded and received. In the words of an international logistics officer, "Anything elections want, they get. If they want 100 mobile phones, they can have them, tomorrow. All of our resources are at their disposal. Democracy is our top priority for Bosnia." She was not necessarily pleased with the leverage elections wielded, but she was following high-level orders and policy. However, the Election Department also dealt with the problem of being a short-term project in a larger universe of ongoing processual programs emphasizing human rights and democratization. "Why," an ambassador once asked a regional electoral officer, "should 'casual labor' get special treatment?"

The Polling supervisors and their local support staff made up the bulk of personnel, but the Election Department also included international election officers and support staff at each field office and senior election officers and support staff at each regional center. Further, the department's head office housed more than 100 people in branches such as Voter Registration, Political Party Services, Out-of-Country Voting, Election Supervision, Joint Operations Center (i.e., security and operations), Election Services, Election Information and Civic Education, Professional Development, Database and Program Development, Quality Assurance, and Legal Counsel. Other agencies were also extensively involved during the election period, including the Swiss Support Unit, SFOR, the UN International Police Task Force, and the European Community Monitoring Mission. The Swiss Support Unit, which assisted the OSCE in transportation and medical care, delivered 150 tons of material, including training kits, polling stations posters, ballots, furniture, and voter information material during the April 2000 election period. SFOR was also heavily involved in elections, mostly in the communications and security realms. SFOR liaison officers spent several days and nights parked outside regional election offices during the election period, monitoring VHF radio channels and providing security.

The electoral effort is exemplary on all fronts of social visibility: personnel, money, resources, and advertising. Thousands of workers spent their per diem cash on food and drink, rent, and curios. Institutional money was funneled into Bosnian pockets as drivers, interpreters, assistants, and professionals were temporarily employed. International Presence saturated city streets: it was nearly impossible for supervisors stationed in medium-sized towns to walk into a bar or café without seeing other supervisors; private vehicles sported temporary OSCE signs in their windows; short-term accommodations had to be found for the influx of supervisors; electoral advertising filled the airwaves.[12] Sheer Presence, whether in people or money, and the consequences of accommodating that volume of people and currency are mechanisms of international governance and of Bosnia-Herzegovinian democracy through social visibility. Visible numbers were meant to symbolize international commitment to and caring for Bosnia-Herzegovina. The numbers, a strategy for transformation, were part of a larger mechanism seeking changes in systems of governance.

Mere Presence

They'd take a monkey if it spoke English.
        —An international, commenting on
          electoral personnel policies, 2000

The existence of mere Presence as a mechanism of international intervention in Bosnia-Herzegovina and of Bosnian democracy came to me slowly, in bits and pieces. After all, action justified international existence not passivity. Why, one might ask, should foreign offices or agencies send internationals if they do not do anything? However, internationals and nationals alike gave importance to internationals' mere existence in Bosnia-Herzegovina. People repeatedly told me that Presence was important in nonwork ways, in passive ways, and in ways that had nothing to do with action. Not all internationals acknowledged this purpose, but such acknowledgments can nevertheless be heard in many of their statements about the point of their jobs and in the organization and implementation of their job duties. This is not to imply that all internationals had vaguely defined tasks or that their responsibilities were few and far between. In reality, the levels of work varied: some internationals seemed overburdened with tasks and responsibility, some seemed underburdened, and some faced apparently just the right amount of work. Further, as is the case in many employment situations, daily work varied depending on deadlines, service requests, and pressures from colleagues. However, mere Presence constituted one significant aspect of their role and work.

The monkey quotation speaks to a wry acknowledgment of and frustration with perceived personnel policies in the international organizations. The speaker's statement accepts the need for staffing vacant positions yet expresses a sentiment I heard many times over—that it seemed that some jobs were often filled without regard for qualifications. Although most internationals I interviewed understood the funding problems and difficulties of diplomatic politics that personnel offices negotiated, many commented that it appeared to matter more that a position was filled than that it was filled competently. It is not that attempts were not made to find qualified people but rather I would argue that the definition of *qualified* was quite broad and depended crucially on Presence. While large segments of electoral workers complained about incompetent international colleagues and joked about who might be best suited to head the "Do-Nothing Department," many also acknowledged that much of the (international) labor was "unskilled." Many positions could be filled by interchangeable international bodies—because the position was not terribly difficult, because it simply required an international body and the skills presumed to be attached to that body, or because the skills needed were easily learned or sufficiently technical that they could be learned on the job.

Internationals circulated frequently within the pool of positions available for internationals in Bosnia-Herzegovina. The high rate of job circulation within international organizations suggests that an important qualification for many international positions was that they be filled by internationals. It was not at all uncommon for internationals to have held three to five different positions, in different fields, all requiring some degree of "technical" (i.e., not managerial) knowledge. Among my informants was an international who became in succession an election officer, a personnel officer, and a human rights officer. Another served as an election supervisor, a coordinator for rebuilding housing, and then a policy analyst. A third had worked as an election supervisor, an election trainer, an ambassadorial assistant, a security and logistics officer, a democratization officer, and an executive secretary.[13]

Despite a work environment considered hectic and stressful and requiring long hours, international staff from a variety of job classifications commented on the redundancy of their positions. Some internationals, realizing they had little work, struggled to find things to do and thereby to give meaning to their existence and activities. Internationals commonly believed that there was little work to be done, that jobs had to be self-created, and that they were engaged in constant struggles to justify their existence in Bosnia-Herzegovina. These comments were sometimes framed in a manner that suggested a purpose for having internationals around despite the lack of concrete and consistent duties. An entry from my fieldwork journal details one worker's frustration and self-realizations:

> I had coffee with Guy today. Guy has just realized he doesn't really have a job. And only has [had one] for about 3 months of the 16 months he's been here. There isn't really much for him to do; someone else is either handling it, or could be. I told him about my Presence theory and he said, "I'd agree with that." He also believes that he is a foreign policy strategy: bolstering internationals.

These sentiments grew over the period of my research. As institutional reforms gave more direct responsibilities and tasks to national officials and employees, internationals increasingly found that a large part of their job was to oversee and verify the work of others. However, within election supervision, the change was less stark because a large part of the job description always involved oversight. As early as 1997 and 1998, supervisors complained about their redundancy. In some cases, others did not consider these positions redundant but rather believed that the passive Presence of these internationals created substantial obstacles for Bosnians intent on committing electoral fraud. In other cases, however, particularly in the area of logistics, many observers felt that Bosnian employees could do the required work effectively. Others, however, questioned the capabilities of Bosnian workers. Could Bosnians, for example, be effective human rights officers? Would they be considered impartial? Could they be impartial? Would a logistics officer give contracts only to his family and friends? Debates regarding the necessity for or redundancy of internationals in particular positions were a constant source of tension and point to the importance given to mere Presence in the transformations of Bosnia-Herzegovina.

While many internationals bemoaned their lack of work, complaints about ambiguous, unfocused, and unnecessary tasks were also common. Many Municipal Election Commission (MEC) supervisors made remarks along these lines during exit interviews and in journals they kept:

I believe that with more planning and scheduling, [we] could have effectively performed our duties in a much shorter time frame—three or four weeks—instead of six.

We felt we had to create a role. Our sense was that there was little planning, it was all built up as we went along.

[My] gloomy mood was much eased when my [international] friend Gabrielle telephoned to suggest she drive down for a drink. We spent some three hours chatting in the upstairs bar at the National Theatre. She asked me what a MEC [supervisor] does. I did not really have an answer.

[Today] was another wretchedly meaningless day.

In particular, many medium-term election staff like the MEC supervisors (i.e., in country for approximately six to eight weeks), felt that they often received busywork to keep them occupied. Out of frustration, many attempted to expand the scope of their work (sometimes to the extreme annoyance of their immediate supervisors) or to take on more responsibility. However, as in any bureaucracy, it was professionally prudent to avoid stepping on people's toes, to avoid engaging in turf wars. Thus, in some cases, superiors soundly squashed attempts to expand the scope of the supervisor's job. In other field offices, officers welcomed the assistance but often gave the MEC supervisors tasks that would "get them out of [our] hair." Supervisors also commonly enjoyed their unexpected free time—touring the countryside, having coffee, and socializing. Such activities led some supervisors to experience mild feelings of guilt at not being professionally engaged during "work hours." However, this sense of guilt failed to take into account the alternative work performed by their international body. These comments on the lack of work, ambiguous work, and unfocused tasks suggest that internationals had concurrent, more subtle purposes under the logics of international intervention. These other roles swirled around Bosnia-Herzegovina's landscape, at play both in electoral sites and in the larger community but always centered on the mere Presence of an international. Under this ideology of Presence, the passive work done by an international is significant.

National and international staff alike believed that the mere Presence of internationals had utility. When I interviewed national (i.e., Bosnian)

Election Officers (EOs) in 2000, they repeatedly told me that internationals were useful tools to deploy. Although all EOs felt capable of doing the job themselves and some felt that their international counterparts—the international election advisers (IEAs)—were redundant or did not know why they existed, the EOs still admitted to an "international usefulness," saying that "the authority of the international is easier" to establish. One EO, faced with an offer of another colleague, exclaimed, "I'd rather have an IEA than another national EO!" The IEA, an international position created in 1999 when the EO position was nationalized and filled with, at least on the first pass, former EOs, was considered better able to pressure, convince, and/or force Bosnian election officials to "do their jobs," "implement the tasks given to them," and "follow given procedures and regulations." The international-as-tool held within his or her body the authority of the international community as well as an assumed set of particularly defined and produced skills or values: expertise and knowledge, democracy, and neutrality. At least three utilities were granted to internationals' mere Presence, including acting as a catalyst, evoking goodwill and postwar reconciliation, and implicitly enforcing rules and proper conduct. Each utility was reckoned to function through the international's bodily tool kit.

First, international bodies were thought to be more effective tools in prodding reluctant officers to comply with international demands. The international body was felt to carry with it an essence able to promote productivity on the part of Bosnian officials. At a minimum, both internationals and nationals I interviewed believed that in most areas of the country, an international would always have more success than a national in forcing an issue to completion or resolution. Several EOs told me that when a topic or task given to the (local) election commissions became particularly contentious and was not going to be done correctly or at all, they would send in their international counterpart. The utility of international mere Presence as a catalyst came out clearly during a trip I took to the Vrata Grad MEC with Igor, an EO. Vrata Grad (a pseudonym), a now ruined and desolate town, was considered one of the most problematic areas in all of Bosnia-Herzegovina in terms of noncooperation with international administrations, violence toward returning refugees and displaced persons, political corruption, and continuing ethnic hatred. Under Croat control at the time of my fieldwork, internationals were no better liked than returning Serbs and Bosniacs. The population in 1999 was 22 percent of its prewar populace and its ethnic makeup had almost entirely shifted—from 79 percent Serb to 76 percent Croat—although the statistics hide severe drops in absolute numbers (International Centre for Migration Policy Development 1999). Bosniacs remained a relatively stable population as a percentage (18 percent compared to 23 percent) but their overall numbers dropped from 2,200 to 600. The city clearly suffered tremendous physical, social, and demographic destruction both during and immediately after the war. Voter registration information from 1997 suggested that only 5 percent of registered voters were residents of Vrata Grad before the war.

I had arranged to interview Igor as part of my research schedule; he graciously invited me to observe his day, correctly assuming that I would be interested in more than just an interview. His task on this day was to push the ethnically mixed MEC to agree on the formation of the polling station committees. As we drove toward Vrata Grad, Igor gave me the background for our trip. The MEC had already been discussing this matter for some weeks with no progress, and the deadline for choosing committees had already passed. The MEC had not only failed to choose individuals but was still debating the ethnic composition of the polling committees, a deadline far gone. The ethnically mixed commission, he said, was notoriously uncooperative. The chair, a Croat, had previously proposed an ethnic distribution of four Croats, one Serb, and one Bosniac for the six-person polling station committee. Unacceptable to the Bosniac and Serb members of the commission, (who were strategically aligned against the Croats in Vrata Grad), the issue remained unresolved. Our meeting was, however, remarkably short and hardly worthy of the 90-minute drive to get there. As soon as we sat down, with little fanfare or discussion, they agreed on a distribution of three Croats, two Serbs, and one Bosniac, with a Croat always serving as chair. Igor was prepared, he remarked to me on the drive home, to threaten them with arbitration by the countrywide Provisional Election Commission, which would have likely resulted in two members from each ethnic group. He said that the commission members knew that he had this ultimatum in mind and thus were ready to make some compromises. That is, the agreed upon distribution kept an equal balance of power between the ethnicities with a gesture toward the political power of the Croats. An even split of two members per ethnicity would have been overly disadvantageous to the Croats. But as we continued our drive, he repeatedly expressed surprise at how smoothly and quickly the negotiations had proceeded—and he attributed this phenomenon entirely on my Presence as an international and a researcher. (I had been introduced as a university student researching elections.)

> They knew you were studying elections and . . . were embarrassed to not be able to reach an agreement. Your presence helped.

In this example and others like it, such as the effectiveness of the IEAs described earlier, an international's ability to provoke a decision does not stem from his or her conflict management or mediation skills or from professional expertise (although he or she may have both) but from bodily presence. In this case, I had no official authority or coercive power; I was not even employed by the Election Department. Igor could have reached the same result with the MEC by himself, but, he surmised, not as quickly or as peacefully.

The mere Presence of an international was not always remarkable in its ability to goad people into action or to reduce tensions. What was remarkable was its dominant place in strategies of intervention and in attempts to implement democracy in Bosnia-Herzegovina despite its checkered efficacy. Daniel's story highlights his (an international's) inability to provoke the correct action on the part of a MEC. His fury, confusion and annoyance suggest that things were not working the way he thought they should—that is, not the way a model of Presence would prescribe. In fact, the overriding sense of frustration felt by many internationals arose because their (implicit) model was not functioning according to plan: their Presence was often not enough. Daniel's journal, about his experiences as an MEC supervisor edited for anonymity and clarity, details how the MEC's members said that they would do something but did not.[14]

> The computer consultant [brought in by the MEC to assist in number crunching for the optional spreadsheets and the obligatory final results forms] was in my estimation a lying, hypocritical worm if not skunk, and his behavior aroused in me more inward anger than anything else that has happened during this relatively unhappy mission.
>
> I have delayed writing about the computer fiasco since I still feel angry and kick myself for believing that people mean what they say and generally tell the truth. During the day, the MEC were giving good data on turnout from computerized results of

information called in by polling station chairs. When the counting stations began to bring in their results forms, I arranged for the MEC member overseeing the computer elements to introduce me formally as an MEC supervisor to the two people there for input. I asked if they were using the OSCE software, and the man assured me they were going to do so.

At 5:15 in the morning, the IEA called me. He wanted a final voting total and turnout and the number of tendered ballots cast. In all innocence I went to the computer room [with my interpreter] and found the wicked consultant/professor. I asked my questions; he returned a basilisk gaze. He could not tell me anything since they were doing input of polling station results. I glanced at the screen and realized that he was not using the OSCE spreadsheet but his own footling listing of results by polling station that would mean a hard copy of several hundred pages.

My MEC stalwart was now on duty checking returning counting stations; the MEC president had gone for a nap; the women MEC members said they did not know the computing arrangements. The MEC stalwart did appear very quickly and we went back to the computing room. He had been with me early in the evening when the input assistant had confirmed clearly that he would use OSCE software. Now in front of his boss, the evil professor, he denied this statement. (He had the grace to whisper an apology to me as I went to leave the room.)

The professor was whining that he could not access the OSCE computer or the password. I put on the voice of quiet severity that heads of state use to recalcitrant ministers (and I have worked with a few heads of state) and said, "I shall inform Sarajevo," and strode out. Of course I could inform nobody, except the IEA, and I could go no further than the next room. However, my hunch not to argue but to play the king was sound. Just as I was calling her about the dirty tricks, my MEC stalwart came in with a great smile on his face.

The OSCE computer was magically accessible. There on the screen was the OSCE spreadsheet. There was the professor keying in data, with an unctuous smile and saying meekly to me was he doing it correctly. The worm had turned.

Here, the MEC supervisor believed that his presence had enough authority that the correct procedures would be followed. And, indeed, it eventually did—but not before the MEC members tabulated the results the way they wanted to.

Second, supervisors resoundingly believed that one of their major contributions to elections and democracy in Bosnia-Herzegovina was simply being a congenial foreigner. Responses to survey questions asking what polling supervisors felt was the most gratifying and most important part of their job or time in Bosnia-Herzegovina suggest that they believed that the most positive element of their jobs was their mere Presence as a goodwill ambassador.[15] Further, they believed that their relationships, contacts, camaraderie, interactions, and exchanges with Bosnians had positive and transformative effects. When asked specifically about their work and presence, supervisors often commented on their role as goodwill ambassadors.

> It showed local people that the international community cares about them, and I assisted in continuing to build the bridge between local people and the international community.

> Our job encompassed far more than just registration; our presence brought an insight of the outside world to the locals.

> Not so much because of the supervision I performed, but more because of the contacts and relationships that were developed with the locals. I really believe that these were valuable and significant.

> [I was only useful] in the counting process. Otherwise, I was only an ambassador trying to be nice and improve relations between my country and this one.

Supervisors downplayed their technical assistance efforts—the primary rationale for their job position—but instead judged that their usefulness lay in their empathy and interpersonal skills.

One American MEC supervisor, Mara, fluent in Serbo-Croatian and with extensive aid experience in Bosniac areas, rarely mentioned her official work with the MEC in her journal. Rather, she focused on the context in which she found herself, the stories of the people she met, and her interactions with her colleagues and friends. She offered little information about what she "did" as an MEC supervisor. However, she commented repeatedly that "touching the lives" of Bosnians was her most useful and productive task. She believed that her Presence as a facilitator or mediator contributed to the country's social reconciliation. She described visiting a Muslim area where she had worked in previous years:

> Neither of my [Bosnian Serb] colleagues had been to Jezero Pelo before, and [they] didn't have the highest opinion of the place. But after being there and meeting all of my [Bosniac] friends, they are very impressed and now look forward to going there. I'm very glad about this. Perhaps of all the things I will do here, that is the most important.

In her view, the technical assistance she provided the MEC was auxiliary, if not offensive, since she considered the MEC experienced and competent. She saw herself as merely an assistant. Her few references to the election work comment negatively on the controlling nature of the bureaucracy, its inflexibility, and its incompetence. Instead, her diary testifies to the tragic stories of all Bosnians and her individual attempts at bringing about reconciliation and recovery.

> One of my best memories that I will take home with me is that of Suzana's younger daughter teaching [Bosnian Serb] Zdravko how to pray Muslim style! Meanwhile, Suzana and Danko compared their understanding of the Bible and the Koran and found them similar. They said that perhaps the war could have been averted (at least in Bosnia) had everyone been encouraged to practice and then share their religions. We'll never know, of course, but it is an interesting theory based on the basic premise of "love your neighbor" and "killing is a sin."

> [By] reaching out and touching lives of individuals, we make far more difference than forcing a democratic process on a people who are not ready. I'm convinced that economic and social stability are crucial prerequisites to democracy, and without these people will have no true freedom of choice. It casts into doubt all of our work here, which is uncomfortable, but we need to be realistic.

Although most supervisors lacked Mara's linguistic skills, historical and political knowledge, and Bosnian friends, most still emphasized their role as an agent of reconciliation. Supervisors believed that their role extended past the polling station and into the community.

Third, the supervisors felt that the simple, passive Presence of an international prevented or deterred voter and committee fraud, added legitimacy and objectivity to the process (and hence made the voters and opposition or minority parties trust the process), and gave confidence and confirmation to the local Bosnian staff, as the following quotations from supervisors highlight.

> Supervisors prevented fraud and kept certain groups from claiming that the "other side" was cheating.

> [Supervisors were] important as a political symbol—presence prevented the worst fraudulent practices.

> [Local] staff feel more confident in this postwar time when a foreign objective monitor is staying with them all during the period.

> It is very good for the local staff members to know that someone is there, to do his job in an absolutely impartial/honest/fair way. They see us as a guarantee.

Supervisors believed that they carried a specific authority rooted in impartiality and neutrality.[16] Rather than being rooted in impartiality, however, their (perceived) authority was actually based on a commitment to bureaucratic and technical rationality. Supervisors generally believed in following the rules. Like law, rules were conceptualized as apolitical and impartial, as affecting all persons equally. Decades of social research have shown that seemingly neutral or equitable rules and laws affect people unequally (see Danielsen and Engle 1995; Lazarus-Black and Hirsch 1994). However, especially given supervisors' distance from the creation of the rules and often from the political situation and debates, they were implicitly encouraged to continue believing in the overlapping nature of neutrality and rules. Their role was to enforce compliance with established rules and to ignore or avoid the politics behind and potential effects of the rules. Their bodily Presence served to coerce and legitimate "proper" behavior—that is, behavior conscious of universality before the law if not under the law.

"Masquerading" internationals and debates regarding nationalized positions further illustrate the perceived and actual power of international bodies through their implicit comparison with national bodies. Masquerading internationals were those who had Bosnian heritage—that is, they were not truly foreign. Some were actually binationals, born and raised in, for example, Germany to Bosnian parents. An Australian-Croat working as a (national) EO said that Bosnians often assumed that she would be biased toward her ethnicity; her half internationalness did not aid her struggles to be perceived as neutral. But she was not convinced that the situation would differ at all if she worked as an international. As an international, she felt, her Croat background would taint her. With the intent of preempting exactly these perceptions of bias, a Croat-Canadian international socialized primarily with international colleagues, effectively hiding her national linkages. These two binationals were one generation removed from Bosnia. Those raised in Bosnia but with dual nationality were especially problematic for internationals. An Italian-Serb raised in Bosnia-Herzegovina was discredited in his international position; colleagues saw him as an impostor. A Norwegian election supervisor was discovered to be a Bosniac emigrant after she confessed great discomfort and reluctance at being stationed in Bijeljina, a town in Republika Srpska. Her supervisor roommates suggested that she was not yet sufficiently removed from Bosnia to count as an international. They reported that she feared for her safety and would not leave their temporary residence except to go to the OSCE office. She essentially remained a national despite her ability to pass as an international through her passport.

Debate continued voraciously throughout my fieldwork on whether a national could adequately do an international's job even as international positions were nationalized. As one manager chastised his staff,

> I believe the root of the problem is [your contention that] "being one of the ethnic groups jeopardizes the integrity of the job being done." This is arrant nonsense, and I will hear none of it. This is no more true of Bosnians than of internationals. Our hiring policy is that we hire nationals for all positions, regardless of ethnic identity. Please make [this] extremely clear to all, and those who do not accept it should find jobs elsewhere in the mission or in the world. We are here to fix this problem, not institutionalize it.

This memo was resoundingly not implemented, and two years later, some jobs remained marked as international while others were labeled national. Later managers swung to the opposite side of the debate, saying that because the organization was an international one, hiring primarily internationals made sense. Efforts to increase the visibility and anthority of nationals were decidedly mixed.

In 2000, efforts occurred to increase the number of national observers in polling stations as the number of international supervisors decreased. For example, a Bosnian NGO with U.S. Agency for International Development funding, the Center for Civic Initiatives, coordinated the presence of 4,280 national polling observers in May 2000 and 5,449 the following November (Center for Civic Initiatives 2000a:1, 2000b:5). Political party observers had always been allowed in the polling stations (two per party per station), but there had been no organized civic presence prior to the center's involvement. The group members (and the international election bureaucracy) considered their mobilization and presence a resounding success. Despite these feelings, however, an election officer told me during a postelection follow-up interview that the Center for Civic Initiatives

> is good, but I don't know how seriously they are taken. They have an effect, but not to the same degree [as a polling supervisor]. Without a doubt it is the polling supervisor as an international who has effect.

Mere Presence, like sheer Presence, is a strategy of international interventions, used to prod Bosnians toward governmental, social, and liberal cooperation and compliance. The passivity of mere Presence interacted with more action-centered practices yet was considered a transformative agent in its own right. This Presence must be international; internationals and Bosnians alike considered only purely foreign bodies to carry authority, expertise, democracy, and neutrality within themselves.

Peer Presence

Our presence trains them, sometimes through observation, sometimes by actual training. . . . Both inside and outside work, people see the international community and how we work and behave.
                    —a U.S.-educated Italian international, 2000

An American woman, Edith, related a long story about her managerial role during the registration of voters. Her job was to oversee and ensure the proper functioning of the office. She was not tasked with the functions themselves but rather with supervising them. During her eight weeks of service, however, when overcome by fits of boredom or frustration with the staff, she would sit down to participate in checking forms. Although she was in part looking for a way to keep herself occupied, Edith explained that she was also explicitly trying to show the staff members that the work could be done faster and more efficiently than they were doing it. She posted daily productivity reports and compared her completion rate to the average rate of the Bosnian workers. Her strategy was not subtle. Here and in other locales across Bosnia-Herzegovina, internationals engaged in explicit demonstrations of (and debates regarding) the way to comport oneself "professionally." Was it professional, an anguished colleague asked me, for her to hire someone who desperately needed a job rather than the most qualified candidate? She desperately wanted to do the right thing but was torn between good business practice and altruism. Internationals, through peer Presence, attempted to demonstrate what needed to be done so Bosnians could become liberal, neoliberal, and modern peers.

Internationals involved in election work believed that they were demonstrating professional and democratic behavior through their commitment to the electoral rules and regulations and in their administrative and bureaucratic techniques.[17] Supervisors and other election staff did not always agree with the rules but almost always obeyed them. In this, they believed that they were demonstrating how to be democratic. This point of view included a commitment to rules and an emphasis on administration/bureaucracy as well as on democratic values such as tolerance and inclusiveness. Internationals explicitly stated this pedagogical impulse in their responses to questionnaires asking about the importance of their supervisory role:

> I think it was important that the registration had been supervised. It's the best training the national teams can receive . . . to do it themselves with somebody who watches and explains.

> [My] strict adherence to the rules provided confidence in the integrity of the registration election process.

Polling supervisors consciously negotiated the demands of electoral regulations and the necessity of following the rules as a pedagogical device, even as many of them recognized the arbitrary nature of the regulations.

As a polling supervisor in 1997, I had experience with demonstration and with trying to forge peer relationships. My experience mirrors the narratives I heard from other supervisors. I shared the responsibility for polling station performance and results with a four-person polling station committee during the 1997 Republika Srpska presidential election (see also Election Day). There was a fine line in determining who was in charge of the polling station. Officially, the polling chair was the ultimate authority, but the supervisor had many tasks and responsibilities that made it clear that the supervisor had overriding powers. For example, supervisors filled out all forms, kept and secured all sensitive material, transported the ballots, and were tasked with polling station management and "advising" the chairs on any and all electoral processes. The rules and regulations explicitly stated that the chair was "in charge," but the wording still left supervisors with powers that effectively negated much of the chair's authority:

> Polling station committee chairs are responsible for the conduct
> of the process. Polling supervisors maintain the authority to take
> an active role whenever necessary.

The dual nature of authority in the polling station led to disputes on proper polling conduct, with supervisors always referring back to the electoral rules and regulations. At the station I supervised, the polling station committee feared that I would discount all the ballots after I discovered that one man had received two ballots. The committee members claimed that his wife also wanted to vote but had not come to the polling station. Issuing two ballots to one person represented a clear violation of the rules and regulations, and in addition to noting the infraction in the poll logbook, I made a rather large and loud fuss about it, stating that the integrity of the elections was in jeopardy. As a supervisor, I had been told that unless all the rules and regulations were followed exactly, the results could be nullified and that it was up to me to enforce and judge voter and polling station committee adherence to those rules. Did this one irregularity constitute an offense worthy of closure and censure? What if it was just one of many but the only one I had seen? In making a scene about this inconsistency, I was concerned about the polling committee's trustworthiness and integrity as well as about demonstrating my integrity as a democratic subject and about how my performance would be evaluated if I failed to prevent breaches of democracy.

The packing of polling materials and results was another instance of demonstrating proper behavior and adherence to rules. There were seven different envelopes or bags to fill with materials for these elections, down from fifteen used during the municipal elections held two months earlier. The process was so confusing that the chair asked me to do it. I attempted to pack correctly and insisted that the other members of the polling station committee help. Although it was eleven o'clock at night, we were all cold and exhausted after the tension of accurately counting ballots, and we all wanted to go home, it was important to me to let them know that the job had to be finished and done correctly. I refused to let them leave (among other carrots and sticks, I was carrying their salaries in my wallet) until I determined that we were done.

Just as internationals distrusted the local election officials and questioned their motives, the polling committee distrusted and questioned the "neutral" representatives of democracy. After the close of polls on the first day, we sealed the ballot box, put sensitive material into sealed bags, and began to put them in my vehicle, in accordance with directives for closing the polling station. I thought everything was fine until the committee members told me that the ballot box would not leave their control—they would transport it to the storage area. They did not trust me. After twenty minutes of debate, I pulled out a copy of the rule stating that the international supervisor was to transport the ballot box, but they refused to yield. I then radioed the OSCE field office and explained the situation. The international EO verified that the international polling supervisor had the sole authority to transport the ballot box and that the Local Election Commission had agreed to this rule. If my committee members disagreed, I was told, they should contact their Local Election Commission. The committee and I consequently agreed that I could transport the ballots to the storage area but that I would be escorted by two cars, one in front and one behind. They wanted to verify that I too followed the rules and regulations. All of these rules are flexible as well, however. For example, I allowed a different counting procedure than the one prescribed, and Helen, another supervisor, accompanied her chair but allowed him to transport the ballot box. As Michel Foucault reminds us, discipline is always negotiated. This flexibility, however, did not negate the pedagogical impulse inherent in the supervisors' Presence. They still had the power to enforce, determine, and promote "professional" and "democratic" conduct and to judge and sanction deviance.

These three modes of Presence—sheer, mere, and peer—are subsumed within the more active practices of internationals and the international community. Sheer, mere, and peer Presence make up a mechanism of international governance—a way through which international and global interventions conduct their transformative missions. Although the forms, salience, and intensity of Presence changed during my field-work from 1997 to 2000, it continued to exist. Presence faded somewhat, but its ghosts and contrails continued. Bodies may have been fewer in number and had less influence, but under this logic, the previous bodies had allowed the reduction of bodies. The transformations of Presence had been at least partially realized and structurally internalized in Bosnian institutions and society.

DEMOCRATIC
GOVERNANCE

ELECTORAL THICK DESCRIPTION

My introduction to implementing democracy in Bosnia-Herzegovina was, in a colleague's words, as a paper pusher par excellence. Within three hours of my arrival in Sarajevo, I was on the job—watching the movement of voter registration forms around a room. The Processing Center had four rooms, about thirty staff members, and ten high-speed optical mark scanners hooked up to computers and was divided into five task-defined sections: receiving, opening, scanning, error fixing, and storage. We received packets of forms, opened the packets, scanned the forms, fixed mistakes on the forms, placed the forms back in their original packets, and then stored the packets on shelves. Here, in the Processing Center, I got my first inkling that elections were far more than just a way for voters to choose their political representatives.

In June 1997, the OSCE hired me to be a registration supervisor in Bosnia-Herzegovina for the municipal elections planned for the weekend of September 13–14. Voters were required to register during a six-week period that ran from May 5 to June 16, and the registrations were already in full swing by the time I arrived. I had been hired in an attempt to have the Processing Center keep pace with the flood of registrations coming in: when I arrived, a two-week backlog existed. Bosnia-Herzegovina had a total of 420 voter registration centers, each of which was staffed by a three- or four-person committee and an international registration supervisor. When someone arrived at a registration center, he or she produced identification documentation and filled out a form, designed and produced for the OSCE's Election Department by a data specialist company located in Milton Keynes, England (fig. 8). That form was delivered to the Processing Center, where it was scanned and its information was added to an electronic database.

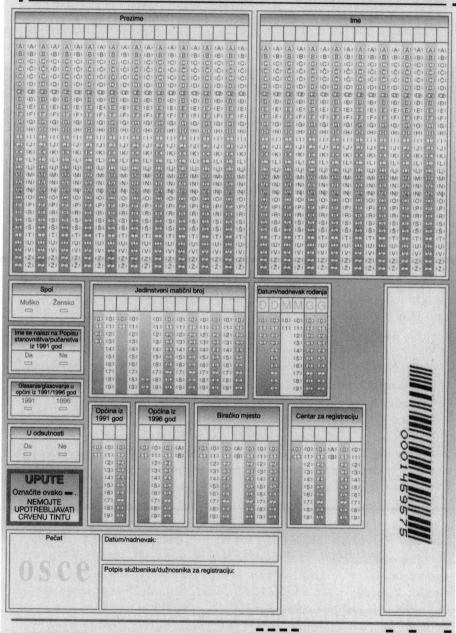

Fig. 8. A voter registration form, 1997. *(Courtesy of DRS Data Systems Limited.)*

The forms were developed to be read by machines as well as humans. Potential voters (I refer to them here as registrants) filled in the forms by hand, with assistance from the voter registration center staff. In addition to printing the required information, they had to "bubble" in the information so that the special optical mark scanners could read the information. The form asks for the registrant's name, birth date, identification number, address, municipality of residence, and chosen municipality of voting (the registrant's current residence, his or her pre-war 1991 residence, or, in a few cases, where he or she was planning to reside in the near future).

Swiss soldiers delivered mounds of packets filled with forms to the Processing Center twice a day. We felt sorry for the Swiss soldier-drivers: How exciting could it be, we pondered, to drive around the country picking up packets of registration forms and delivering them to us? The Swiss soldiers (with help from the men in the Center) carried the packets up two flights of stairs and dropped them into big boxes. We received between 200 and 300 packets, each with 200–300 forms, every day. My first impression of the Processing Center was one of mountains of packets. White plastic packets stretched as far as I could see—delivery piles, opened piles, waiting-to-be-scanned piles, scanned piles, in-need-of-corrections piles, corrected piles, and completed piles.

When all the packets had been carried up the stairs, another registration supervisor or I verified the delivery with our signature. A national could not sign for them. The second step was to slit open the tops of the plastic packets with scissors. Each packet's forms were then removed and examined. Would the scanner accept the stack of forms? Were any forms crumpled, upside down, or ripped? Were they neatly stacked, with all the edges aligned? Was the top form a batch sheet (which supplied information for the scanner such as the number of forms in the batch, the range of their serial numbers, the municipality from which the forms had come)? Was it filled out properly? Batch forms were supposed to be followed by spoiled forms, those that had been filled out improperly at the voter registration center. (Since all forms had to be accounted for, spoiled forms could not just be thrown away.) Good forms came next in the sequence, and then forms with some sort of attached documentation, such as a request, a commentary, or a birth certificate. Attached documents signaled to us that a registrant's data were somehow irregular. For example, a registrant who did not appear in the 1991 census (the main measure for proof of citizenship) would attach a document that verified his or her citizenship. Because the machines could not read such documents, any form with anything attached to it was sent to a different department. We did not want to see it—we were interested in maximizing the number of forms read by the scanners each day, not in verifying citizenship or making judgments on the merit of any particular registrant. On some occasions, we threw away small attachments we deemed unnecessary. We got bolder as it became apparent that registration supervisors at the voter registration centers were attaching what we considered completely meaningless documents or notes to the forms, such as notes asking for the correction of an improperly spelled registrant's name on the census. We could not perform those types of tasks or any tasks other than our specialized one.

After the forms were separated, the batch was registered as "in process" on a tracking form and put into a scanner stack. Scanning involved putting the forms on top of the machine and pushing a button to start it. Accepted forms went to the left, and rejected forms went to the right. Rejects were run a second time to weed out misreads by the machine. When all the forms in an envelope were scanned, the accepted forms were put back into the plastic packet and the rejects were put on top of the packet with the batch sheet and an error log created by the scanner. If none of the forms had any errors, the packet was stapled shut, recorded as scanned on the tracking form, and put on a storage shelf.

Most packets went into an enormous error pile that threatened to overwhelm our office space. Staff members worked through the rejected forms, attempting to resolve the problems identified by the scanner. Most errors were bubbling problems: double bubbles, missing bubbles, and wrong bubbles. All of these bubbling mistakes could be fixed. We could not fix incorrect data, just incorrect bubbles. We had to assume that the written information was correct. After the errors were rebubbled properly, the offending forms were scanned again. If the second scan resulted in a 100 percent acceptance rate, we could complete the batch, staple the packet shut, record it as processed, and put it on a storage shelf. If forms were still rejected, they were either sent to a machine for manual computer entry or put in a pile to run "without checks." Each form went through a small series of computer verification checks (e.g., that the municipality listed was a valid municipality, that the stated birth date was numerically possible). Removing the checks that the scanner performed on the forms would often result in acceptance. Of course, this did not mean that the data were correct but simply that the form had been processed and its information entered into the database of registered voters. If the form was not processed and the information not entered into the database, a registrant had not registered, even if he or she had filled out a form.

The process was nauseatingly boring. However, I was not alone; I discovered that elections had more than enough tedium to go around. Other registration supervisors were also bored. International trainers (on hand for the entire registration period to assist with problems and policy changes) told me that they were bored. And, the Swiss soldiers were bored. However, for the election to take place, there had to be voters; voters required a voter list; and the creation of a voter list required forms to be filled out, delivered, and processed. So we processed. On average, 70,000 forms per 16-hour workday passed through the scanners, and into the database, representing a total of 2.1 million Bosnian voters.

During my time in the Processing Center, I absorbed information and knowledge about many different aspects of the implementation of elections in Bosnia-Herzegovina: voter registration, political party development and registration, out-of-country voters and voting, fraud, and election supervision. My understandings of those aspects later deepened, and I also learned about the practices of and perspectives on election implementation and administration in sites such as field offices, election training centers, and voter education classes. As I moved through different electoral sites, I confronted theoretical questions about the intersections among democracy and the contexts and contents in which it is produced. The following four chapters give ethnographic detail into both the production and productions of democracy, examining how technical, bureaucratic, and pragmatic objects and practices contribute to the constitution of particular meanings of democratic governance, such as neutrality, inclusiveness, accountability, universality, fairness, freedom, and transparency.

ELECTION DAY

I arrived at the polling station with my designated driver and interpreter, at 7:00 A.M., as instructed by the *Polling and Counting Manual* and reiterated by the election core supervisor. Of course, no one else was there. My driver and interpreter had tried to convince me to arrive later—say, around 7:30—telling me that the committee would certainly not arrive on time. But I had stuck hard to the instructions, feeling like my authority would diminish significantly if I failed to follow the rules myself. As we waited in the chilly predawn air for the members of the polling station committee to arrive I became increasingly frustrated. They ambled in at 7:35. When we opened the station to voting, some 30 minutes late, I felt vindicated in my argument that their lateness would prevent the polling station from opening on time. However, there were no voters waiting for us to open the polling station, and none arrived for at least another half hour. That first day, during 12 hours of polling (minus the 30 minutes lost at the beginning), 41 precious voters trickled in. My fury dissipated throughout the day as I realized how few voters were going to appear.

What is the relationship of an election day to democracy? Many political theorists view them as nearly synonymous, following Joseph A. Schumpeter's (1947) classic, still dominant, minimalist, and institutionalist definition of democracy. Although scholars and practitioners seeking to incorporate social and economic conditions, influences, and aspects into the analysis, evaluation, and implementation of democracy have launched a deep and sustained critique of this narrow formulation, a general consensus holds that elections remain the central feature of democracy. Democracy should be more than elections, but it cannot be

?. Demokratsi?

less (Pastor 1998). They are the centerpiece of democracy but not its sole criteria (Schmitter and Karl 1991). As legions of political science students can tell you, they are necessary but not sufficient. The most common understanding of the term—despite over a decade of debate— defines *democracy* as free and fair electoral competition with minimal civil rights guarantees. The importance of civil rights and liberties, is acknowledged, but done so within a framework of the procedural minimums necessary for meaningful electoral contestation (Caldeira and Holston 1999). However, whether using narrow defi-nitions of democracy or broader definitions that acknowledge social and economic conditions and/or processes, an electoral focus remains at the core. The primacy of elections, however, contributes "to the development of a distorted picture of democratic transition: the poll itself has become the focus of attention, acquiring an importance that has no basis in either democratic theory or practical politics" (Elklit and Svensson 1997:34).

Bosnia-Herzegovina during the period of my research featured a checklist approach to democracy assistance (akin to procedural minimums) criticized by, among others, Newburg and Carothers (1996) as erring toward a standardized model and failing to see, let alone confront, relations among social attitudes, state structures, and democratic processes. Elections were at the top of the to-do list. In fact, they are a top priority for many international interventions, as seen by their codification into many peace agreements. Marina Ottaway (2002), criticizes this "democratic reconstruction model," arguing that,

> A common feature of these [peace] agreements is that they were to be sealed by democratic elections with a period of time that was dictated more by the international need for a quick exit strategy than by real consideration of how much time was necessary to undertake all preliminary steps required for successful elections. A two-year period became codified as the length of time needed to prepare post-conflict elections, no matter what the initial conditions were. (Ottaway 2002:3)

The "democratic reconstruction model," now routinely prescribed as a means to peace, follows the assumption that democratic systems provide reconciliation mechanisms and are the best guarantee of a lasting peace (Ottaway 2002; cf. Gowa 1999; Ray 1997). Elections, thus, are now central to peace agreements and their to-do checklists.

Rather than referring to democracy in minimalist terms or even in maximalist terms that include civil society features, state institutions, and political accountability, I turn to an alternative conceptualization of democracy. With an eye toward the easy reification of democracy, its contingent nature, and its implication in power relations, I refer to *democracy* as a set of practices and artifacts. This analytical approach focuses attention on both democracy's constructedness and its inherent place in the social sphere. Furthermore, this definition offers some distance from modernist, a priori, and singular models of democracy. I do not mean this perspective to deny differences between, for example, authoritarian and democratic regimes. Rather, this approach includes the myriad of social institutions and practices that accompany those criteria most often used in defining democracy. However, this approach allows for better understanding of how regimes cast themselves as democratic even though others may not consider them as such. Jennifer G. Schirmer's (1998) analysis of the cloaking of Guatemala's military regime as democratic is an example of where this perspective might be productive. Under this formulation—democracy as a set of practices and artifacts— the mechanics and technicalities of democracy can be attended to and seen as consequential.

Anthropological studies of democracy have been broad and indirect. They rarely focus on democracy as a political regime, instead couching the discussion within other frameworks, including, for example, social movements, civil society, and human rights (Paley 2002). However, by more often focusing on the societal or cultural aspects of democracy, anthropologists miss the cultural and societal in those domains explicitly defined as politics. A conviction that politics can be found in domains outside of the political should not limit anthropological investigations. The specificity of politics should not be forgotten (Barry 2002:269) but instead should be scrutinized and examined. Leaving the specialist activity of politics to political science codifies disciplinary boundaries and contributes to the narrowing of analyses of societal and cultural phenomena. I label the missing aspect of democracy—or politics more generally— technical democracy or technical politics. By technical, I mean practices and actions that are commonly considered instruments of or for democracy. For example, electoral laws, polling stations, election officials, and ballots are underexamined as constitutive of democracy and as producers of the truth and authority that democracy claims. By treating Election Day as a technique of democratic government rather than as a functional condition of liberal democracy, we can see how it normalizes and naturalizes particular modes of conduct and participation.

A classic anthropological move would be to treat elections and specifically Election Day as a ritual. Such an approach focuses attention on the function and meaning of the election. For example, as a state ritual, an election legitimates state and governance institutions, binds individuals to their political society, and emphasizes particular processes of dispute, discussion, and resolution. It reinforces the values of inclusion and equality through the mass participation of citizens and the translation of their choices into political authority (Kertzer 1988). The relationships between ritual and political institutions have long been studied. The issue of divine authority has, for example, been central in ritual scholarship, analyzed in terms of both how ritual maintains kingly authority and social order and how the symbolic action of ritual constructs royal power and authority (Bell 1997:83).[1] Political rituals are a loose genre of rituals that "can be said to comprise those ceremonial practices that specifically construct, display, and promote the power of political institutions (such as king, state, the village elders) or the political interests of distinct constituencies and subgroups" (Bell 1997:128). In this manner, it appears anthropologically obvious to use ritual to understand democratic authority.[2]

Although the concept of electoral ritual highlights the legitimacy of the state and democratic modes of governance and gives meaning to participation, among other things, election ritual does not account for techne. In fact, ritual scholarship often ignores action viewed as technical or instrumental, viewing ritual as nonutilitarian action. This genre of scholarship does not look at the production of the structure that allows actors to act, to be, or to hold authority. Focusing on the technology of politics—analyzing the technical and institutional forms that politics takes—shows us how democracy is made. Looking at democracy's component parts, objects, and processes demonstrates how it is put together and how it can be understood in the ways that it is indeed understood. Democracy can be decontextualized, seen as neutral and objective (like science), because it reifies its technicality. I do not argue that democracy is universally considered neutral or objective but simply that there is an easy slippage toward idealism based on democracy's technical center. This phenomenon was particularly acute among the election workers with whom I engaged in Bosnia-Herzegovina. Furthermore, although democracy is easily reified, it cannot be understood separately from society or the social sphere, which it simultaneously works to reify, too, through its concoction of the will of the people. The social is an effect.

I propose that an election is less like the ritual of Catholic mass and more like a scientific laboratory. While Catholic mass evokes religion, laboratories produce science. As Rayna Rapp states about her research on the impact of amniocentesis,

> Tracking the dense circulation of personnel, technical artifacts, reagents, biological tissue, and machines through a collaborative protocol whose outcome is a pictographic and alpha-numerological diagnosis eventually led me to think of the lab as a factory for fact construction. (1999:192)

The diagnoses to which Rapp alludes are facts that doctors and parents used to determine the viability and future of pregnancies. Elections produce democracy in much the same way. While the technologies and techniques may be different—substitute a Bunsen burner or a logbook for a ballot box and a voter register—in both cases, human and nonhuman actors combine to collectively represent as well as act on specific contexts and produce specific facts. Thus, rather than looking at the meanings of electoral practice and symbols (e.g., voting, campaigning, party logos and slogans) and how they legitimate governance and create political identities, my approach analyzes the practices and actor networks of elections to better understand the construction of democratic reality, democratic facts, and democratic order. I do so by carefully considering actions commonly perceived as instrumental or technical and thus often ignored in scholarship. Shaheen Mozaffar and Andreas Schedler (2002), for example, remark that electoral governance (i.e., the technical activities that create and maintain the institutional framework) is a "neglected variable" in the study of political democratization. Seeing politics as a set of technical practices, forms of knowledge, and institutions reinserts material devices and forms of knowledge into the frame of political action (Barry 2002). This is important as persons can act as political agents only through the existence of technical processes and items. Similarly, political processes depend on technical devices.

Scholars of science have repeatedly commented on the need to carefully recognize material and technical objects and processes in the making of science and to document their role in the constitution of science and scientific authority (e.g., Barry and Slater 2002a; Callon 1998; Callon, Rip, and Law 1986; Latour 1999; Latour and Woolgar 1979; Rapp 1999). Following from this attention to the technical and the nonhuman, science scholars have called for a dismantling of the subject/object dichotomy. Actors can be nonhuman: objects have agency and act on, cause, and influence processes. A corollary to the nonreductionist agenda within science studies is the removal of a society/science dichotomy. Science is social. Here, the argument goes further than seeing society as an influence on or context for science. Rather, the false separation into two distinct realms is problematic—"There is no outside world" (Latour 1999:15; Barry 2002). A distinction between the technical and the social only furthers the idea that the technical is somehow not social or, perhaps worse, that the technical is influenced by or influences the social but is somehow a distinct and separate, isolatable category (Barry and Slater 2002b; Callon 1998; Latour 1988, 1999). The creation of technical and material processes and objects is also social. Thus, science studies calls for attention to the (social) content of science, not just its (social) contexts. The technical and mundane create facts and knowledge.

Latour and Woolgar (1979) and Latour (1988, 1999) demonstrate how a detailed description and analysis of science's inner workings, such as quotidian laboratory life, can demonstrate the networks and practices on which the "sciences" depend and on how what some observers dismiss as technique or the technical creates facts, knowledge, and order. For example, in *The Pasteurization of France* (1988), Latour demonstrates that what is now attributed and credited to Pasteur—the defeat of a terrible disease through the discovery of microbes and creation of inoculation—actually depended on a conglomeration of forces, human and nonhuman:

> I had to reestablish, all too briefly, the innumerable crowds and the direction of their general movement in order to deprive the great war leaders, Napoleon or "Pasteur," of the power of performing all these wonders. . . . Pasteurism is *made up* of all this credit. This statement can surprise only those who forget the allies that a science must find in order to become exact. These allies, of which the science is sometimes ashamed, are almost always outside the magic circle by which it later, after its victory, redefines itself. (59–60)

Rapp (1999) and Paul Rabinow (1999) also highlight technology, forms, and machines in their research, offering theoretical perspectives that account for how the interplay of nonhuman and human phenomena makes those phenomena more or less conceivable or possible. We can fruitfully take these ideas and move them into the realm of electoral and democracy studies and in so doing can see the forces subsumed into and taken over by democracy but on which it depends. As in science, the networks, practices, and technicalities that create democracy's accomplishments and possibilities must be recognized and made visible. Reductionism only serves to legitimate and bolster their latent authority and power.

The analogy between science and democracy is not simply methodological: as in science, "there are few serious contemporary challengers to the normative and institutional dominance of democracy" (Squires 2002: 132). Furthermore, both democracy and science bear the weight of many expectations. Humanity has placed its faith in the promises of science, from reducing hunger and disease to improving our ability to predict and control natural disasters, and in the promises of democracy, from diminishing the likelihood of war and human injustice to promoting individual freedom and economic growth (Shapiro and Hacker-Cordón 1999). As hegemons, both science and democracy are constitutive of reality.

Viewed less than two years after the signing of a peace treaty, the "building" of Bosnia-Herzegovina appeared to be a large project staffed primarily by logisticians, managers, and support staff. It was a supremely technical exercise, but we were all engaged in what I considered a supremely political enterprise. Reflecting a few years and five elections later, I realized that I had often had no idea what each election was contesting (e.g., the races or issues), even while I was deeply embedded in the "election effort." After an election, I was sometimes hard-pressed to tell anyone which political party had won or held the majority. I wish that my ignorance had been the exception rather than the norm, but I and many international election workers with whom I spoke failed to learn the results of almost every election in which we participated. For us, as electoral officials, having results was more important than what those results were.

This lack of political knowledge is a symptom of the emphasis on Election Day and technicality rather than on politics and election results. This is not to say that election results were not important in postwar Bosnia-Herzegovina but simply that they were not very important to many electoral workers; the fact of Election Day always overshadowed the political issues. One international worker stated that the role of electoral workers and supervisors was to make the process transparent and efficient, not to engage in politics. "It's not that they don't care or that they aren't personally interested," he said, "but it's not their job." Results were important only in that they needed to be accurate, on time, and able to be replicated. This stress on technicality downplays the political and social nature of Election Day and democracy. Larger processes, such as the politics within politics, are obscured thorough an emphasis on apolitical technical procedures and decontextualized actions. Voters and their democratic voices—the apparent hallmarks of an election—form only one small piece of the puzzle.

Election Day

Election "Day" is a fiction. Electoral practices spread out over weeks and months. Even polling and counting practices, the mainstays of Election Day, temporally bleed into other days, both before and after Election Day itself. In Bosnia-Herzegovina, for example, polling occurred earlier than Election Day as refugees and other out-of-country Bosnians mailed in their ballots. Counting ballots and formulating results started on Election Day but continued on for many days thereafter. Complete counting lasted weeks, since not all ballots were counted at polling stations. Although regular ballots were counted at the polling stations after they closed and counting commonly lasted between three and eight hours, absentee, out-of-country, and tendered ballots were counted at centralized facilities during the weeks after Election Day. Simultaneously, results—tabulated on accounting and result forms and entered into computer databases—had to be verified and audited. Like science, Election Day masks many networks and practices on which it is built.

Election Day represented the zenith of the efforts and the end point of the goals of the electoral administration in Bosnia-Herzegovina, which well knew the work put in during the election period. In some cases, post–Election Day activities and personnel, such as counting, auditing, and associated staff, did not appear in budgets or received short shrift during planning meetings. Ad hoc space and personnel had to be quickly added and finances carved out of existing budgets. For example, counting supervisors were forgotten about in one election; they simply did not appear in planning documents. It was not uncommon to ask supervisors to stay on for a few more days to cover new duties. In one case, I boarded a bus that was taking 50 departing supervisors to the airport to ask for 3 volunteers to get off the bus to work for 7–10 more days. I checked their airline tickets right there on the bus to see whether their airline reservations allowed modifications. In another case, a crucial software program was not approved until after the election, not because the program was unimportant but because Election Day activities had garnered higher spots on to-do lists. In a third case, the day before I was scheduled to return home, I was asked to "stay on" a while longer to finish the project I was overseeing. Project timelines and personnel commitments did not always match.

The collapsing of time has effects. It emphasizes the constituency's participation as the primary facet of elections, ignoring the technical procedures and decisions that also affect elections (e.g., rules that govern what ballots or markings can or cannot be counted, the throwing out of results as a result of major accounting errors, seat-allocation formulas, political party qualification criteria). Democracy should be analyzed and understood in a nonreductionist framework, with full consideration given to the layers of networks and practices that create and sustain it. When democracy is reduced to Election Day, as when science and the processes of discovery are celebrated without recognizing the multiple networks and technicalities on which they stand, the effect is a legitimation and reification of democracy. Technicalities' ability to affect democracy is well known in political science and the election community, but the emphasis on Election Day overshadows the political and technical effects. For example, as explained in Hyper-Bosnia, many internationals were dismayed by continued resistance by Bosnians and Bosnian politicians to an election law. Over and over again I heard rhetoric, personal and official, that Bosnia-Herzegovina needed an election law to move forward, to join Europe, and to become a modern, democratic state. Most of this rhetoric ignored the fact that Bosnians did not like the content of that particular election law—they were not necessarily rejecting any election law, just that particular measure. The emphasis on Election Day, with its ritualistic participation of voters, neatly obscures the political structuring of democracy behind the scenes.

Processes occurring both before and after the election are important, but the emotional buildup to Election Day blurs the drawn-out, lengthy, unbounded processes that govern democratic elections and democracy. The collapsing of time condenses a sense of the elections themselves. This sense figures, for example, into the announcement or publication of results. In Bosnia-Herzegovina, there was always an explicitly lengthy process of counting ballots and announcing results. People knew that final results would not be known for days or weeks after Election Day because large numbers of absentee, mail-in, and tendered ballots needed to be sorted, verified, and counted. Even after all votes had been

tabulated, public announcements were often staggered to reduce potential protests and unrest. However, anxiety still existed about getting the
results out as quickly as possible.[3] For example, regular ballots were
always counted immediately after the close of polls, to the detriment of
cold, bored, tired, and worn-out polling station committees and staff.
For some committees and supervisors, this procedure lacked logic, given
that the counting of all the other ballots (up to 50 percent of the total)
would take weeks. "Why can't we at least sleep a bit and start counting in
the morning?" they asked superiors. This false need for instant
gratification and knowledge ignores or deemphasizes the work that must
be done to verify and account for the results.

Elections correspond to no single temporal unit; likewise, an election
has no single location. Although the most public face was the polling station, important election sites also included storage facilities, municipal
election committee offices, the desks and phones of election officers and
support staff, and counting centers. Counting took place in several locations, and polling was not confined to the polling station as out-of-country voters received and sent back their ballots through the mail, homebound voters cast their ballots via the services of mobile polling staff, and
disabled voters unable to enter polling stations had staff members meet
them outside. Results tabulation, a neglected facet of elections, took
place in municipal offices, computer databases, and mathematical formulas. Election Day—marked most predominantly by the polling station—is temporally and spatially multisited.

In the remainder of this chapter, I describe an Election Day in 1997 from
a polling station site in Bosnia-Herzegovina, focusing on the extensive
technical practices deployed by the polling station committee and by me
in the role of an international polling station supervisor. Each polling station was assigned a supervisor, all of whom were volunteers from OSCE
member countries—people from Western and Eastern Europe, the
United States, Canada, Korea, and Japan. I emphasize the techne of politics to demonstrate that Election Day involves not only democratic values
such as tolerance and inclusion or the participation of national subjects
in the nation-state but also the construction of an election as an acultural
and apolitical event. The forms of authority and social relations promoted via this model of democracy take the apparently neutral form of
techne, which is in fact tremendously social and political. Polling stations,
then, are places, like laboratories, where experimentation and engineer-

ing take place and attempts are made—some failing and some succeed-
ing—to achieve results and to promote certain types of knowledge.

Democratic Laboratories

I arrived with my interpreter and driver at 7 A.M., the committee and
political party observers arrived together around 7:30, we greeted each
other (me somewhat less pleasantly given my annoyance), and began to
set up the polling station. The committee members opened and began
to look through the polling station kit I had brought. To know exactly
what tasks needed to be accomplished, we turned to the chapter "Before
Voting Begins on Polling Day" in the *Polling and Counting Manual* (mine
in English, the committee members' in Serbian). Although we all knew
generally what needed to be done, having attended training sessions
(where we received the manuals), the *Manual* laid out the details and
step-by-step instructions. Supervisors had been told during their training, which was separate from that of the committee, that the *Manual*
would be useful for following the Rules and Regulations as well as for
enforcing or pointing out the proper course of action to an errant chair
or committee member. Thus, even if a chair failed to bring out his or her
Manual on his or her own (as mine did), the majority of the polling station supervisors I spoke with reported that they requested "their" chairs
use it as a guide.

Polling stations were normally located in schoolrooms, municipal
offices, or halls. Potential locations in religious centers, bars, or sites
associated with political parties or war activity, such as detention centers,
were banned. Size varied, as did accessibility. However, all of the sites
would eventually contain desks and voting booths to accommodate the
soon-to-arrive voters. Supervisors received written descriptions of their
assigned polling station along with a crude map of its location and a list
of emergency radio and telephone numbers.

> Polling station in poor condition . . . located at a paved road, but
> other than that it has no significant utilities. There is no water,
> electricity, [bathroom], doors cannot be locked and there are no
> windows as well.

I was warned by the election officer at the OSCE field office not to walk
anywhere that was not paved with asphalt because the area was completely mined. This was not surprising once I saw the town—it no longer

existed. There were no residents and none of the partially standing houses were habitable. Recently rehabilitated, the building-cum-polling station stood alone amongst a destroyed and deserted town. It seemed prudent not to leave the asphalt. When I visited the building the day before Election Day, it was empty but had window glass, door locks, and electricity, and the polling station chair was busily fixing broken furniture. Polling stations had to be physically constructed as well as articulated through electoral actants.

We began by opening the polling kit and taking out its contents, verifying the material against a packing list as we went along—marking the existence of boxes, seals, tags, bags, notebooks, signs, envelopes, instructions, identification cards and holders, batteries, lamps, calculators, candles, pens, scissors, string, ink stamps, and other items. Although supervisors were nominally supervising rather than performing these tasks, most supervisors with whom I spoke reported that they assisted more often than not. This involvement became a problem in later elections, when the supervisors were told to reduce their active role in setting up, filling out forms, counting ballots, and providing leadership. A more passive supervisory role was in place by the 2000 elections, in harmony with the international programs of nationalization and ownership. After years of microcontrol, many polling station supervisors found it difficult to reduce their role from leader to onlooker.

Two committee members constructed voting screens by folding two flat cardboard pieces along the premarked indentations. Making a three-sided voting booth by placing the cardboard structure on a recently refurbished table, the committee members used tape to ensure that the screens stayed up—that they remained screens rather than cardboard shapes. The two screens were placed directly opposite each other to ensure privacy for future voters. Likewise, after a group discussion among the chair, the other committee members, and me, the table and voter screens were placed as the sole objects at the far end of the room against a wall without windows so that, in accordance with the *Manual*, no one could look into a voter's private space from the outside. After the screens were taped down, they tied pens to them with string, again following the *Manual*'s detailed instructions and using the materials provided in the kit: "Place a pen, tied securely with the string provided, at each Polling screen." We used the pens to punch holes in the cardboard so that we could tie the string to the screen.

Several members wanted to construct the ballot box next but were told by the chair to wait because there were many protocols to follow in regards to the ballot box. It would be better, he told them, if we all did it together so that there would be no questions regarding the box's legitimacy. Instead, he gave them signs to put up in and around the polling station. Meanwhile, I walked around the station looking for violations of election rules. Were there any political posters within the designated 50-meter boundary? I had little real knowledge about how far 50 meters was, so instead I walked to the nearest crossroad. Finding no propaganda, I ensured that the polling station signs, including entrance arrows, the number of the polling station, messages indicating that weapons and smoking were not allowed, the sample ballot, and ballot instructions were prominently and accurately displayed in the polling station room and outside on the building's porch. At this point, my teenage male interpreter asked me the first of a series of (from my perspective) inappropriate questions about my age, sexuality, and intimate relationships. He was clearly fascinated, perhaps understandably, by the opportunity to talk to an American female about sex, but my ability to speak with the polling station committee was ultimately severely affected by both his lack of interest in elections and my increasing annoyance with questions about my personal life.

Four chairs were placed against the north wall for political party observers and the Bosnian policeman who arrived to provide "security" for us. Although Article 61 of the *Rules and Regulations* clearly stated that "police personnel shall vote in an orderly and expeditious manner, and shall not remain in the Polling Station any longer than required to exercise their right to vote," we negotiated a chair for him just outside the room, in the hall. Any coercion he was going to introduce to the atmosphere would only be minimally mitigated by his displaced presence, but I wanted him out of sight (and out of mind). The committee forcefully argued that it was cold outside and that no one cared whether the police were around. The first argument was far more convincing than the second. The rule was followed in law, if not in spirit.

After the desks, chairs, and signs were laid out, we began to examine more closely the material I had brought: ballots, forms, the final voter register, the supplementary voter register, silver nitrate ink, and the tendered ballot stamp. This material was considered sensitive—tampering with any of it had the potential to alter the election results—and was the sole responsibility of the international supervisor. For example, the silver nitrate ink could be exchanged with water, rendering the check for repeat voters ineffective, or the final voter register could be tampered with by presigning voters' names or tearing out pages, with the effect of giving a ballot to someone who was not entitled to one or denying someone his or her right to vote.

The blank ballots, in pads of 50, garnered the most attention. They were fondled and examined closely. The order of the candidates was remarked on, and, even if recording the serial numbers had not been required, I had the sense that the staff would certainly have noted them. The two political party observers present wrote down the starting and ending numbers in little pocket notebooks—268651 and 268950—and the chair wrote them in box 2b of the daily accounting form (fig. 9). The total number of ballots (300) was recorded in box 2a. We did not count them but relied on the accuracy of the preprinted serial numbers to achieve the mathematical result (i.e., subtracting the starting number from the ending number plus one). The daily accounting form acted as our mechanism of truth and transparency, a techne of accounting and accountability.

To fill in box 1 of the daily accounting form, we had to determine the number of voters listed in the final voter register. As with the ballots, there was great interest in the booklet of names—members crowded over the chair as he counted each name, sliding his thumb down the page as each name entered into his cumulative count. The other members kept mental tallies, verifying the thumb's simultaneous movements with the chair's rhythmic chant of numbers. One hundred ninety-one was the number recorded in box 1 and in the notebooks carried by the two political party observers.

The displaced authority (Yablon 1992) behind the daily accounting form required only one more number before voters arrived: box 3 called for us to enter the serial number of the seal that would later cover the drop slot of the ballot box. Thus, it was time to construct the ballot box. Made out of cardboard, the ballot box was quickly assembled through a series of folds and flap maneuvers. A polling station committee member picked up the box, turned it upside down, shook it, and showed its empty insides to each of us. He folded over the top flaps to shut the box and covered the four side slits with long serialized stickers. The fifth seal was saved for the drop slot, which would be sealed at the close of polls still some twelve hours away. We placed it back in the kit and recorded its number in box 3. The box was then placed on top of a table in the center of the room. We were almost ready to admit voters.

All that remained was to initiate the poll book by writing down the polling station number and municipality name, the date, and the names of all the persons present. The chair recorded this information, asking

PART I: BEFORE FIRST VOTER VOTES ON DAY 1

1.	Number of Voters on FVR		1.
2a.	Number of Ballots Received		2a.
	2b. Serial Number Ranges	From: To:	
3.	Serial Number of "Drop Slot" seal	Box Seal No.	

PART II: DURING POLLING ON DAY 1

4a.	Additional Ballots Received		4a.
	4b. Serial Number Ranges	From: To:	

PART III: AT THE CLOSE OF POLLING STATION ON DAY 1

5.	Number of Signatures on the FVR	5.
6.	Number of Signatures on SVR +	6.
7.	Total Number of Voters on Day 1 (line 5 + line 6) =	7.
8.	Ballots received on Day 1 (line 2a + line 4a)	8.
9.	Number of Declined Ballots (from Packet 3)	9.
10.	Number of Spoiled Ballot (from Packet 3)	10.
11.	Ballots USED (add Line 7 + 10 Only)	11.
12.	Total Ballots UNUSED (minus line 8 - 11)	12.
13.	Record Serial No: of Plastic One-Way Seal for overnight storage: Seal No.	
14.	Signature of Polling Station Chairperson	
15.	Signature of International Supervisor	

PART IV: BEFORE FIRST VOTER VOTES ON DAY 2

We, the undersigned attest that we have taken steps to verify that 1) the Final Voters Register and Supplemental Voters Register have not been altered or defaced overnight; 2) the Ballot Box and "Drop Slot" seal affixed on Day 1 remain intact; 3) same number of unused ballots remain unchanged since the polls closed on Day 1.

16. Confirmation signature of Polling Station Chairperson	
17. Confirmation signature of International Supervisor	

Fig. 9. A daily accounting form, 1997. *(Courtesy of the Organization for Security and Co-Operation in Europe, Mission to Bosnia and Herzegovina.)*

my interpreter how to spell my name. The chair then remembered that we were also required to sign polling station pledges and codes of conduct. Although this task was not specifically listed in the *Manual* under "Tasks before the First Voter Votes" or "Arranging Your Polling Station," he remembered from his training course that we needed to tear out and sign the pledge and the code, which were located in the *Manual*'s appendixes. We all tore out our copies, signed them, and placed them in the poll book. Like contracts hurriedly signed unread, we all glanced only briefly at the code and pledge before putting them—following the letter of the law—in the poll book. According to the *Polling and Counting Manual*, the code of conduct is "designed to encourage" polling station committee members and observers "to carry out their duties in a manner of integrity and neutrality," and the polling station pledge is "designed to govern their actions and behaviour, as well as to encourage the highest standards when carrying out their duties." Despite their absence from the *Manual*'s zealous step-by-step instructions, failure to sign these two documents was grounds for withholding their salary of 80 deutschmarks. At the time, the average monthly salary in this region of Bosnia-Herzegovina was 76 deutschmarks (UN Development Programme 1998:32, 72).

We sat down to await voters.

The ideal polling station layout should facilitate an efficient flow of voters and ballots (fig. 10). Voters enter the room through a door, located on the upper left of the image. Behind the imaginary door are directional and instructional signs and posters and a potentially long line of voters, which explains the need for the queue controller, who controls access to the polling station and ensures order and calm. In most of the Bosnia-Herzegovina elections the queue controller also held the role of ultraviolet light checker (left side, fig. 10). Potential voters had their fingers checked for fluorescent silver nitrate ink, which the ballot issuer sprays on each voter's right index finger later in the process; thus, anyone with the ink on their finger has already voted and should be refused entrance.

In reality, many factors undercut the effectiveness of the light check. According to supervisors and trainers, it was difficult to see the ink during the daytime; many ultraviolet lights had poor batteries; phosphorescence from fertilizers stuck to farmers' hands, giving off a similar glow to

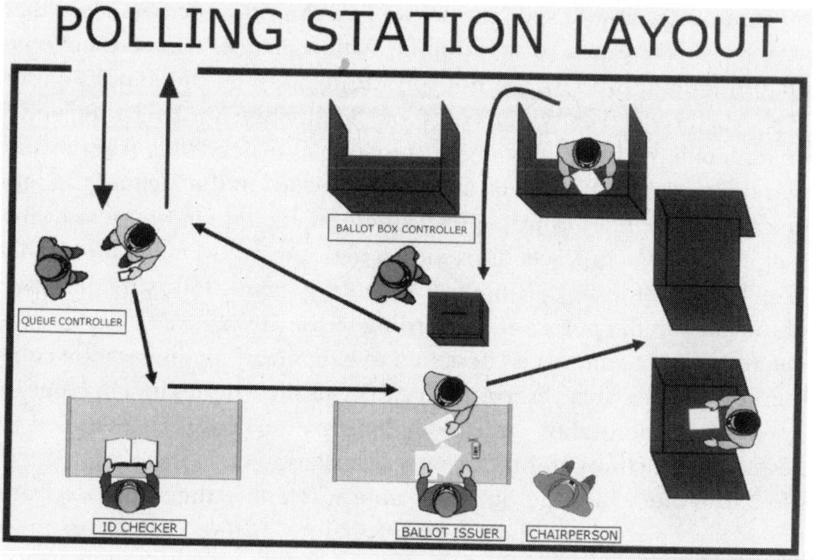

Fig. 10. Ideal polling station layout, 2000. This PowerPoint slide was used in training exercises to show the roles of polling station staff as well as briefly to explain the spatial placement of desks, booths, and boxes and the efficient flow of voters. The 1997 version of this image (in the Polling and Counting Manual) is very similar but has no labels, the chair is seated elsewhere, and there are only two voting screens. *(Courtesy of the Organization for Security and Co-Operation in Europe, Mission to Bosnia and Herzegovina.)*

the ink; and staff members were apathetic. My fieldnotes document the deployment of the light in my polling station:

> Due to the small voter list, we were not ever very busy and often the committee and observers, and myself to a lesser extent, were smoking, drinking, or eating in the other room. Whenever a voter arrived, we sprang into action. The first stage in the voting process, often skipped because that committee member did not spring into action as quickly as the rest, was to check the potential voter's right index finger.

Across Bosnia, few voters were ever turned away as a result of the ultraviolet light check.

The ink check disappeared from the *Rules and Regulations* in 2000. My colleagues and informants expressed little concern with the removal of this check against voter fraud. No one, including relatively high-level electoral staff, could tell me why the change had occurred. Guesses included that there was now only one day of voting, that the election budget had been severely reduced, that voters were more trustworthy, and that it had been ineffective. One senior electoral staffer relayed my question to a head election official in Sarajevo and was told that there were three reasons for the change. First, doing so would "regularize the process and remove restrictions." This type of ink was not commonly used in elections in other countries and was felt to be insulting to Bosnians. The logic appeared to be that the Bosnians now deserved to be trusted and that the ink check was restrictive because it was based on physical rather then identificatory evidence. Second, according to the official, the ink check did not appear in the *Rules and Regulations* (overlooking the fact that it had explicitly been written into the *Rules and Regulations* for the three previous elections). The tautological nature of this answer suggests that electoral officials thought of themselves only as technicians, implementing the rules without thinking about who created them, how, or why. The third reason given was budgetary concerns. I was unable to learn how much money was saved by cutting ink, bottles, ultraviolet lights, and batteries from the budget, but various cost-saving measures were frequently tried. For example, cutting the tenure of polling station supervisors by just one day would have reduced costs by USD$90,000 in per diem payments alone. Removing the cost of the ink and ultraviolet lights was not as likely to be as cost-effective.

These explanations speak more to the normalization of certain standards and expectations within democracy and elections and less to concerns about ineffectiveness or voter fraud. These explanations omit—and perhaps staff members were not aware of—the existence of greater degree of control over other aspects of voter identity and action. Fluorescent ink was needed less because other checks, such as identification checks, were better integrated into the electoral and governmental structure. Greater control over citizen identification (by the Bosnian state) and the voter register (by the OSCE) translated into less need for control over voters' bodies (or at least the perception of such). This bothered at least one Bosnian, who, after learning that I was studying the elections, launched into a litany of complaints, starting with the removal of the ink check, which she believed left the polls wide open to fraud. "Anyone could pretend to be anyone without a physical mark!" she exclaimed. Her sentiment was exactly the opposite of that inside the election bureaucracy. Election staffers felt confident linking government-issued photo identification cards to voters, believing that state control over identification was an effective instrument to limit fraud. She disagreed, supporting bodily rather than identificatory marks.[4] Whether the check worked did not necessarily make a difference in how voters perceived its effectiveness. The mechanism led them to trust the process and, at least until the transition to trusted government identification documents, was a key determinant of fairness in Bosnia's postwar elections.

After passing by the queue controller/ultraviolet light checker, voters continue to the ID checker (lower left corner, fig. 10). This member of the polling station committee affirms each voter's identity by matching the presented identification document with the person and looking up each voter's name on the polling station's voter register (an excerpt of the full voter register). Voters were required to produce not just any identification but an acceptable form. The list of acceptable documents shifted with each election, moving from a rather extensive 13-item list in 1997, to a smaller and more rigid list of state-sanctioned and state-produced photo ID documents in 2000 (table 1). The 1997 list took into account such things as fears among voters over state control of personal information, the loss of identification as a result of war damage, and inability or unwillingness to get a new state-issued identification card. The shrunken list used during the last internationally administered election (November 2000) brought Bosnia-Herzegovina's "identification process in line with established democratic norms": a state-sponsored identification document with an attached photograph. Furthermore, the state had to be recognized as a state; thus, identification documents issued by the unrecognized war governments of Herceg-Bosna and the Republic of Bosnia were phased out, although documents from states such as Austria, Serbia, Canada, and Sweden were deemed acceptable.

The voter register listed names, state identity numbers, gender, registration numbers, and residence locator information and had blank boxes reserved for signatures. The excerpt shown in figure 11 lists persons living in municipality 006 (Bosanska Krupa/Krupa Na Uni) registered as constituents of municipality 004 (Bosanska Krupa) who are instructed to vote at Polling Station 006B3501. Each voter signs next to his or her printed name before continuing on to the ballot issuer, who theoretically gives a single ballot to each voter along with verbal instructions on marking the ballot. The ballot issuer then sprays each voter's right index fingernail with the silver nitrate ink. Voters next proceed to the cardboard voting screens. There they are to mark their ballots "in secrecy," rather than engaging in nonelectoral or fraudulent activities,

TABLE 1. Acceptable Identification Documents, 1997–2000

1997 General Registration	1997 General Polling	1997 Republika Srpska	1998 Municipal	2000 Municipal	2000 General
ID card	National ID card	National ID card	ID card	ID card	ID card
Citizenship certificate	Citizenship certificate	Citizenship certificate	Citizenship certificate	Citizenship certificate	Passport
Passport	Passport	Passport	Passport	Passport	Driver's licence
Birth certificate	Birth certificate	Birth certificate	Birth certificate	Birth certificate	Military ID
Resident certification	Resident certificate	Resident certificate	Resident certificate	Driver's license	Valid identification document issued by a host country
Driver's license	Driver's license	Driver's licence	Driver's license	Military booklet	Refugee card issued by a host country or other international organization
Military booklet	Military booklet	Military booklet	Military booklet	Residency certificate	
Health booklet	Health booklet	Health booklet	Health booklet	Passport issued by a foreign government that permits dual citizenship	
Certificate of registration of change of name	Certificate of registration of change of name	Certificate of registration of change of name	Certificate of registration of change of name	Refugee card issued by a host government or other international agency	

TABLE 1. Acceptable Identification Documents, 1997–2000 (cont'd.)

1997 General Registration	1997 General Polling	1997 Republika Srpska	1998 Municipal	2000 Municipal	2000 General
Passport issued by a foreign government that permits dual citizenship	Passport issued by a foreign government that permits dual citizenship	Passport issued by a foreign government that permits dual citizenship	Passport issued by a foreign government that permits dual citizenship	Displaced person card	
Declaration	Displaced person card	Displaced person card or refugee card	A refugee card issued by a host government or other international agency		
		Declaration	Displaced person card		
			Declaration		

Note: These lists were taken from the training manuals, which summarize the *Rules and Regulations* established by the Provisional Election Commission for each election. I have kept the original wording as much as possible.

Općі izbori 2000 – Birački spisak
Općі izbori 2000 – Popis birača
Општи избори 2000 – Бирачки списак

006 БОСАНСКА КРУПА / КРУПА НА УНИ				006Б3501
Презиме и име	Рег. број			
Матични број	Пол	Нас. мјесто	Рег. број	Потпис

Општина за коју гласа	Комбинација гласачких листића број
004 БОСАНСКА КРУПА	**01**

АЈДУКОВИЋ, МИЛЕНА	0527106214			
0104975116069	Ж	104205		
БЈЕЛАЈАЦ, НИКОЛА	0451530356			
1607962111055	М	104507		
ВОЈИНОВИЋ, РАЈКО	0451484951			
04.02.1935	М	104191		
САЛКИЋ, САБИРА	0268168138			
29.06.1963	Ж	104094R		

Број имена на списку: 4

Страна 1 од 2

Fig. 11. Voter register sample, 2000. Bar codes were scanned during the counting period after Election Day to create an electronic list of voters. The list was checked before accepting a submitted tendered ballot to ensure that a voter was not attempting to vote multiple times. *(Courtesy of the Organization for Security and Co-Operation in Europe, Mission to Bosnia and Herzegovina.)*

Fig. 12. Vote casting, Kosovo, 2001. Ballot boxes in Bosnia were constructed by PSC members out of cardboard during the early elections. Later, the OSCE bought permanent blue metal boxes. The Kosovo ballot boxes, more typical of internationally observed or supervised elections around the globe, were made of clear plastic.

such as putting ballots in their purses or vandalizing the voter screen. After leaving a voting screen, voters walk up to the ballot box and, under the watch of the ballot box controller, slide their ballots through the small top slit (fig. 12).

Of course, not all people appearing to vote existed as entries on a polling station's unique excerpted voter register. In such cases, voters could fill out and sign both a supplementary voter register (providing their name, ID number, date of birth, gender, and voting municipality) and a special envelope with the same information (fig. 13). These voters were then allowed to vote but the back of their ballots were stamped with a *T* (until it was found that the ink leaked through to the front, making it hard to read the ballot; in the next election, ballot issuers were asked to write a *T* on the back of the ballot). After voters marked their ballot, they placed it in the envelope on which they had previously filled out identifying information. The envelope was then cast into the ballot box.

Polling Station Number

Tendered Ballot Envelope

1   Registration Number

2   National ID Number

3   Family Name

4   First Name

5   Date of Birth

6   Sex

M   F

7   Municipality where normally resident

8   Settlement Number where normally resident

9   Electoral Unit Code

For Official Use Only

Confirmed   Denied   Code

Fig. 13. Text on tendered ballot envelopes, 2000. A member of the polling station committee, generally the chair, filled out the supplemental voter register and tendered ballot envelope before the voter proceeded to the ballot issuer. An efficient polling station layout (see fig. 10) might also have a desk for these tendered ballot activities.
(Courtesy of the Organization for Security and Co-Operation in Europe, Mission to Bosnia and Herzegovina.)

The presence of the identifying information allowed a central office to later verify the voter's registration status. If the envelope's information was verified, it was opened and its ballot was counted. The *T* marked on ballot's backs was meant as a mechanism to prevent accidental and strategic attempts to cast tendered ballots as regular ones: if a ballot with a *T* was found in the ballot box, it was not to be counted.

Tendered ballots had a checkered history in Bosnia-Herzegovina. When used in September 1997, the ballots were promoted as a means through which potentially disenfranchised people could still participate in their country's decisions. That is, if a person came to a polling station but could not be found on the voter register, he or she could still vote. The mechanism accounted for (or acknowledged) the possibility of errors in the organization of the voter register. Tendered ballots were sent to a processing facility where staff used a database program to check if the person was a valid voter and had voted in the municipality for which he or she had registered. As a result of concerns about the fraudulent use of tendered ballots and a sense of confidence in the accuracy of the voter register, however, officials decided that for the November 1997 election, tendered ballots would be issued only to voters who had a notation after their name that said "Duplicate" or "Tendered Ballot Required." The electoral administration had tracked such people as being listed more than once in the database and thus probably also being listed on multiple polling station voter registers. The use of tendered ballots would mean that if these people voted more than once, the fraud would be discovered. However, the restriction of the circumstances under which tendered ballots could be used left voters not found on voter registers without recourse, except perhaps to try all the polling stations in town (if there was a town), looking for their names on the numerous registers. This change created enormous tumult on the first day of polling and led to the restoration of the original tendered ballot practice on the second day.

Three years, and two elections later, a midlevel electoral official told me that tendered ballots primarily constituted a mechanism to accommodate returning refugees. Refugees normally voted by mail, sending their ballots from their foreign homes to a facility in Vienna. However, this official informed me, refugees in the process of returning or visiting home during the election period sometimes needed or wanted to vote in person. They could go to any polling station in the country with the contingency that they vote by tendered ballot so that the nonduplication of a mailed-in ballot could be verified and double voting could be prevented.

The bar scan (seen in fig. 11), a technique introduced in 2000, allowed for a high-tech check against double voting in which people voted once by the regular method and once by tendered ballot. While the ink check had served this function in earlier elections, the new system relied on control over identification. However, it could not prevent persons voting for or as different persons, which probably occurred. (The OSCE received complaints from people attempting to vote but discovering that someone else had already signed their name.) In 1997, a written memo warned supervisors about this masquerade voting:

> A great deal can be done fraudulently. Make sure nobody signs someone's name in the [final voter register] and/or gives someone more than one ballot. Remember, the Local Staff will know who has registered . . . but will NOT be coming to vote. That vote could be used fraudulently by someone else. Any person could sign the [register] for that person when the Supervisor is not looking. BE CAREFUL!

The new bar code mechanism could only stop persons from voting (as themselves) more than once. More accurately, because the bar codes were not scanned until the postelection auditing and counting phases, the new procedure could prevent a person's second (tendered) ballot from being counted. The mechanism was unable to distinguish between double voting by one person and fraudulent voting by a person masquerading as another. It also relied on heavy technical and labor power as each barcode (corresponding to a signature on a polling station's voter register) had to be scanned by hand.

At the same time, supervisors were being told to use tendered ballots as a pacification mechanism. Many trainers encouraged supervisors to give angry or belligerent voters tendered ballots because they represented a quick and easy way to restore calm and order in the polling station. The person would still receive a ballot, although whether it would be counted was uncertain. This way, the trainers continued, supervisors were not charged with the responsibility of deciding who was a valid voter and who was fraudulent. That responsibility was shifted to nonhuman databases and their executors.

Bosnians as a whole vehemently distrusted the tendered ballot mechanism, with some political parties and groups claiming that such ballots were thrown away and never counted. Others claimed that it singled out particular individuals, violated the secret ballot, or constituted merely a

mechanism for masking the fact that the voter register was poorly organized. In September 1997, fewer than 25 percent of tendered ballots sur-
vived the computerized verification process. It will never be clear if such
a low rate resulted from attempts to vote by nonregistered persons, persons attempting to vote multiply or in different municipalities, or the
database's failure to match voter and registrant information (either
because of inconsistencies in information or because of organizational
and logistical difficulties). Bosnian voters and political parties disagreed
with international electoral administrators on the intent behind tendered ballots, their necessity, and their effectiveness.

Polls closed at seven o'clock in the evening. Like all other aspects of the
voting process, the activity was regulated and ordered. According to
chapter 8 of the *Polling and Counting Manual,* an announcement was supposed to be made fifteen minutes prior to closing. Then, at seven o'clock
sharp, if there was a queue of waiting voters, a polling committee member would take a position at the end of the line. We had no such queue
at our polling station; in fact I had seriously considered—or fantasized
about—closing for at least the preceding two hours. It was dark, cold,
and deserted. But we remained open. I did not verbalize my secret
desire, and no one approached me with the temptation.

At seven o'clock, we sealed the top of the ballot box, making sure that
the number on the seal was the same one previously written down on the
daily accounting form. The chair decided that I would fill out the
accounting form, since as he said, according to my translator, the form
came from my people, my organization. Did this mean that I understood
it better, that the form would be trusted more with my writing, or that he
wanted to excuse himself from any charges of fraud? Regardless of his
rationale, I readily accepted the chore thinking I could ensure its accuracy more readily if I controlled it. The daily accounting form (fig. 9)
required us to sum up two objects—signatures and ballots—and to classify them in a variety of ways: supplemental signatures, declined ballots,
spoiled ballots, and unused ballots. We calculated each in the order prescribed by the form. First, we counted the signatures in the final voter
register. As we had hosted few voters during the twelve hours of polling,
this process did not require the same attention as the morning's count of
names. This time, the chair turned the pages faster, without his thumb as
a guide, simply noting and summing in his head the few signatures on
each page. Coming to a total of 38 and adding the 2 signatures of the vot-

ers who had been issued tendered ballots, I entered 40 in box 5 on the form.[5] However, when reading the instructions for box 6, we found that two signatures for tendered ballot voters from the supplemental voter register were supposed to be counted and recorded there, so I crossed out 40, replaced it with 38, and entered 2 in box 6. The sum of boxes 5 and 6 was entered in box 7. Box 8 was a repeat of box 2a, the number of ballots received. That left the number of declined and spoiled ballots (both found in envelope 3). Finding the envelope empty, I entered a 0 in boxes 9 and 10. Adding up the figures in box 7 and box 10, we recorded the number of used ballots used in box 11 (40 signatures plus 0 spoiled/declined ballots equals 40 used). Unused ballots were to be recorded in box 12, and the form instructed us to subtract the figure in box 11 from the figure in box 8 to get this number (300 received minus 40 used equals 260 unused). Later, during ballot counting, these numbers should reconcile with the number of ballots in the ballot box. However, they did not. We had only 259 ballots left over. One of the committee members discovered that we had 9 ballots left on the pad, which meant that we had issued 41 ballots, not 40. Shocked and annoyed, we again counted the signatures on the final voter register, with each of us keeping a separate count as the chair slowly turned pages. This time, we counted 39 signatures in the final voter register. It was fortunate that we checked. If a recount had taken place and had shown 40 signatures but 41 used ballots, we would have faced accusations that we had issued multiple ballots to one person, failed to require everyone's signature, or engaged in other potentially fraudulent behavior.[6]

Fortunately, given our mistakes, I had been filling out these numbers on a sample worksheet (fig. 14), and I now neatly transferred the information to the official daily accounting form. We then began to pack the election materials for overnight storage in preparation for the second day of polling. We placed the unused ballots and ballot stubs into a sealed transport box; placed the voter registers, poll book, daily accounting form, and envelope 3 into a clear plastic bag, sealed it with tape; and then placed the transport box and clear plastic bag into a white tamper-evident bag, which we sealed with #1812015 (recorded in box B of the daily accounting form). The chair wrote the polling station number on the bag in heavy black marker, and we began to turn off the lights and leave the room.

At this point, the chair and I disagreed about who would transport the bag to the overnight storage center. As I interpreted the instructions,

DAILY ACCOUNTING FORM

Municipality Name: Trebinje   Polling Station Number: _____   Unit Number: (if applicable) _____

Instructions for completing Form:

Complete ALL parts of the Daily Accounting Form. This sheet is to give specific instructions for those Lines that need clarification:

Line 5: Count and record number of signatures on FVR

Line 6: Count and record number of signatures on SVR

Line 7: Calculate and record total number of voters on Day 1 (add line 5 + line 6)

Line 8: Calculate and record total number of Ballots received on Day 1 (add line 2a + 4a)

Line 11: Record the quantity of the USED Ballots that were issued to voters during first day of Polling (add line 7 + 10 ONLY)

Line 12: Record the quantity of UNUSED Ballots (line 8 minus line 11)

Line 13: Record the number of the Plastic One Way Seal used to secure the White Tamper Evident Bag for overnight storage

Line 16: The Polling Station Chairperson must sign this in the presence of the International Supervisor attesting that they have ensured the figures and serial numbers have not been altered or disturbed during overnight storage

Line 17: The Polling Station Chairperson must sign this in the presence of the Polling Station Chairperson attesting that they have ensured the figures and serial numbers have not been altered or disturbed during overnight storage

Distribute the copies as follows:

OSCE HO Sarajevo: Put Original into Packet 7 for the International Supervisor to take to the Field Office

Local Election Commission: Put into Packet 6 to be given to an LEC representative for the LEC Chairperson - Green copy

Tendered Ballots Material: Put into Packet 5, then place with the Tendered Ballots in the Coloured Tamper Evident Bag for transportation to Counting Centre - Blue copy

Polling Station Chairperson: The Polling Station Chairperson will keep after signing the original - Pink copy

White	Copy 1
Green	Copy 2

Original to OSCE HO Sarajevo (Packet 7)
Local Election Commission Chairperson (Packet 6)

Copy 2 Blue   Tendered Ballot Materials (Packet 5)
Copy 4 Pink   Polling Station Chairperson (given at PS)

PART I: BEFORE FIRST VOTER VOTES ON DAY 1

1.	Number of Voters on FVR			1	191
2a.	Number of Ballots Received	268451	To: 268750	2a	300
2b.	Serial Number Ranges	From			
3.	Serial Number of "Drop Slot" seal		Box Seal No. 34401		

PART II: DURING POLLING ON DAY 1

4a.	Additional Ballots Received			4a	
4b.	Serial Number Ranges	From	To:		

PART III: AT THE CLOSE OF POLLING STATION ON DAY 1

5.	Number of Signatures on the FVR	5	38 31
6.	Number of Signatures on SVR	+ 6	3
7.	Total Number of Voters on Day 1 (line 5 + line 6)	= 7	3041
8.	Ballots received on Day 1 (line 2a + line 4a)	8	300
9.	Number of Declined Ballots (from Packet 3)	9	0
10.	Number of Spoiled Ballot (from Packet 3)	10	0
11.	Ballots USED (add Line 7 + 10 Only)	11	4041
12.	Total Ballots UNUSED (minus line 8 - 11)	12	260289
13.	Record Serial No: of Plastic One-Way Seal for overnight storage:	Seal No. 18206	
14.	Signature of Polling Station Chairperson		
15.	Signature of International Supervisor		

PART IV: BEFORE FIRST VOTER VOTES ON DAY 2

We, the undersigned attest that we have taken steps to verify that 1) the Final Voters Register and Supplemental Voters Register have not been altered or defaced overnight; 2) the Ballot Box and "Drop Slot" seal affixed on Day 1 remain unchanged; 3) same number of unused ballots remain unchanged since the polls closed on Day 1

16.	Confirmation signature of Polling Station Chairperson	
17.	Confirmation signature of International Supervisor	

Fig. 14. Daily accounting form worksheet, 1997. There is an error in the instructions for line 17, which should read that the international supervisor had to sign the document in the presence of the polling station chair. The polling station number has been removed to preserve anonymity. (*Courtesy of the Organization for Security and Co-Operation in Europe, Mission to Bosnia and Herzegovina.*)

the polling station supervisor was supposed to transport the material. However, in an inversion of trust (or in a duplication of the lack of trust), the chair refused to allow me to transport the electoral material, telling my interpreter to tell me that he would take it. Loudly debating through the moderating voice of Boris, our disagreement was only resolved after I radioed the Election Office to ask for clarification. The voice on the radio told Boris to inform the chair that if he had a problem, he should talk to his superiors on the Municipal Election Commission, who had agreed to this procedure. We placed the tamper-evident bags in the back of my driver's van and drove in a convoy to the storage center.

The next morning, the majority of the practices repeated themselves. I still got to the polling station on time, dragging Boris and our driver with me, after stopping by the storage center to recover the polling materials safely ensconced in their tamper-evident bags and guarded during the night by police officers, election staff, and international supervisors. During this pickup, supervisors were milling around, waiting to receive their bags and reading updated instructions. The most significant change was that the tendered ballot policy had been reversed. We were to now offer tendered ballots to anyone not found on the voter register rather than to just the people with a mark next to their name on the voter register. The polling station committee met me, as on the first day, approximately a half hour before opening. However, on the second day, we had fewer opening tasks and I had fewer anxieties about the need to open on time. Our main duties involved verifying that material had not been tampered with. Because the bags looked okay, we signed the daily accounting form, attesting to our verifications. I broke open the seal of the ballot box, and the chair announced to no one in particular that voting had begun.

The second day passed much as the first had—waiting for voters— although we were warmer, having left the space heater on all night. With plenty of time between voters, we spent time socializing on the porch, eating, and drinking. The chair's wife had packed a buffet picnic for us (since the town had no facilities), complete with homemade cheese, smoked pork, bread, cubes of solidified fat, and homemade plum brandy. As seven o'clock in the evening came and went with nary a voter in sight, we grumbled about electoral regulations, bonding in our boredom. (We had been informed by radio a few hours earlier that polling had been extended an hour; we were now to close at eight o'clock, not seven o'clock. Someone had decided that another hour of polls would resolve some tensions or problems with voters trying to reach polling sta-

tions. We certainly did not have that problem at our polling station.)
Eight o'clock eventually arrived, and we sealed the top of the ballot box
and began to clear the desks in preparation for counting the ballots.

Technical Democracy

Without social and technical electoral artifacts and practices (actants, as
Latour would call them) to frame the action, Election Day would be
impossible. Democracy and the knowledge it creates rely on a complex
web of actant relationships. The creation of political figures (e.g., presidents, council members, parliamentarians) is not simply a translation or
the measure of the sovereign will of the people. Underneath this purportedly single translation from opinion to leader lies a substantial network of material and knowledge practices. Andrew Barry briefly comments on this phenomenon in light of the November 2000 U.S. electoral
debacle:

> Consider the question of the capacity of persons to act as voters.
> The design, distribution and counting of ballot papers requires
> constant and substantial investments. The frame of representative
> democracy breaks down when these investments are not properly
> made, and the frame made secure; when questions can be raised
> about the marks made on ballot papers, registration of voters and
> the distribution of polling booths. . . . It is rare, as the case of
> American presidential election of 2000 demonstrates, that this
> framing is challenged and disintegrates as each technical compo-
> nent is scrutinized. (2002:269)

Before 2000, U.S. voters rarely if ever considered the possibility that the
technical aspects of an election could affect whether their voices were
heard and their votes counted. Although people at times grumbled
about the oddity of the Electoral College in determining presidential
elections, American voters remained woefully ignorant about the existence of invalid ballots, the subjectivities of counting, and, as Mozaffar
and Schedler phrase it, the routine or unacknowledged margin of error
that exists in all elections. They argue that, "in Florida, a statistical dead
heat produced by the closest presidential race in over a century sharply
accentuated the otherwise negligible effects of routine electoral errors
on the final result" (2002:6). What was widely considered a debacle actually represented elections as usual. This is not to say that elections are

usually debacles but rather that the interplay of electoral objects, networks, and practices always has elements of uncertainty, ambiguity, error, and subjectivity. The myth of democracy hides the reality of democracy making.

In Bosnia-Herzegovina, the reality of democracy making was still near the surface; it was still contested in some domains. The international election effort thus involved the building of trust as much as of democracy. Officials sought to create trustworthy elections in Bosnia-Herzegovina by professionalizing and technicalizing their work (cf. Lynch 2005; Rubin 2005 on the debates over computer technology and trust vis-à-vis computer voting). This chapter has not looked at whether or how Bosnians trust the system but rather at the processes thought to build trust—that is, an adherence to structured, rigid, written, bureaucratic practices. Trust, then, is a form of antipolitics, limiting the possibilities of debate and confrontation through its use and normalization of technical procedures (on antipolitics, see Barry 2002; Ferguson 1994).

> In general, legislation and technical regulation have the effects of placing actions and objects (provisionally) outside the realm of public contestation, thereby regularizing the conduct of economic and social life, with both beneficial and negative consequences. (Barry 2002:270)

Technicality, because it is thought of as nonsocial and noncultural, calls forth trust. As one official remarked in a public speech to Bosnian election officials,

> The major challenge is not the technical aspects of [electoral] administration—Bosnians can count and open a polling station—the major challenge is the confidence of the election. Voters need to know that you are a trained professional, not just that you have the job because you are a member of a particular political party.

Here, she effectively removed the social and the contingent from technical electoral actants and framed politics where it traditionally resides—in the power games played by people and political parties. Confidence-increasing measures she advocated included holding meetings open to the public (so citizens would not think that officials were trying to hide anything) and continued use of safeguards and security measures that ensure "free and fair" election machinery. Nationalization was also considered a confidence builder because it would give authority back to Bosnians rather than having important political decisions made by foreigners, who were often seen as having their own political agenda and as undermining Bosnia-Herzegovina's self-determination. Internationals reveled in the idea that they were simply technical administrators—neutral, objective, and efficient—but occasionally admitted that their reputation was not all that they wished. They too, sought to depoliticize elections, increasing trust and confidence by emphasizing the technicality of election work.

Technicality also confronted democratic values. Tolerance, liberty, pluralism, and inclusion are predominantly considered democratic values but were placed into contention with "technical democracy," which simply provides a forum for the contestation of power and authority. As one supervisor cattily remarked, "If the people want to vote in bastards and xenophobes, is that not their right under 'democracy'?" This question was asked often in Bosnia-Herzegovina as the 1996 elections, held less than a year after the signing of the peace agreement, had given governing mandates to political parties and politicians preaching ethnic nationalism and to those who had been in power before and during the war. Many internationals, given these electoral results, remarked that Bosnians were not yet ready for democracy in 1996. This sentiment was widely shared among my informants in Bosnia-Herzegovina and can be seen in peacekeeping and democratization scholarship. In a written report evaluating the 1996 elections, the International Crisis Group, a prominent research-oriented organization that generally promotes increased international authority over Bosnia-Herzegovina, concluded that instead of furthering reconciliation,

> elections held under the current conditions may in fact . . . advance the likelihood of violence—either when on election day a large number of voters cross the former confrontation lines that were hitherto hermetic, or when the time comes to install newly elected leaders to areas from where they have been cleansed. Instead of taking a step in the process of democratisation, the Parties, especially Republika Srpska and "Herzeg-Bosna," have manipulated the registration process and additionally suppressed freedom of expression and association. Thus the run-up to the elections has exacerbated not reduced instability. When voters are directed to vote according to the wishes of the ruling political par-

ties, elections cannot be described as stabilizing. (International Crisis Group 1996b:22)

Proponents of delayed postconflict elections, such as International Crisis Group, advocated using that time to build civil society and encourage pluralism—that is, to focus on democratic values. Technical democracy, like Election Day, does not in itself effect or create democratic values. The mass participation of Bosnian citizens in choosing their leadership does not in and of itself promote tolerance, equality, and an inclusive community.

This chapter has worked to place politics and culture in techne. Techne is not opposed to the social or the political; they are one and the same. Counting ballots and opening polling stations are cultural and political, too. Making distinctions only naturalizes particular constructions of authority and knowledge and allows for a problematic reification of democracy. Despite evidence to the contrary, including that presented here, democracy enjoys an exalted place in the political imagination. Thinking of democratic techne, increasingly exported via cadres of international elite, as simply instrumental fails to account for either its own social and political articulations or its wider social and political implications, in Bosnia-Herzegovina as well as in other sites of democracy promotion around the world.

ELECTORAL ACTANTS

Translating Voter Will into
Political Authority

Just weeks before one of the elections in Bosnia-Herzegovina, I and a few other international electoral technicians had dinner with Margaret, one of the upper echelon of international electoral officials. We went to a restaurant popular with internationals and mere steps from her office. She said it was the only restaurant she frequented because she essentially had "no life," given her workload and the constant political negotiations between international diplomats and Bosnian political parties. In response to a now-forgotten question, she laughingly responded that she and other top international election officials avoided any *F* word: free, fair, or fraud. Margaret's juxtapository play speaks to the difficulties of implementing free, fair, and nonfraudulent elections, particularly in postwar settings. Electoral officials engaged with these issues every day in their routine bureaucratic tasks, yet such matters also hovered uncomfortably and elusively as morality-laden phantasms.

Free and *fair* have become the adjectives of choice to describe valid, democratic elections and to distinguish them from elections held in nondemocratic states (such as totalitarian or authoritarian regimes).[1] Without this designation, governments do not gain international legitimacy. The question, then, is how rather than whether to be democratic; few alternatives exist now that the cold war has ended. In a pro-Western worldview, *free* and *fair* are qualifiers meant as measures or standards of real democracy. An election gains internal and external legitimacy with "free and fair" designation: it will be viewed as a true statement of the will of the people and thus have a mandate for government. However, "free and fair" contributes to a narrowing of the field of being for democracy. There are fewer and fewer ways to be democratic than ever before.

The anxieties and realities behind the joke about the three *F*s suggest that elections might be better thought of as existing on a continuum rather than as fulfilling (or not) discrete, categorical criteria; elections would thus be able to include pragmatics as well as the contextual conditions "fair enough" and "free enough." Jørgen Elklit and Palle Svensson (1997) argue this position, calling for assessments that take into account the local situation (e.g., postconflict status, infrastructure limitations, demonstrations of progress toward greater freedom). Observers could then declare elections "acceptable" even if they fell short of the "free and fair" criteria. Elklit and Svensson provide a checklist to serve as a guideline for election observers, although the authors caution that this list is not exhaustive, does not indicate the relative importance of individual criteria, and does not specify how the criteria can be measured as fulfilled or what to do with partial compliance (1997:36). The "free" checklist contains items such as freedom of movement, speech, assembly, and association; freedom from fear in connection with the election; an absence of impediments to standing as a candidate; equal and universal suffrage; and legal possibilities of complaint. The "fair" checklist contains items such as a transparent election process; impartial treatment of candidates by the police, the army, and the courts of law; an electoral system that grants no special privileges to any political party or social group; impartial voter-education programs; equal access to publicly controlled media; no misuse of government facilities for campaign purposes; secrecy of the ballot; effective design of ballot papers; proper counting procedures; proper treatment of void ballot papers; proper precautionary measures when transporting election materials; official and expeditious announcement of election results; impartial treatment of election complaints; and acceptance of election results by everyone involved (37). These criteria measure freedom and fairness before polling day, on polling day, and after polling day. If the criteria are implemented or satisfied, then an election can be declared "free and fair."

I am interested in precisely the problem of measuring these criteria: how something might be measured or evaluated also suggests its meanings. How are "freedom of movement" or "impartial voter-education campaigns" constructed? To what does the "proper" in "proper counting procedures" actually refer? How do specific components or criteria acquire their status as delimiters of freedom and fairness? In this chapter

I demonstrate that the "free and fair" designation comes into being through electoral objects and their deployment. The processes associated with these measures of democracy are born out of electoral objects and their social and spatial deployment. Their representation as apolitical and technical measures allows democracy to be thought of as external, distinct, or separate from its creations, but freedom and fairness are part of the system. They are not merely external measures of democracy but social productions of democracy. As technical and bureaucratic objects—predominantly thought of as apolitical—electoral objects give meaning to freedom and fairness.

This technicality appears apolitical but in fact frames political action. As Andrew Barry argues, technicality permits politics to be political, permits politics to exist, to be conducted.

> The political actor does not come isolated into the political arena
> any more than the consumer comes isolated into the marketplace.
> He or she comes with a whole array of material devices and forms
> of knowledge which serve to frame political action. (2002:269)

Paradoxically, although techne frames and articulates politics, it is often directed toward antipolitical ends. That is, politics can be antipolitical if its effects suppress potential spaces of contestation or place limits on the possibilities for debate and confrontation (270). Elections, through the measures of freedom and fairness, are exactly this antipolitical political event. Freedom and fairness, as forms of knowledge, establish democracy as an arbiter of morality but do so without acknowledging their contingent social and political nature.

Other theorists, in contrast, claim that freedom and fairness are external measures or judgments of democracy and its conditions. Freedom opposes coercion, while fairness is closely related to impartiality. But freedom also entails something offered. While there must be a choice and there should not be repercussions directly related to the act of making that choice, voters can choose only from among the given options, those options allowed by the electoral system (see Bachrach and Baratz 1970; Dahl 1961 on unacknowledged "dimensions of power" behind standard definitions of politics). Similarly, fairness depends on particular, bounded, and predetermined constructions of impartiality, equality, and reasonability. Thus, while a working characterization of fairness can be constructed that emphasizes equal treatment, the regular and unbiased application of rules, and the reasonable distribution of resources (see Elklit and Svensson 1997:35), picking apart the practices and meanings that make up the terms is relevant to any cultural analysis attendant to structures of naturalized power.

My point is less to show how "free" is not really free or how "fair" is limited in substantial ways. Although ferreting out the inconsistencies between democratic ideology and democratic reality is important work, this chapter focuses more on the substance and tensions within the ideology of democracy, with attention given to how *free* and *fair* receive and make meaning on the ground. Thus, although I note some inconsistencies, I do so less as a mechanism for pointing out places for improvement and more as a commitment to an understanding of the acquisition of meanings. Freedom and fairness may be measures of politics, but they cannot be thought of as separate, apolitical, or inert concepts. Rather, they are firmly entrenched social actants that frame and articulate political activity.[2]

This chapter details the creation of freedom and fairness through the production and deployment of three exemplary electoral objects and processes: voters, ballots, and results. These three objects—better phrased as actants because of the processes that go into making them and because of the processes and influence they subsequently wield— are crucially linked together. They act as translators within a process of transference whereby voters' wills are translated first into ballots and then into results. Voters, presumed to have a singular and extractable opinion, transfer that opinion to a choice on a ballot. The ballot is joined with other ballots and becomes, through a process of counting and tabulating, results. The results are subsequently massaged through electoral system formulas into the appointment of political authorities. I look within each actant to analyze how it came into being in Bosnia-Herzegovina; how it incorporated particular meanings of freedom and fairness while simultaneously denying forms of authority embedded in its form, such as hierarchical relations and apolitical representation; and how complexity was repeatedly reduced as voter will was transformed into political authority.

Voters

Participation is a key discursive domain in democracy, purportedly built into democracy through its call for governance legitimated by the people (see Dahl 1971). Elections are the principal opportunity for citizens to participate in their own governance. Through voting, they choose their political leaders (i.e., representation). Elections call on voters to come to the polls to cast their vote. However, this analytical focus presumes that voters exist a priori and that all that is needed is to harness their will (Barry 2002; Rose 1999). In reality, much work goes into the creation and maintenance of the subject category "voters." Democracy requires educated citizens able to rationalize and calculate their interests within particular logics.

> Citizenship should be studied at the level of the practices, technologies, and mentalities within which citizens were to be formed, not simply as moral subjects that philosophical deliberation seeks to equip with abstract rights and freedom, but as the subjects of governmental technologies, ethicalized individuals capable of exercising self-mastery, discipline, foresight, reason, and self-control. (Rose 1999:226)

How are voters created, and what capabilities are they assumed to have? To what governmental technologies are they subjected?

Voters are those persons who express or act on the election. That is, the election expresses and synthesizes their wills. It creates a collective will and, as politicians are apt to phrase it, a mandate for government. However, voters are also created and acted on by the election process. They allow an election to go forward, but they are also created through the election process and manipulated by electoral practices. Like science's neutrons or soil samples, voters can be thought of as created through their interactions with electoral administrators (cf. Latour 1999). They come into being only through a complex articulation and mutual authorization (Latour 1999:113–44). However, when thought of as objects, as already existing opinion holders, voters as social beings lose their complexity and agency.

Voting is a voluntary activity in most countries. Although a few countries require citizens to vote, it is more generally conceptualized as a civic responsibility and right rather than a duty. It is usually an activity reserved for adult citizens in good standing (i.e., some criminals are denied the franchise).[3] This subset of adult citizens chooses (or not) to register as voters, to become participants in state governance. They simultaneously submit to and legitimate state authority through their registration and participation in polling processes. Furthermore, through registering, voters declare themselves constituents of particular political entities, most often based on residence location. For example, a U.S. citizen living in Ames, Iowa—barring illegality, fraud, or mobile living situations—can register to vote only in Ames, Iowa. In so doing, she declares herself a constituent of the United States of America, the state of Iowa, the municipality of Story County, and the city of Ames.

In Bosnia-Herzegovina, registration and constituency were also structured by citizenship and territorial residence. However, because the war had displaced more than half the population and the international postwar intervention sought to return the displaced to their prewar homes/houses, the process of voter registration was complex. Dayton specified that refugees and internally displaced persons had the right to vote in their original place of residence. Indeed, it was the hope that they would do so: "A citizen who no longer lives in the municipality in which he or she resided in 1991 shall, as a general rule, be expected to vote, in person or by absentee ballot, in that municipality" (Dayton 1995, Annex 3, Article IV). As a result, Bosnian citizens over 18 years of age and listed on the 1991 census had three options regarding their constituent status. They could choose to vote in their prewar area of residence (as determined by the 1991 census), their current residence (as determined by residence documentation between April 6, 1992, and July 31, 1996—essentially the war years), or, although this option was later rescinded, in a future residence (as determined by proven connection to the municipality, such as family living in the area). The determination of constituency specified for whom registrants could vote at local, municipal, cantonal, entity, and state levels, and was interpreted as a statement of residential intent and political engagement. For example, a displaced Bosniac from Srebrenica living in Sarajevo could decide to vote where she currently lived (Sarajevo) and then have the ability to vote for Sarajevan municipal and cantonal candidates, parliamentary candidates of the Federation of Bosnia-Herzegovina, and presidential and vice presidential candidates for Bosnia-Herzegovina. To election officials, this constituency choice meant that she did not plan to return to her home town. Rather, she was opting into decisions that might directly affect her material and residential life. Alternatively, although resident in Sarajevo, she could choose to vote as a Srebrenica constituent and would then vote for Srebrenican municipality seats, the Republika Srpska National Assembly, the Republika Srpska president and vice president, and the Bosnia-Herzegovina president and vice president—she was choosing political involvement and engagement with a territorially distant community. Internationals interpreted this as a statement of intent to return;

in doing so, continued to emphasize the spatial assumptions embedded in democratic governancy yet increasingly challenged by diasporic communities. Finally, she might be planning to move to Mostar, where her daughter lives. She could then choose to vote as a Mostarian might, but from Sarajevo, with the expectation that she would eventually move to Mostar and vote for and from there. Refugees (those displaced outside of Bosnia's borders) could vote only in their prewar home. These constituency options formed a crucial part of the international plan to promote refugee return, introduce neoliberal property regimes, and orchestrate ethnic physical, social, and psychological reconciliation.

Although Dayton has been criticized for its codification of ethnic divisions and ethnonationalist territories as well as for operating with underlying nationalist assumptions about the relationships among identity, territory, and political space (e.g., Campbell 1998, 1999; Dahlman and Tuathail 2005; see also Malkki 1994), most internationals with whom I spoke believed that they were working to reverse the war's effects (cf. Campbell 1999). To this end, data were mined from refugee return rates and voter registration forms to measure and predict demographic shifts as well as to plan electoral logistics such as ballot printing and delivery, polling station locations and security, and counting timelines. A breakdown of how applicants chose to vote in 1997 (table 2) demonstrates that 60 percent of the internally displaced Bosnians who registered chose to vote as constituents of their new residences and 40 percent selected their old residences. However, displaced Serbs (now living in Serb-dominated areas) were more likely to vote in their new residences than were displaced Bosniacs and Croats. That the majority of registrants declared themselves residents and constituents of their newest residential location depressed the electoral official who gave me the raw numbers that later formed the basis of the table in an Office of Democratic Institutions and Human Rights (ODIHR) electoral report. As the official interpreted these numbers, they belied a common assumption about voters: that they have a primarily political allegiance to that territorial political entity. However, we should not discount a host of other rationales for the decision about where to register, including the desire to have a say in the political structure of their temporary home or reaping symbolic and material benefits of a public declaration of allegiance. Such was the case in Bosnia-Herzegovina, where local officials sometimes coerced displaced persons to register in their 1996 locations to receive aid and welfare benefits or simply to avoid being branded as traitors. As Julie Y. Chu (2005) reminds us with her analysis of the market for U.S. immigration papers among elderly Chinese in China with no plans of migration but a desire to be buried rather than cremated, documents may have a very pragmatic life far outside of their official intent, function, or purpose (cf. Riles 2006). As false as an isolatable political will, the documentary designation of a person as a constituent through voter registration relies on tenuous assumptions of political participatory desire and presumed relations between identity and territory.

Eligibility to vote was determined by three factors: citizenship, age, and residency. People were eligible to vote if they were citizens of Bosnia-Herzegovina over the age of 18 by the date of the election. However, the designation of these factors was not a matter merely of declaration but also of evidence and proof. Those eligible could present themselves and their proof of identity, citizenship, and residency to voter registration staff during a registration period. Much work was involved in this process. The first steps of registration involved setting up an intensive and complex bureaucratic and institutional infrastructure; determining a time period for registering citizens; setting up and staffing voter registration centers with local personnel as well as international monitors; and announcing the process to citizens through media advertisements. Only after these steps had been completed could citizens appear in person at a designated site with their evidence. At this point, the applicant was petitioning various government structures to be designated as a voter—the state authority is in charge, and the effect is to empower the state as well as the voter as effective actors. To verify an applicant's identity the applicant needed to produce one of several "acceptable documents" to the voter registration staff, the same lists described in table 1 (in the chapter "Election Day").

After someone had applied, the registration staff would attempt to

TABLE 2. Voting patterns, 1997

Entity	Voting and Resident in 1991 Municipality	Voting for 1991 Municipality via Absentee	Voting for 1996 Municipality	Total
Federation of Bosnia-Herzegovina	1,036,271	235,544	55,854	1,331,670
Republika Srpska	587,372	347,636	221,943	1,177,556
Total	1,623,643	583,180	277,797	2,509,226

Note: The numbers are approximations of voter registration constituency allegiances based on OSCE figures as of September 1, 1997.
Source: ODIHR 1997

find his or her name in the 1991 census records accessed through a database software program. The prewar 1991 census was important to international organizations because it was considered relatively legitimate and accurate—the work of a still-functioning state apparatus—since it had been collected before tensions actualized. For voter registration purposes, the census information could prove both citizenship and 1991 residence location. If applicants existed on the 1991 census (normally checked via an indexed lookup feature using the applicant's identification number), then citizenship and residence could be confirmed. Registrants not conforming to the expectation of 1991 constituency selection or of existence in the 1991 census often found themselves mired in complex and fraught processes of information acquistion, verification, and authentication. Residents now living in different municipalities could choose to register at their current residences provided they could prove they lived there. If applicants were not on the census (or could not be found on the census), they began a process of proving their existence, citizenship, and residence by collecting official documents and submitting a claim to the Election Appeals Subcommission. They were required to provide, using a form prepared by the OSCE, a citizenship certificate issued prior to 1991 or a receipt from a municipal authority stating that the applicant was recorded as a citizen in an official municipal record book prior to that year. This could be difficult if the 1991 municipality was non-cooperative or if the record books were damaged or missing. The 1997 *Rules and Regulations* stated that the only forms of acceptable proof were a residency receipt issued by the appropriate municipal authority, a displaced person card (e.g., issued by the UN High Commission for Refugees), or a state identity card.

However, one report noted some controversy regarding the strict application of acceptable proof of residency:

> The Rules and Regulations left too little room for judgment, in that a very precise list of documents were defined as the only ones accepted; although it is recognised that this was a response to the situation in 1996 when massive fraud in manipulating the electorate took place. (ODIHR 1997:12)

The report further noted problems with registration outside of the formal confines of the voter registration centers:

Among the significant irregularities reported by observers was the linkage of registration with, for example, the provision of human-itarian aid, the issuing of public documentation, or with employ-ment or property questions. The second issue that came to the attention of the observers was the use of more general intimida-tory statements and practises to encourage people to register, or to register for a particular place. (ODIHR 1997:11)

Voters, articulated by the electoral voter registration system, were also put into place by the mediations of social circumstances, including coer-cive, symbolic, and pragmatic practices.

In 1997, at the end of this process, applicants received a voter receipt, and their forms were packaged with the other forms processed that day and sent as a batch to the processing center, where, as detailed in the introduction to part 2 of this volume, much technical work goes into forming voters as actants. Each day, the processed forms had to be appended to the computer database of voters. When the database was complete, the names needed to be checked against the list of indicted war criminals (from the International Criminal Tribunal for the Former Yugoslavia), duplicated names removed, and mistakes in bubbling of individual names fixed. The data subsequently needed to be sorted in a variety of ways to create municipal-level and polling-station-level voter registers and to estimate the number and type of ballots needed. The articulation of voters through this process creates a sense of the voter as independent and as already existing prior to registration—all that is needed is to register them. However, voters materialize only through specific technical, legal, and political practices. Furthermore, the voter's political will, its existence, and its forms of expression are crucially artic-ulated by all of the formal and informal, legal and extralegal, pragmatic and symbolic social practices that swirl around that voter.

Publicity campaigns aimed at advertising both the registration period and the benefits of voting urged residents of Bosnia-Herzegovina to become voters and partake in the transformation and governance of their new country. Citizens were repeatedly told that their will mattered and that they were responsible now for the care of Bosnia. But how does a voter technically make a choice? A variety of forums were used by the election administration to shape their knowledge and conduct. Brochures, posters, and booklets informed voters how to mark ballots, how voting day worked, where to vote, how their votes would be counted, and how the eventual results would be tabulated. Deciding upon a choice is not enough; the choice also must be made materially. Bosnians were told how to act as voters as well as how to be voters when the time came. For example, in 2000, polling station committee staff members were directed to hand a flyer to each voter waiting in line. Addressing the voter directly and personally, the flyer specified the six steps of voting:

1. Having the finger checked for an ink mark
2. Presenting identification
3. Signing the voter register
4. Having the finger marked with ink
5. Taking the ballot
6. Going to the voter screen to vote

Descending into minute detail, the instruction flyer even informed waiting voters that, "in every voting screen you will find a pen to use for voting, but if you prefer you can use your own pen." Like Latour's actants, defined by what they do, voters needed to be told how to act and how to perform what they were meant to do. Voters vote, of course, but they can only do the work required of them with the assistance of a great deal of other articulation.

Voters are the purported centerpieces of an election, but they are strangely displaced. As one election supervisor pithily put it, echoing the complaints of many others,

> It bothers me that it seems that the focal point of my role is to ensure smooth elections—not for the sake of future democracy in Bosnia-Herzegovina/Republika Srpska, but for the sake of being able to say that the elections they organized were successful.

His comment came after a push by the election administration to be more "service oriented" toward voters. In the effort to have impartial and standardized elections with equal treatment under the law (and bureaucracy), the needs and real complexities of persons had been erased. Service was sometimes sacrificed for efficiency and control, such as a decision in one election to limit tendered ballots to particular polling stations. A tendered ballot is specifically a mechanism designed to allow voters not found on a voter register to cast a ballot. It made little sense, in terms of voter convenience, to permit this contingent ballot only at particular polling stations. Were voters supposed to travel to this special polling station after being turned away at another station? What if they lacked the time or means to travel to another polling station? Why punish the voter for what might have been an administrative error? In terms of electoral efficacy and control, however, the idea is masterful. It simplified the distribution of resources, such as ballots, specialized envelopes, and accounting forms. Given the number of voters in Bosnia casting ballots for other municipalities other than the one they lived in, were all 3,223 polling stations supposed to receive the full complement of municipal, cantonal, district, entity, and federal ballots? Was it logistically feasible to distribute resources this way? Was it cost-effective to account for all possibilities? Normally, polling stations are places of certainty and control. Voters are not free to turn up at any polling station but may vote only at a polling station specified by the electoral administration. Thus, the electoral logistics interpolate them and their participatory frame. For example, in Bosnia-Herzegovina, voters planning to vote for the prewar (1991) constituencies were funneled to polling stations that carried only absentee ballots. The voter register specified which type of ballot the voter should receive. Voters could not change their earlier decision regarding constituency. Their "will" was, in substantial ways, shaped and set in conjunction with bureaucratic rationalities. The election framework renders freedom and fairness (and voters) accessible and visible. Freedom and fairness, if they are measures, assess the degree of successful erasure of politics from democratic knowledge and democratic techne.

Ballots

Along with voters, ballots are quintessential electoral objects. They are, after all, the objects on which voters mark their intent. As referents (Latour 1999), the ballots act as the isolated voter will since voters are physically and bureaucratically detached from their vote after it is cast. The ballot now stands in for the voter and is a material guarantor of the moment he or she specified their "will." However, until the ballot is placed in the ballot box, the voter and the concomitant mark are entangled in a social world. The complexity of the voter's investments in the process or outcome becomes invisible through the translation of complex decisions into an isolated, specified and sanctioned, anonymous, technical ballot. Moreover, a ballot is not free-form. The innovation of the Australian secret ballot in 1856 was government printing of the ballot rather than voter- or party-supplied ballots. In contemporary democracies, voters mark their choice or choices from a given list of candidates or parties. Although, many electoral systems allow for the possibility of write-in candidates, such was not the case in Bosnia-Herzegovina. However, even when write-in candidates are permitted, the form of the ballot dictates the proper protocol for writing in a name but does so at the expense of voter will and, in at least one case, can unleash debates regarding the relationships among democracy, the law, and voter intent. In November 2004, Donna Frye ran a late but coordinated and highly publicized write-in campaign for the mayorship of the city of San Diego. The race was expected to be close; however, few observers expected the contest to be as virulent and legalistic as it became. The incumbent was originally declared the winner after ballots with Frye's name misspelled were discounted. Legal action reversed both these decisions, but further legal action led to the discounting of 5,000 ballots after a judge ruled that the city's laws required that the ballot have the write-in candidate's name *and* the bubble filled in. The other candidate thus won the race by 2,000 votes. Even when trying to allow openness for unregulated voter intent, the form and aesthetic of voter marks is regulated. Some marks signify intent, while others do not. Any ballot has an overabundance of meanings as well as things that are unsaid and said; like more recognizable forms, ballots are indeterminate in their blankness (Yablon 1992). The ballot does not, for example, specify the rules to which the mark will become subject, the rules regulating the appearance of candidates' names, or the rules that will articulate the single marks into cumulative results. The ballot gives the voter power but attempts to technicalize and apoliticize its own power. Without visible power, the ballot becomes part of the regime of freedom and fairness. Only when the frames of power are disrupted does the previously uncontestable become thinkable. Conceptualizing ballots as actants, however, allows an analysis attendant to the legitimating work put into ballots as well as the work they later legitimize.

Bosnian-Herzegovinian ballots can be distinguished into three sections. First, a titular section provides information about the particular electoral race. In the case of figure 15, a ballot from the November 2000 elections, the race determined representatives for the Parliament of the Federation of Bosnia-Herzegovina from Constituency Region 1. The race was numbered 511 as part of a larger numbering schema for the electoral races in Bosnia-Herzegovina: 500 for a race for the House of Representatives for Bosnia-Herzegovina, a 10 for the constituency of the Federation of Bosnia-Herzegovina (versus a 20 for Republika Srpska), and another 1 for electoral region 1 (of 5).[4] Underneath the titular information is a brief statement (in the blue band across the top) urging voters to read the instructions on the back of the ballot. Second are sets of boxes framing, marking, and delimiting political parties and their candidate lists. Each party and each candidate within that party's framed box has a blank square next to his or her name. Third, an instructional section appears on the back of the ballot, providing details on the electoral region and on how properly to fill out the ballot. In figure 15, the ballot specifies that Constituency Region 1 includes the municipalities Velika Kladuša, Cazin, Bihać, Bosanska Krupa, Bužim, Bosanski Petrovac, Sanski Most, Ključ, Drvar, Bosansko Grahovo/Grahovo, Glamoč, Livno, Kupres, and Tomislavgrad. It then explains, in both Latinic and Cyrillic script,

How can you fill out the ballot correctly?
　You can mark the empty box by the name of ONLY ONE political party or coalition or independent candidates' list or ONE independent candidate.
　Also you can mark the empty box by the name of one or more candidates but ONLY ON ONE LIST of the political parties or coalitions or independent candidates' lists.
　A mark by the names of candidates from your chosen political party or coalition or independent candidates' list will be taken as the vote for that political party or coalition or independent candidates' list.
　IF YOU MARK NAMES OF CANDIDATES FROM MORE THAN ONE POLITICAL PARTY OR COALITION OR INDEPENDENT CANDIDATES' LIST, YOUR BALLOT PAPER WILL BE CONSIDERED INVALID.

This brief instruction on the back of the ballot was the last in a long series of instructions to which a potential voter was exposed, from posters plastered on the walls of buildings to television advertisements to leaflets handed to them while in line at the polling station.
　On this ballot, political parties receive top billing, the entities framed or enclosed by a square. The name of each party is noted in a bold font and has an attendant medium-sized square. Below each party name is a

PROČITAJTE UPUTE NA PREDNJOJ STRANICI!   **ПРОЧИТАЈТЕ УПУТСТВА НА ПРЕДЊОЈ СТРАНИ!**

СОЦИЈАЛИСТИЧКА ПАРТИЈА РЕПУБЛИКЕ СРПСКЕ
1. ЂАКОВИЋ ЈОВО
2. ДУБАЈИЋ НАДА

STRANKA DEMOKRATSKE AKCIJE
1. BORIĆ ADEM
2. EGRLIĆ ASIM
3. JUSIĆ ENISA
4. ALIJAGIĆ MEHMED
5. MISALJEVIĆ BEĆIR

LDS - LIBERALNO DEMOKRATSKA STRANKA
1. TERZIĆ FEHRET
2. AMIDŽIĆ REDŽEP

HDZBiH - Hrvatska demokratska zajednica Bosne i Hercegovine
1. TOKIĆ MARKO
2. BAKOVIĆ MIRKO
3. KRIŠTO BORJANA
4. ŠANTIĆ VID
5. MARIĆ NEVEN

СНСД - МИЛОРАД ДОДИК
1. ЗРИЛИЋ ВЛАТКО

GRAĐANSKA DEMOKRATSKA STRANKA BiH
1. OSMANOVIĆ KARMELA
2. GRADINČIĆ EDIN

SDP - Socijaldemokratska partija Bosne i Hercegovine - Socijaldemokrati
1. ŠARGANOVIĆ SENAD
2. BRDAR ŠTIPO
3. ĆEHAJIĆ DUSANKA
4. HADŽIĆ NURIJA
5. DUPANOVIĆ ĆERBA

Demokratska narodna zajednica BiH - DNZ BiH
1. ĐEDOVIĆ IBRAHIM
2. KNEŽEVIĆ DUŠAN
3. RIZVIĆ REFIKA
4. MAŠINOVIĆ ZUMRET
5. PRATLJAČIĆ TOMISLAV

DEMOKRATSKA STRANKA PENZIONERA BOSNE I HERCEGOVINE
1. KLEPIĆ JOSIP
2. PEČENKOVIĆ VERA
3. TOPČAGIĆ SABIRA

NOVA HRVATSKA INICIJATIVA - NHI
1. ČULO FRANO
2. DŽAMBO PERO
3. BANOVIĆ SLAVICA

STRANKA ZA BiH
1. PURIĆ MIRSAD
2. IBRAHIMPAŠIĆ MUHAMED

KRAJ LISTE.
КРАЈ ЛИСТЕ.

Fig. 15. Ballot sample (*obuka*) for the open-list selection method, used for most municipal, cantonal, and parliamentary races beginning in 2000. *(Courtesy of the Organization for Security and Co-Operation in Europe, Mission to Bosnia and Herzegovina.)*

list of candidate names, each with a smaller square. The ballot offers a graphic synthesis and representation of the choices given by the open-list proportional representation voting system. Proportional representation is an electoral system in which single districts elect multiple legislators based on the vote share each party garners within that district. Under a list system, authorized political parties submit a list of candidates in an order selected by the party. In a closed-list system, if a party wins five seats in Parliament, the first five candidates on the list would fill those seats. In an open-list system, however, voters may modify the list by marking their preferred candidates. Thus, upon final tallying of ballot markings, those five seats could be filled by the 3rd, 4th, 23rd, 7th, and 1st candidates instead of the first five persons listed.

The logic of the list lends itself to the designation of fairness: everyone can be included on a ranked list, even those who are not desired. The list is potentially endless and thus fully inclusive. Like the matrix described by Annelise Riles (2000:152–61), one of the general features of the electoral list form is that the ordering of rectangular boxes allows a potentially endless number of units to be stacked on top of each other without altering the form or elucidating context and content. The list categorizes and orders—in this case, names of candidates—flattening other potential social facts and referents. Candidates are aesthetically equal on the ballot. The logic of the list suggests the comparability of the units, however mythical in reality. It makes no allowances for the representation of differing resources or support, the depiction of relationships (such as informal alliances or similar ideological or policy goals) within and between units, or the incorporation of rejected items.

Listed parties are also sanctioned. Their presence means that they have followed the regulations and consequently have been deemed acceptable candidates. In 2000, in Bosnia, this meant that candidates had not been indicted for human rights crimes, obstructed Dayton, or been charged with electoral fraud or illegal house occupancy. Further, their parties had presented a certain number of signatures of support (between 100 and 10,000, depending upon the size of the political unit [entity, canton, municipality]); signed statements of conduct; written a political platform in accordance with the guidelines; paid a registration fee (between 500 and 1,000 KM, or roughly $250 to $500); created candidate lists for the races they planned to contest; and provided an address for their party headquarters (and, in some cases, information about candidates' ethnicities). The logic of the list gives equal allocation to listed items, but the order of the list can never be equalizing. In

Bosnia-Herzegovina, the ballot list order of political parties was determined by lottery draw.[5] The device of randomness and publicly determined fate gave weight to the perceived fairness of the ballot layout.

Furthermore, the ballot completely hides the seat allocation formulas and distributions. Instead, the ballots simply list parties and candidates. How these parties and candidates win their seats and achieve political authority is not foretold either by the instructions or through the ballot layout. In race 511 (fig. 15), 11 political parties were vying for 12 seats, with the seats themselves determined by a formula. All 140 seats of the Parliament of the Federation of Bosnia-Herzegovina were open to contestation, with 12 of them allocated to Constituency Region 1. Thirty-five open "compensatory" seats were also available to parties receiving overall (cross–constituency region) high numbers of support. In race 600 (fig. 16), six candidate pairs competed for one paired position, the Republika Srpska president and vice president. Although the ballot has a similar layout to the one for race 511—lists, blank boxes, equal font sizes for names—the way in which ballot marks were translated into results was completely different. Ballots themselves do not suggest, imply, or detail how their referents will translate into results or what the markings should look like.

Without instructions, it is difficult to determine the appropriate aesthetic of marking. In race 600, the markings were supposed to be sequential numbers (i.e., 1, 2, 3, 4, 5, 6). Voters were asked to rank candidates in order of preference. If a candidate received more than 50 percent of the votes, he or she would win. If no candidate won a majority, voters' second choices would be counted. Subsequent choices (third, fourth, fifth, etc.) would be counted until a candidate received more than 50 percent of the markings. However, second choices would be counted only on ballots whose first choice had come in last—that is, the candidate ticket that finished sixth would be excised from the race, and the second preferences of those ballots that ranked the sixth-place slate as their first choice would be counted, as if it were a five-person race.

Ballots and their attendant processes and practices, such as design and layout, guides for marking, distribution, and presentation of candidates, help set the concepts of freedom and fairness in motion. "Free" and "fair," following this logic, come into being and meaning through the neutralization of politics and the dominance of seemingly neutral bureaucratic and technical processes and relationships. Thus, for example, the presentation and ordering of candidates on a ballot legitimates and sanctions the politicians as viable, equal candidates for a position. A

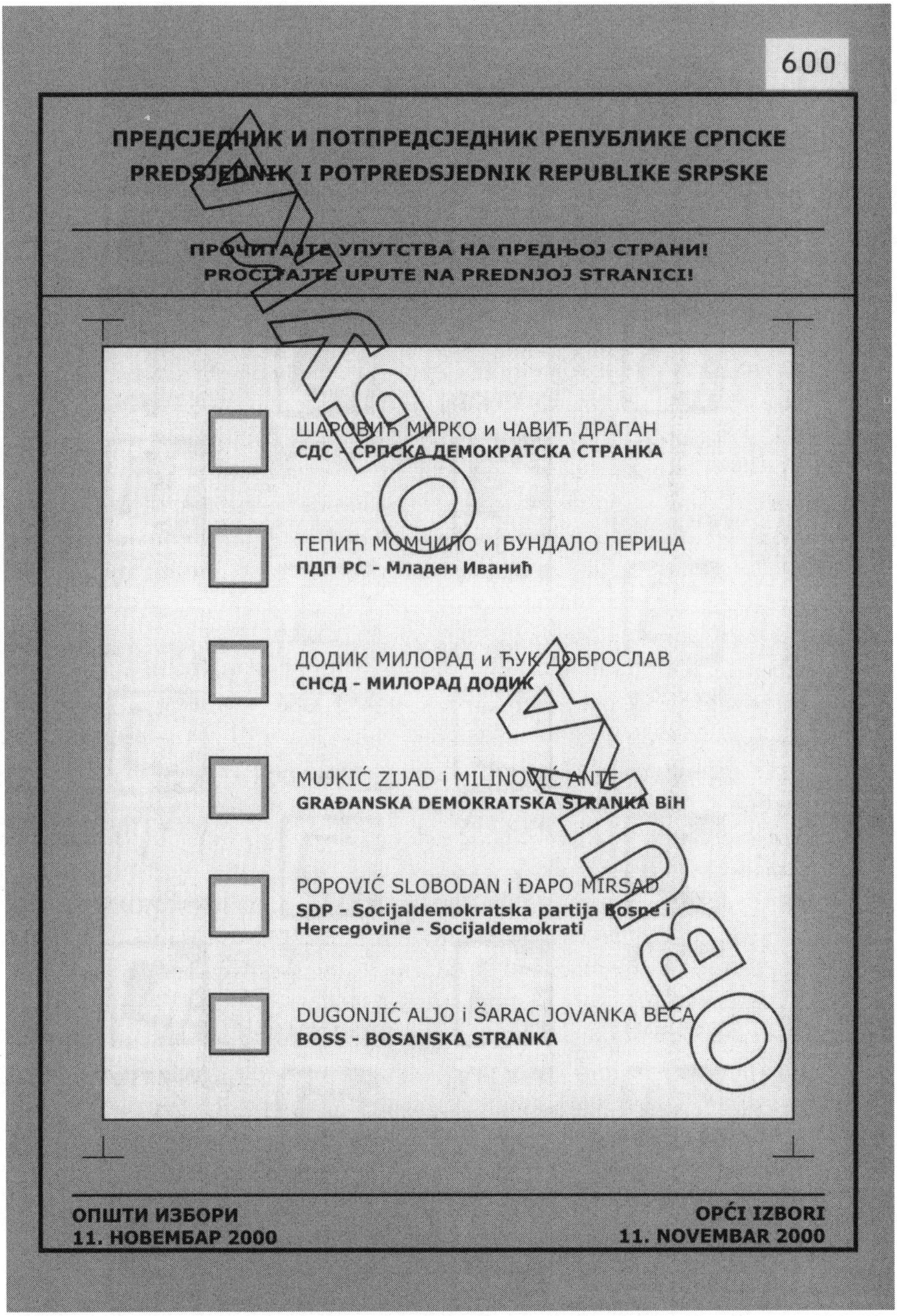

ПРЕДСЈЕДНИК И ПОТПРЕДСЈЕДНИК РЕПУБЛИКЕ СРПСКЕ
PREDSJEDNIK I POTPREDSJEDNIK REPUBLIKE SRPSKE

ПРОЧИТАЈТЕ УПУТСТВА НА ПРЕДЊОЈ СТРАНИ!
PROČITAJTE UPUTE NA PREDNJOJ STRANICI!

☐ ШАРОВИЋ МИРКО и ЧАВИЋ ДРАГАН
СДС - СРПСКА ДЕМОКРАТСКА СТРАНКА

☐ ТЕПИЋ МОМЧИЛО и БУНДАЛО ПЕРИЦА
ПДП РС - Младен Иванић

☐ ДОДИК МИЛОРАД и ЋУК ДОБРОСЛАВ
СНСД - МИЛОРАД ДОДИК

☐ MUJKIĆ ZIJAD i MILINOVIĆ ANTE
GRAĐANSKA DEMOKRATSKA STRANKA BiH

☐ POPOVIĆ SLOBODAN i ĐAPO MIRSAD
**SDP - Socijaldemokratska partija Bosne i
Hercegovine - Socijaldemokrati**

☐ DUGONJIĆ ALJO i ŠARAC JOVANKA BEĆA
BOSS - BOSANSKA STRANKA

ОПШТИ ИЗБОРИ
11. НОВЕМБАР 2000

OPĆI IZBORI
11. NOVEMBAR 2000

Fig. 16. Ballot sample (*obuka*) for the preferential vote-selection method, used for the president and vice president of Republika Srpska race starting in 2000. *(Courtesy of the Organization for Security and Co-Operation in Europe, Mission to Bosnia and Herzegovina.)*

ballot activates voters, drawing them into its systematic logic and the implicit legitimation of its authority and power. The voter does not and cannot act outside the scope of the ballot. Moreover, voters' participation in the technologies of the ballot obscures their often complete participatory absence from events and decisions prior to Election Day.

Counting Marks and Marks That Count

Turning ballot markings into results is a tricky business that can be compromised by sleep deprivation, subjectivity, formulas, districting, acceptable error rates, and invalidity. Political issues or debates are seen as outside of counting, but counting too is political. In Bosnia-Herzegovina, technical measurement and counting procedures were created, codified, and institutionalized even though they were arbitrarily chosen in some cases and strategically chosen for political effect in others. Barry (2002) discusses how calculation regimes can be antipolitical but argues that they also often open up space for contestation and alternate modes, demonstrating the fragility of metrological regimes and inventiveness of measurement. In my research, calculation and measurement were most often represented as neutral and apolitical. Strict counting procedures assisted in antifraud efforts. However, deviations from the established practices—no matter how trivial—were considered irregular and potentially a threat to the legitimation of the election results. In this way, counting became an antipolitical device through its demand for strict adherence to a particular form of techne. For example, during the 1997 Republika Srpska presidential election, I worried about whether I should allow an alternative form of counting from the one detailed in the training manual (which formed part of the Rules and Regulations). I could not envision any problems with the way championed by the polling station chair but worried that perhaps I was not taking all the possibilities into account. In my mind, the designated procedures had been tested and approved as free, fair, and transparent. Who was I to change them? Many polling station supervisors I interviewed were similarly reluctant to allow any deviation from the established counting procedures, even though other procedures could have been equally capable of ensuring accurate tabulations (or, better phrased, were equally arbitrary in terms of accuracy, error rates, and bias). Reluctance stemmed from fears about allowing and/or unwittingly participating in antidemocratic action. During our conversations, polling station supervisors emphasized that they believed that many of the polling station committees were trying to follow the designated procedures but needed assistance in understanding them (and the importance of following them) as well as in resisting temptations and/or coercive threats to modify calculations and totals. The process of counting, or the measurement of opinion, displaces debate and contestation, the hallmarks of politics. What is counted is crucial; participant observation in polling stations and election training suggested that how counting occurs was equally crucial.[6]

Counting of ballots began in the polling stations after the close of voting, generally at eight o'clock in the evening in Bosnia-Herzegovina. Regular ballots cast at the polling stations during Election Day were counted at those polling stations, while absentee, tendered, and out-of-country ballots were delivered to a centralized counting center. In 1997 and 1998, these counting centers employed hundreds of Bosnians to hand count ballots; by the November 2000 election, ballots were machine scanned with human intervention used to adjudicate ambiguous or unclear (e.g., faint) ballot marking, to open and sort ballots, and to provide logistics.[7] At the counting center and at polling stations, a series of steps specified the designated procedures through which ballots could be counted to produce free and fair results (table 3). However, even with counting broken down into steps, achieving accurate results was very difficult. In spring 2000 training exercises for election officers and polling station supervisors, many groups failed to get the correct results when practicing on already marked ballots. As the election trainers joked to the supervisors, "Don't forget that next time you won't have me to tell you that you've counted wrong." Freedom and fairness hope for but do not require accuracy; rather, they relate more to the adherence to a particular, technical, and codified practice of calculation.

   The ballots, some as large as a size A3 piece of paper (approximately 16.5 by 23 inches), had hundreds of boxes and names on them. It was difficult to see all of the check marks, let alone count and keep track of them. To that effect, systems for controlled and orderly counting were put in place. In 2000, this process comprised three major counting tasks: reconciliation, first count, and second count. Reconciliation consisted of opening the ballot box, separating the tendered ballots from the regular ballots, counting the tendered ballots twice, stacking the regular ballots into groups of 25 ballots, recounting the piles to verify the number, totaling the number of groups to come up with an overall number of ballots, and recording the total number of regular and tendered ballots on the summary of overall results form 1. Only after a total number was determined was it proper to start with the first count.

I and the other election trainers stressed to the polling supervisors during their training that order—of protocols, of steps within protocols—should be strictly followed. The first count resolved the degree of

TABLE 3.   Summary of Steps to Follow When Counting a Full Ballot Box at a Polling Station

1. Open the ballot box and empty it onto the top of the counting table.
2. Ensure that the ballot box is empty.
3. Separate the tendered ballots from the regular ballots. Count the ballots into piles of 25.
4. Double count each pile.
5. Add up the total number of piles (of 25 ballots) and add the remaining ballots to the total.
6. Record the number on the result form.
7. The chair announces the result.
8. Sort the ballots into piles by political party.
9. Make a separate pile for doubtful ballots (i.e., invalid).
10. Count each pile into stacks of 25, double-checking the mark and validity of mark.
11. Double count all stacks in each pile. Bind each stack with a rubber band.
12. Label each stack (of 25) with the name of the political party and have both counters sign it.
13. Bind the combined stacks of each political party together, record the total number of ballots on a label with the party name and the signatures of the counters.
14. The chair examines the doubtful ballots and adds any valid votes to the appropriate pile, amending the label.
15. Record the totals on the result form.
16. Place invalid ballots into specified envelope.
17. Start with one political party pile.
18. Choose two members to be readers and two to be markers.
19. One reader will read out loud the names on the ballots one by one, while the second reader confirms the name.
20. Each marker will place a mark next to the name of the candidate on their tally sheet using the crosshatch method.
21. After a stack of 25 ballots has been read, the markers will confirm that they have the same number of tally strokes.
22. Move to the next column on the tally sheet to read the next stack of 25 ballots.
23. Repeat reading and marking and comparing for each stack in the political party pile.
24. Each marker should transfer the results from each tally column to the summary of tally results form.
25. Compare the summary tally results forms.
26. Repeat the procedure (from #17) for each political party.
27. Markers sign tally forms.
28. Transfer summary tally totals to final results forms.
29. The chair and deputy sign the results forms.

Note: The list is distilled from the April 2000 *Polling and Counting Training Manual.* Not all steps, such as those relating to packing materials or to fixing acknowledged errors, are included.

support for political parties, coalitions, and independent candidates, with the results reported on the summary of overall results form 1. The second count totaled the support for candidates within political parties. This process involved three forms, four people, and a lot of time, space, and noise. For the second count, the ballots (still grouped into their piles by political parties and divided into bundles of 25 ballots) were looked at again, but the candidates within the parties were counted rather than the parties themselves. Like the first count, everything was done in groups of 25 and in duplicate. Ballots were counted in groups of 25 to create a manageable number of ballots for counting and any potential recounting. The time needed for a committee to count nine hundred ballots (the maximum allowed at any polling station) had been estimated at between six and nine hours. Since counting began around eight o'clock, there was a sense that strict procedures would be very important in maintaining control of the counting process.

The second count process consisted of one person reading the numbers that corresponded to the candidates marked on each ballot, a second person verifying the first person's accuracy, and two people separately recording the numbers on tally sheets (fig. 17). At the end of reading the numbers of marked candidates in a group of 25 ballots, the two sets of tally marks were added up and checked against each other. If the numbers did not match, the set of 25 ballots was reread and retallied. The correct procedure called for the workers doing the tallying to cross out the incorrect column and use the next column for the recount, not—under any circumstances—to fix mistakes in the original column. After a pile of ballots for a given political party was tallied, the numbers for all the groups of 25 were added up and transferred to the summary tally form, compared again, and transferred to the open list summary of results form 2 (fig. 18). The cycle would then start again with another political party's ballot stacks.

Despite popular impressions to the contrary, not all ballots can be counted (notwithstanding the debates in Florida over the 2000 U.S. presidential race and the disruption to the frames of complicit trust they engendered). It is not always possible to determine voter intent. In these cases—when it is not clear which candidate or party a voter chose—the ballot is declared invalid. Common characteristics of invalid ballots in Bosnia-Herzegovina were multiple marks, no marks, and ambiguous marks. Because voters specified their choices by written mark (versus by hole punches, computer touch screens, or spoken word), ambiguities arose about markings and

Tally Sheet

Candidate Number	Party or Coalition or List of Independent Candidates Name: STRANKA NOVOG POČETKA — Votes	Subtotal	Candidate Number	Party or Coalition or List of Independent Candidates Name: STRANKA NOVOG POČETKA — Votes	Subtotal	Candidate Number	Party or Coalition or List of Independent Candidates Name: STRANKA NOVOG POČETKA — Votes	Subtotal	Candidate Number	Party or Coalition or List of Independent Candidates Name: — Votes	Subtotal	Candidate Number	TOTAL
1	̶H̶T̶ ̶H̶T̶ IIII	14	1	̶H̶T̶ I	6	1	IIII	4	1			1	24
2	̶H̶T̶ I	6	2	II	2	2	IIII	4	2			2	12
3	II	2	3	I	1	3	III	3	3			3	06
4	IIII	4	4	̶H̶T̶ IIII	9	4	̶H̶T̶ II	7	4			4	20
5		0	5	I	1	5	I	1	5			5	02
6	I	1	6	II	2	6		0	6			6	03
7	III	3	7		0	7		0	7			7	03
8	II	2	8	I	1	8	I	1	8			8	04
9	̶H̶T̶ IIII	9	9	̶H̶T̶ ̶H̶T̶ IIII	14	9	̶H̶T̶ IIII	9	9			9	32
10			10			10			10			10	
11			11			11			11			11	
12			12			12			12			12	
13			13			13			13			13	
14			14			14			14			14	
15			15			15			15			15	
16			16			16			16			16	
17			17			17			17			17	
18			18			18			18			18	
19			19			19			19			19	
20			20			20			20			20	
21			21			21			21			21	
22			22			22			22			22	
23			23			23			23			23	
24			24			24			24			24	
25			25			25			25			25	
26			26			26			26			26	
27			27			27			27			27	
28			28			28			28			28	
29			29			29			29			29	
30			30			30			30			30	
31			31			31			31			31	
32			32			32			32			32	
33			33			33			33			33	
34			34			34			34			34	
35			35			35			35			35	
36			36			36			36			36	
37			37			37			37			37	
38			38			38			38			38	
39			39			39			39			39	

Fig. 17. Tally sheet, 2000. (*Courtesy of the Organization for Security and Co-Operation in Europe, Mission to Bosnia and Herzegovina.*)

| OPEN LIST SUMMARY OF RESULTS FORM 2 | | MUNICIPALITY NAME | POLLING STATION NO. |

Political Party or Coalition Name

STRANKA NOVOG POCETKA

Political Party or Coalition Vote Received

NO.	Candidate Name	Valid Votes Received
1.	Nurdin Cengic	
2.	Samir Hanusa	
3.	Jasna Sipovic	
4.	Sabina Resulbegovic	
5.	Dobrina Kusmuk	
6.	Fahrudin Custo	
7.	Mithad Becirspahic	
8.	Adis Pasovic	
9.	Zoran Mitrovic	
10.	Slobodan Buk	
11.	Eldin Vidovic	
12.	Mirjana Traparic	
13.	Nikola Mandic	
14.	Valentina Curic	
15.	Tanja Milisic	
16.	Aleksandra Markovic	
17.	Zoran Petrovic	
18.	Edina Deliomerovic	
19.	Miralem Haskovic	
20.	Orhan Ovadija	
21.	Nedim Babovic	
22.	Izdrif Zubcevic	
23.	Danijela Petkovic	
24.	Javor Popara	
25.	Darko Popovic	
26.	Azer Skaljic	
27.	Mirna Stuka	
28.	Milan Cuk	
29.	Vidoje Milenkovic	
30.	Zdravko Babic	
31.	Milena Kokuric	
32.	Asmir Nikolic	
33.	Amel Kurtovic	
34.	Mirko Malic	
	No Candidate Vote	

Political Party or Coalition Name

STRANKA INTELIGENTNE OMLADINE

Political Party or Coalition Vote Received

NO.	Candidate Name	Valid Votes Received
1.	Nurudin Alender	
2.	Ricard Dzon	
3.	Jasna Sinancevic	
4.	Sabina Hasanbegovic	
5.	Selma Hodovic	
6.	Brajan Stiers	
7.	Mithad Becirspahic	
8.	Zoran Dimitrljevic	
	No Candidate Vote	

Political Party or Coalition Name

STRANKA OMLADINSKOG PROSPERITETA

Political Party or Coalition Vote Received

NO.	Candidate Name	Valid Votes Received
1.	Valija Dedovic	
2.	Nermina Klisovic	
3.	Elma Hajrovic	
4.	Edin Car	
5.	Omer Dzinovic	
6.	Nisveta Goro	
	No Candidate Vote	

| Serial Number of Plastic Seal 1 | Serial Number of Plastic Seal 2 |

CHAIRPERSON (print name + signature) .... Date

DEPUTY CHAIRPERSON (print name + signature) .... Date

Original .... OSCE HQ Sarajevo (Packet 10)   Yellow .... Field Office (Packet 9)   Green .... Municipal Election Commission (Packet 7)   Red .... Chairperson (Packet 8)   Blue .... (Packet 6)

Fig. 18. Summary of results form 2, 2000. (*Courtesy of the Organization for Security and Co-Operation in Europe, Mission to Bosnia and Herzegovina.*)

their locations. For example, did an X in the box mean the same thing as an X over a candidate name—that is, had the voter chosen that candidate in both instances, or only the former (fig. 19)?

What qualified as valid or invalid was the subject of many debates at all levels of authority and decision making. While the official statement was that the "intent of the voter" had to be "obvious," it was clear that *obvious* was contingent and constructed and needed to be defined. However, even specific regulations defining invalidity were not necessarily adequate. For several elections, guidelines were formally printed and distributed to clarify "clear intent" (fig. 20). Supervisors, trainers, and electoral officials—precisely the people verifying the counting process—debated and disagreed with the guidelines. During an audit of supposedly invalid ballots in 2000, a colleague, Greta, and I had multiple disagreements over "clear intent." In particular, we debated what to do when the voter was supposed to rank candidates (1 though 6) but the only mark was a 4 in the blank box next to the fourth candidate listed on the ballot. Because this happened multiple times, I believed that there was some voter confusion about how to mark the ballot. This occurred within a context where some political parties were encouraging voters not to rank candidates but to mark only one candidate. Counting instructions given to polling station supervisors and polling station committees attempted to clarify what to do with single and multiple marks:

> If there is only one mark, in one box next to a pair of candidates, the ballot is valid. It does not matter what this mark is, as long as there is only one mark. If there is more than one mark on the ballot, only the numbers in sequence are valid.

Consequently, I forcefully argued that these voters had marked the fourth candidate as their first preference. The mark was simply a mark, even though it looked like a four. After all, who would mark only their fourth preference, omitting their first, second, and third choices? My argument was both literalist and rationalist. Greta pointed out another sentence in the instructions that specified that "the over-riding principle in determining a valid ballot is that **the intention of the voter is clear.**" She argued that we should not try to guess the voter's intent and that the written four could not be considered just a mark. As always, the guidelines failed to address every situation seen on the ballots. The guidelines could not account for the variance and creativity found in purportedly mismarked ballots.

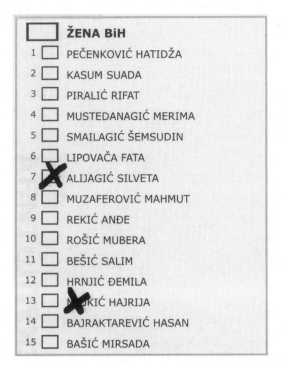

ŽENA BiH
1 ☐ PEČENKOVIĆ HATIDŽA
2 ☐ KASUM SUADA
3 ☐ PIRALIĆ RIFAT
4 ☐ MUSTEDANAGIĆ MERIMA
5 ☐ SMAILAGIĆ ŠEMSUDIN
6 ☐ LIPOVAČA FATA
7 ✖ ALIJAGIĆ SILVETA
8 ☐ MUZAFEROVIĆ MAHMUT
9 ☐ REKIĆ ANĐE
10 ☐ ROŠIĆ MUBERA
11 ☐ BEŠIĆ SALIM
12 ☐ HRNJIĆ ĐEMILA
13 ☐ ✖ KIĆ HAJRIJA
14 ☐ BAJRAKTAREVIĆ HASAN
15 ☐ BAŠIĆ MIRSADA

Fig. 19. What counts as valid, ca. 2000? *(Courtesy of the Organization for Security and Co-Operation in Europe, Mission to Bosnia and Herzegovina.)*

Clear intent is not at all self-evident; rather, it becomes apparent only through specific legal, technical, and social mediations as well as power relationships. Clear intent references a theory of intention where people have clearly defined wills or opinions that they transparently express with marks on ballot papers. Perhaps mismarked ballots can be usefully analyzed as suggesting that no clear relationship exists among intention, choice, and subject. However, the theory of intention guides the entire process. These strict procedures of collecting marks and creating count totals translate individual marks into preferences and knowledge about voters' wills. Technicality, in this way, exemplifies neoliberal governmentality in its creation of, intervention in, and maintenance of the polity through distance, displacement, and autonomous control (Barry, Osborne, and Rose 1996).

The Translation into Results

Even after a polling station committee counts ballots and records the information, a great deal of tabulation is required to create results.

Primjeri glasačkih listića koji mogu biti prihvaćeni kao ispravni

SAMPLES OF BALLOTS that may be accepted as Valid

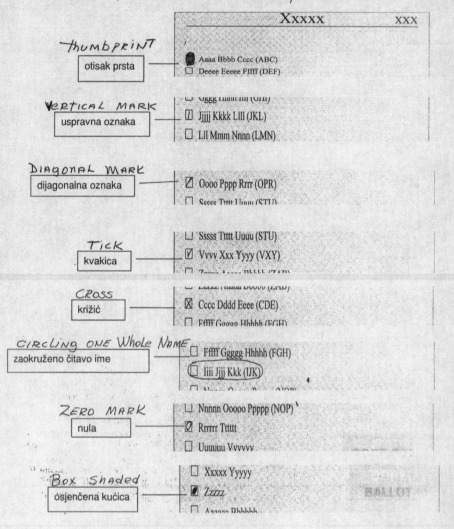

ThUMbPRINT — otisak prsta

VERTICAL MARK — uspravna oznaka

DIAGONAL MARK — dijagonalna oznaka

TICK — kvakica

CROSS — križić

CIRCLING ONE Whole NAME — zaokruženo čitavo ime

ZERO MARK — nula

Box Shaded — osjenčena kućica

Xxxxx   XXX

Aaaa Bbbb Cccc (ABC)
Deeee Eeeee Fffff (DEF)

Gggg Hhhh Iiii (GHI)
Jjjjj Kkkk Llll (JKL)
Lll Mmm Nnnn (LMN)

Oooo Pppp Rrrr (OPR)
Ssss Tttt Uuuu (STU)

Sssss Ttttt Uuuu (STU)
Vvvv Xxx Yyyy (VXY)
Zzzzz Aaaaa Bbbbb (ZAB)

Cccc Dddd Eeee (CDE)
Fffff Ggggg Hhhhh (FGH)

Ffff Ggggg Hhhhh (FGH)
Iiii Jjjj Kkk (IJK)
Nnnn Ooo Ppp (NOP)

Nnnnn Ooooo Ppppp (NOP)
Rrrrr Ttttt
Uuuuu Vvvvv

Xxxxx Yyyyy
Zzzzz
Aaaaa Bbbbb

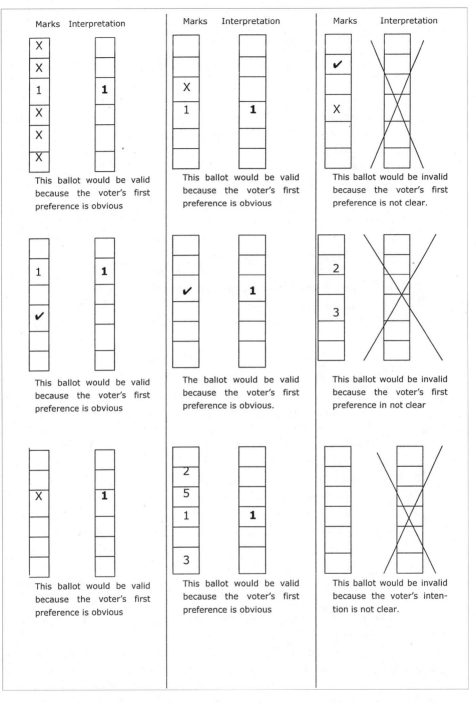

Fig. 20. Sample valid and invalid markings guideline sheets distributed to polling station committees and supervisors, 1997 and 2000. Assumptions of when an X references a positive or negative intent are interesting. Compare the cross on the left with the crossmarks on the right, especially the differences between the various interpretations of crossmarking on the right. *(Courtesy of the Organization for Security and Co-Operation in Europe, Mission to Bosnia and Herzegovina.)*

Counts from polling stations must be combined with those from other polling stations. Those counts must be verified and entered into databases, along with any recounts and the absentee and tendered ballots counts. Counts from and for municipalities must be merged and reconciled to create the raw numbers for each constituent race. Formulas and other forms of calculation and measurement then translate raw numbers into political seats and politicians, numerically putting an electoral system into practice. In some electoral races, especially those in which only one political office is under challenge, the translation from cumulative marks to results is relatively direct: the candidate who receives the most ballot markings wins. Although much work is still subsumed into the process of counting and sorting millions of ballots, the winner is the candidate with the "majority." This simple majority system was used for Bosnia-Herzegovina's postwar presidential and vice presidential races, but the rest of the offices being contested—municipal councils, cantonal assembly seats, and Parliament and assembly seats—used a proportional representation system, under which political parties receive a percentage of seats in the assembly based on the number of votes received in particular constituencies. In these cases, not even counting, sorting, and tabulating produces results, for mathematical formulas translate the raw numbers into percentages and mandates (i.e., political seats in an assembly or other political institution). The achievement of political seats by political parties and/or candidates expresses the people's will only through powerful acts of translation, transformation, and modification.

Electoral systems are increasingly manipulated to promote or produce intended effects, such as representation, proportionality, consensus, or stability. Measuring and tallying groups of votes differently, requiring alternative calculations or comparisons, or changing numerical minimums modify the determinations of winners (see, for example, Taagepera and Shugart 1989). Grouping voters by geographic regions instead of into one group, for example, can create vastly different outcomes. Taagepera (1999:2–3) argues that electoral systems cannot be designed but only evolve from devised starting points through the selection of electoral rules since, more often than not, "design" is not a harmonious process of creation but rather a patchwork of incongruous compromises. He continues by pointing out the danger that with a hubristic sense of design and causal control, expectations may not be met and disillusionment may arise when certain effects are not achieved. Nevertheless, electoral system design is a burgeoning industry and sociopolitical engineering project—see, for example, the Institute for

Democracy and Electoral Assistance's *International IDEA Handbook of Electoral System Design* (1997) or even the International Foundation for Electoral Systems consultant database. Given social science's knowledge about the general relationships between electoral rules and effects, electoral design can never be neutral.

In 1999, the international community began to design an electoral system. Over some months, the Draft Election Law Working Group conducted public opinion surveys and forums, met with election system consultants, ran computer models comparing different scenarios, and produced information campaigns. The resulting system appeared very much like Taagepera's patchwork, mixing ethnic compromises with rules promoting female candidates, small parties, nonethnic constituencies, compromise, moderation, reconciliation, and accountability. It also appeared to take into account international frustration with voters' continued expressions of support for nationalist parties and with elected officials' perceived inability to govern (see also Manning and Antić 2003, Manning 2004). From this bricolage of ways of determining and allocating political authority, the government of Bosnia-Herzegovina was formed (fig. 21).

The system was used during the two elections held in 2000 and was proposed as the election law. It failed to pass the Bosnian legislative bodies on multiple introductions but finally was enacted in August 2001. The design fills its created political institutions and positions with a combination of electoral mechanisms: plurality-majority (first past the post), proportional representation, semiproportional representation, compensatory mandates, and thresholds. For example, the open-list proportional representation was introduced to increase accountability. According to an internally distributed guide to the draft election law,

> Under this system, voters will be able to express their preferences not only for parties or coalitions, but for individual candidates as well. . . . In this way, individual candidates will have strong incentive to appeal directly to voters. At the same time, current political representatives will also have a stronger incentive to be more responsive to the needs of their constituents, since their own record in office will become an important factor in their prospects for re-election.

In theory, accountability would then be linked with individual politician performance rather than political party performance. International

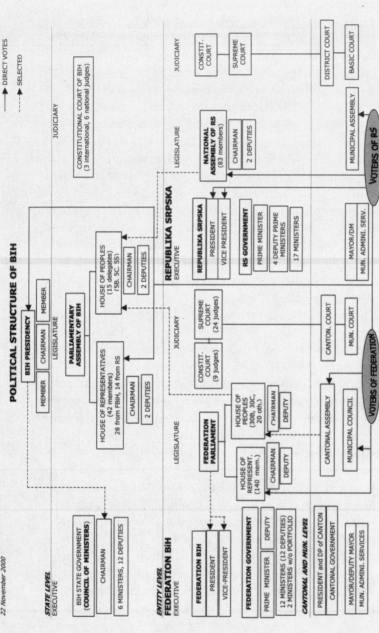

Fig. 21. The political structure of Bosnia-Herzegovina, 2000. The graphical representation displays what political authorities exist but only partially shows how the authority gains its status. It distinguishes between political authority legitimated directly by the voters and that selected by the authorities themselves. However, it leaves out how electoral rules affect voters' "direct votes." *(Courtesy of the Organization for Security and Co-Operation in Europe, Mission to Bosnia and Herzegovina.)*

analysts believed that each of the three main political parties had strong support from a primarily silent ethnic base but that the parties did little in exchange for that support. The reform attempted to change political parties from within, reducing their strong hold over elected representatives as well as their ability to draw strength solely on their perceived ethnic representation. An open-list system could potentially pressure politicians into working for their constituents as well as their party. Furthermore, since the designed system only required candidates to achieve a small threshold of overall votes within the party to achieve seats, a relatively small but active support base could change the order of the party's list. An official reported that in the April 2000 municipal elections, 18 percent of candidates received their seats through the mechanism of open-list voter choice.

This reform also potentially worked toward the goal of moderation in that the system's designers believed that the politicians most likely to work with their opponents to pass legislation or enact projects were moderates and that those candidates most likely to get active votes would be those who had been "held accountable" to voters on local and concrete issues such as water and sanitation infrastructure, job creation, and pensions (rather than abstractions such as cultural rights). Campaign finance limitations (two KM per constituent voter) and compensatory seats allocation also worked toward the goals of politican moderation and accountability. Compensatory seats give political voice to smaller parties who have a wide or dispersed cross-constituency appeal. In Bosnia-Herzegovina, this mechanism assisted opposition parties. Election designers hoped that opposition parties would offer pragmatic alternatives to the three dominant nationalist parties. Of course, opposition parties were not always the pluralists for which internationals had hoped; some of these parties offered messages of inclusion and multiculturalism, but others decried the international community's interventions.[8] The campaign finance limit was also a measure designed to help smaller parties have equal resources and voices (by limiting the resource base of the dominant parties).

In addition to the creation of constituencies and support for smaller parties, other facets of the system promoted moderation. In particular, the preferential vote system for the presidencies of Bosnia-Herzegovina and the presidential and vice presidential race in Republika Srpska allowed voters to rank candidates. A political effect was hoped for: that candidates would move toward moderate positions. In the words of an OSCE election FAQ,

One advantage of the system is that it enables supporters of candidates who have little hope of being elected to influence the outcome of the elections. This system will compel candidates to seek not only the votes of their own supporters but also the second, third, fourth etc preferences. Therefore, in order to attract these preferences candidates must move away from extremist positions and appeal to a wider range of interests outside his or her own constituent peoples.

During the 2000 election, when I saw it in practice, the preferential system failed in that although the top candidate ticket failed to receive enough votes (50 percent), it was so close to that threshold (49.8 percent) that only 1,117 more votes were needed (table 4). But too few of the ballots with markings for the ticket that had come in sixth place (party F) marked a second choice to make a difference. If no second choice was marked (31 percent), a ballot was not considered part of the pool of valid ballots. The absence of a mark meant a no vote, not a nonvote. The reduction of overall counted ballots meant that without counting the second preferences, the top candidate ticket (Party A) won. The total number of ballots decreased, giving Party A 50.1 percent. If the ballots without a second choice had been counted as nonvotes, then the 313,607 ballots would have been divided by the total original number of valid ballots (629,363), and a majority would still not have been reached. A third count would then have been conducted using the ballots from the party with the next-fewest votes (in this case, Party D). It is unclear from the *Rules and Regulations* whether those ballot's second preference or third preference would have to be counted (or if it would be the second preference for the 37614 original party D ballots and the third preference for the 5220 party F-now-party D ballots). Not only are the *Rules and Regulations* ambiguous on the matter but any interpretive logic is already socially and politically mediated.

TABLE 4. **Preferential Vote Transfers during the 2000 Republika Srpska and Vice Presidential Election**

	Party A	Party B	Party C	Party D	Party E	Party F	Total
Total number of votes	313, 572	54,392	161,942	37,614	48,992	12,851	629,363
Percent of total	49.8%	8.6%	25.7%	6.0%	7.8%	2.0%	
Second vote	+35	+42	+212	+5,220	+3,419	−12,851	−3,924
New total	313,607	54,433	162,154	42,834	52,411	0	625,439
New percent of total	50.1%	8.7%	25.9%	6.8%	8.4%	0.0%	

While I was learning about the preferential vote system and its purported benefits, including the economics of collapsing the need for runoff elections into one race, I wondered why the second preferences were counted only from the party with the fewest number of votes. Wouldn't it be better to look at the second preferences on all the ballots? I asked at an information session. The lecturer chastised me for (unwittingly) condoning the De Borda system, which De Borda reformers promote as encouraging compromise and cooperation but which was frowned upon (for unknown reasons) by the election administration. I thought that counting all second choices would more faithfully mimic a "second round of voting" than the system that had been put in place. Furthermore, if the intent was to "promote programs and policies of compromise" and to have supporters of smaller parties "retain influence over the electoral outcome," then it made more sense to make the parties reach out to the whole political body. It was clear that the 12,851 supporters of the party that received the fewest votes (party F) had not retained any real influence. Support for one party was already so strong in polarized Bosnia-Herzegovina that this strategy of counting and measuring preferences did not promote compromise or reduce radicalism, although it might have done so in a more evenly contested election.

As the measurement of preference has multiple practices associated with it, so does proportional representation. Proportional representation is not singularly defined. The Bosnian system used something called the Sainte-Laguë mathematical formula for seat allocation. This system apportions seats by dividing vote totals by odd numbers until the number of divisors reaches the number of seats allocated. The top numbers among the quotients (the results of the division) then receive seats in accordance with how many were allocated. The designers of Bosnia-Herzegovina's system chose the Sainte-Laguë formula over, among others, the d'Hondt rule, the modified Sainte-Laguë system, or the Imperiali formula. These mathematical procedures are also based on dividing vote shares.[9] According to Taagepera and Shugart (1989:29–34), the d'Hondt rule slightly favors parties that receive larger numbers of votes, although this benefit is reduced as the number of mandates or seat allocations increases. For example, a large party may garner more seats when only 7 mandates are open than when 14 are available. The Sainte-Laguë formula favors smaller parties, and the modified Sainte-Laguë formula favors midsized parties, although like d'Hondt, this bias lessens (approaching pure proportional representation) as the number of mandates grows. The differences occur because of the size of the gap between divisors. In d'Hondt, the vote totals are divided in numerical order (1, 2, 3, 4, 5), so the size of the gap equals 1. Sainte-Laguë uses odd numbers—1, 3, 5, 7, 9—and thus has a larger gap. The modified Sainte-Laguë reduces the favoritism toward the small parties by starting at 1.4. Because by design, the average mandate size of constituencies in Bosnia-Herzegovina was between three and six seats, the benefit to small parties should occur. As table 5 shows, Party C, with the smallest number of votes (75,000), achieves a seat in the Saint-Laguë system but not under D'Hondt or the modified Sainte-Laguë. Party E, the second-largest party, wins two seats under the D'Hondt and modified Sainte-Laguë systems but only one under the Bosnian-Herzegovinian system.

Elections were used in postwar Bosnia-Herzegovina as a tool to change the existing political and social structures. As Carrie Manning (2004) points out, elections were conceived not merely as part of the usual quick exit strategy for international involvement but as an important component in the reconfiguration of political cleavages and interests and the overall transformation of the nature of politics. Elections became tools for reshaping society, albeit with (as yet) limited effect. As with so many transformation-based projects, intent does not necessarily match up with reaction or effect (Scott 1998). While the results of the Bosnian experiment cannot yet be determined, early findings were var-

TABLE 5.   **Hypothetical Seat Allocations for a Six Mandate Election Using Different Formulas**

6 mandates		Party A	Party B	Party C	Party D	Party E
Sainte-Laguë	1	(1) 220,000	(4) 180,000	(5) 75,000	(3) 195,000	(2) 210,000
	3	(6) 73,333	60,000	25,000	65,000	70,000
	5	44,000	36,000	15,000	39,000	42,000
	7	31,429	25,714	10,714	27,857	30,000
	9	24,444	20,000	8,333	21,667	23,333
D'Hondt	1	(1) 220,000	(4) 180,000	75,000	(3) 195,000	(2) 210,000
	2	(5) 110,000	90,000	37,500	97,500	(6) 105,000
	3	73,333	60,000	25,000	65,000	70,000
	4	55,000	45,000	18,750	48,750	52,500
	5	44,000	36,000	15,000	39,000	42,000
modified Sainte Laguë	votes	220,000	180,000	75,000	195,000	210,000
	1.4	(1) 157,143	(4) 128,571	53,571	(3) 139,286	(2) 150,000
	3	(5) 73,333	60,000	25,000	65,000	(6) 70,000
	5	44,000	36,000	15,000	39,000	42,000
	7	31,429	25,714	10,714	27,857	30,000
	9	24,444	20,000	8,333	21,667	23,333

Note: bold numbers in parentheses indicate *the order in which seats were won.*

ied. For example, while legislative carrots and sticks changed political parties' actions and assisted in the creation of moderate alternatives, Bosnians continued to vote for the wartime nationalist parties, which consistently earned twice as many votes as their nearest rivals (Manning 2004:67). Indeed, it is difficult to measure success or failure as concrete categories. For example, international groups had sought to incorporate more women into politics through a requirement that each party's candidate list be at least one-third female and that women be evenly distributed throughout each candidate list (i.e., women had to be listed third, sixth, ninth, and so forth). However, because open lists were used and voters could choose specific candidates, it was possible for voters to ignore female candidates. As a result of the 1998 election, which had included a similar gender provision but with a closed list, women held 26 percent of the seats in Parliament, up from 2 percent in 1996. In the 2000 elections, with one-third of the candidates female and voters given the option of selecting individual candidates, women won approximately 18 percent of seats in municipal, cantonal, and entity assemblies. This disparity demonstrates that voters indeed used the open-list system to avoid selecting women. Conversely, if the requirement that parties include women on the lists had not been put into place, women might still hold only 2 percent of seats.

Technical Transformations

How do clearly social and political processes become depoliticized? The techniques embedded in the electoral system were explicitly and strategically used with particular effects in mind. The international community was transforming politics (both visible and unacknowledged political practice) through technicality. This chapter has detailed the process of creating voters with wills and the subsequent flattenings and sleights of hand that occur as will is translated onto ballots, and then counted and massaged into results and political authority. It has illustrated the political nature of seemingly apolitical technical practices. Freedom and fairness are measured through these technical practices even as visions of accountability, representation, and the pragmatism of compromise and moderation are put into practice through them. As an OSCE fact sheet on multimember constituencies and compensatory seats declares,

> Because of the vagaries of the Multi-Member Constituencies, there is a chance that some parties might not be awarded with

their proportional share of seats under the Multi-Member Constituencies. In other words, some parties might show strongly in elections across their entity or [Bosnia-Herzegovina], but never quite finish high enough to win a mandate through the Multi-Member Constituencies. These parties would not receive their fair proportion of mandates. Therefore the Rules and Regulations revisions include Compensatory Seats, which will be given to those parties that are underrepresented in Parliament. . . . Entity-wide proportionality will be maintained.

"Fair proportion" meets "representation" and "accountability." The desire for local and direct accountability threatened representation, so the system was tweaked some more. Accountability, representation, moderation, and reconciliation are knowledges created and promoted through technical matters. Once these knowledges and their political effects become codified into law, they will appear more and more technical and less political. Normalized, political ends are achieved through the power of techne.

EMBODIED TRANSPARENCY

The Eyes and Ears of the
International Community

Transparency is touted as a key component of democracy, and of free and fair elections. A report by the International Foundation for Electoral Systems, a leading organization that provides electoral assistance and expertise, defines transparency as "the term for a clear and open process, which is understandable and accountable to the electorate" (2002:2) and locates transparency at the core of free and fair elections: transparent procedures encourage participation, promote public confidence, eliminate the appearance of impropriety, and limit the possibility of fraud. Transparent procedures should be used in such aspects of elections as organizational meetings, voter registration, candidate eligibility, ballot design, electoral worker training, civic education, observer participation, and security. An ODIHR handbook for election observers emphasizes transparency's relationship to the rule of law, inclusiveness, and visible and verifiable practices:

> The principle of **transparency** requires that the election be carried out according to due process of the law, and according to legal ground rules that are established in an inclusive and open manner. A transparent process limits the possibility for election fraud, and thus the vote count should be visible and verifiable from the level of the polling station, to any intermediate levels of the election administration, and finally to the national election authority. (1999:5)

191

These criteria set the structure of transparency, but its content remains open to design and interpretation. What counts as "inclusive," "verifiable," or "clear and open"? These questions about meaning lead to broader concerns about the interaction and relationships between power and transparency as practiced and made concrete. *Transparency* is not a static or stable term but is culturally and politically infused by power relations and other social mediations.[1] We should be asking not only whether a process is or is not transparent but also what processes and practices fall outside of the purview of transparency. How does something become transparent or not transparent? Whose actions need to be transparent, and whose do not? To whom should something be transparent? When something is made transparent, what remains opaque? Any analysis of transparency must account for its meanings, forms, and politics as well as the practices of its legitimation.

The following sections present a description and analysis of international supervision, a core feature of transparency in five postwar Bosnian-Herzegovinian elections. In Bosnia-Herzegovina, transparency took bodily form through the presence of international polling supervisors. First, I describe the supervisors, focusing on who they were and on their interactions with Bosnia and Bosnians. Although the international supervisor embodied transparency, it is not what it appears to be. Contrary to its claims, transparency provides neither full visibility nor full truth. Rather, transparency is partial, particular, and reliant on specialized knowledge. The polling station supervisors' local-level dilemmas call into question the nature of the ideal sought through the invocation of transparency. The following chapter, "Transparent Forms and Bureaucratic Mechanisms of Watching" takes up a second system of transparency: bureaucratic-technical forms. I discuss how although the two systems existed concurrently, embodied transparency was emphasized in earlier elections but was eventually supplanted by disembodied, bureaucratic mechanisms of transparency. The halting progression from an embodied transparency to a technical transparency shows the logics of democratic governance in action.

Transparency is unstable terrain, influenced by a variety of social and political negotiations and mediations. By looking at how transparency was given meaning and form in postwar Bosnia-Herzegovina, I demonstrate that transparency itself is a shifting category. Furthermore, contrary to its claims, it is an exclusionary category; rooted in notions of vision and truth, transparency excludes other senses, such as hearing, and obscures its embeddedness in existing power relations. However, in all its forms, transparency directs and regulates the conduct of political behavior (as well as many other public and private institutions) (see M. Dean 1999). Transparency especially directs democratic institutions, as it is perceived that through them the people ensure that their will is done. Transparency purportedly allows constituents to see the truth behind the paperwork. But, building on Michel Foucault and other scholars of governmentality (e.g., J. Dean 2000; M. Dean 1999; Rose 1993, 1996, 1999), I argue that transparency does not free truth but acts through the discursive power of truth to shape human conduct. Surveillance, made familiar and natural via discourses and practices of transparency, becomes a conduit for knowledge as well as an instrument for control (Strathern 2000).

Making the invisible visible is part of an anthropological project with which I engage. Denaturalizing what is taken for granted requires a commitment to showing the workings of power. How is it then that I present here a critique of practices that also aim to make things visible? I am not suggesting that we rid ourselves of the process but that we critically examine assumptions about its value, workings, and effects. Haridimos Tsoukas (1997) argues, for example, that transparency undermines the trust needed for expert systems to function effectively. Accountability trumps trust (Power 1994, 1997; Strathern 2000). And, through it all, "the 'real' workings of [any] institution, its social structure, cultural values, modes of organisation . . . are ignored" (Strathern 2000:314). Critique is not necessarily a call to destroy but a comment on knowledge practices and how we come to understand our world.

Visibility and Truth

In the mid- to late 1980s, new internal critiques began to question the anthropological and ethnographic production of authority and knowledge and their representations of cultural and historical truths. James Clifford and George E. Marcus (1986) persuasively argue that part of the legitimacy of anthropological analysis lies in the primacy of participant observation and its paradigmatic use of visualism. Their alternative, textual approach highlights the constructed, artificial nature of cultural accounts rather than treating cultures as scientific objects. To explain their turn toward textuality and away from visuality, they write,

> The predominant metaphors in anthropological research have been participant-observation, data collection, and cultural

description, all of which presuppose a standpoint outside—looking at, objectifying, or somewhat closer, "reading," a given reality. (11)

They reject the dominant hierarchy that places vision at the top of truth over evidence of sound and interlocution, of touch, smell, and taste. While anthropology has to some measure realized that cultural representations and "truths" come out of dialogues, not just observations, transparency and its related visuality remain a dominant category in discovering and ensuring "truth" in contemporary liberal and neoliberal domains (see also science and technology studies scholarship on seeing results of electron movements or gamma ray bursts, e.g., Haraway 1991; Traweek 1998).

The focus on clarity, openness, and understandability in electoral definitions of transparency dovetails nicely with popular understandings and electoral staff practices. Transparent electoral processes can be watched and understood. Like the legal proof given by eyewitnesses to describe a crime or the truth claims of witnessing, electoral processes are understood through watching. Also, processes are considered transparent if they can be re-created to some degree through mechanisms of watching. Supervisors and observers can retell what they saw, for example, and forms can trace the event by tracking voters, ballots, signatures, and results. The visible election is a verifiable one. However, the mechanism that watches and what—and how—it watches vary and become more insidious and subtle as democracy becomes more entrenched. These eyes and the sight they provide are the linchpin in the creation of "facts" and "evidence," but the act of seeing is contingent (Maurer 2001:904). The eyes through which democracy is validated do not see or understand everything. However, democracy legitimates its rule through a mythic image of wide-open, all-seeing, and all-knowing public eye(s).

In Bosnia-Herzegovina, the transparent gaze of democracy was explicitly symbolized through eyes. Although it may appear to be pointing out the obvious—a gaze is made up of eyes—it is important to emphasize how eyes, a body part, are symbolized, disembodied, and made technical. Electoral logos, slogans, and speeches extensively used eyes. In Bosnia-Herzegovina, international polling supervisors were told in welcoming speeches that they served as the "eyes and ears" of the international community in its effort to conduct free and fair elections. The logo (fig. 22) for ODIHR, a major election-monitoring organiza-

Fig. 22. The "eyes" of democracy, as seen in logo for the Office of Democratic Institutions and Human Rights (ODIHR, ironically pronounced by some election administrators as "Oh Dear!") *(Courtesy of the Organization for Security and Co-Operation in Europe, Office for Democratic Institutions and Human Rights.)*

tion, uses the symbolism of eyes to evoke the group's mission of electoral observation. The logo features a tree of eyes or a multieyed person, a bevy of eyes on top of legs and feet, mobile and multidirectional eyes. A Bosnian civic group also used eye imagery in its slogan (fig. 23). Their alliance of NGOs–the Eye Network—trained and organized thousands of Bosnian civil election observers for the two 2000 elections. All these slogans and logos explicitly and graphically link the idea of eyes and watching to democracy and democratic institutions. Based on the symbolism of the watchful eye, the logos and slogans mimic the All-Seeing Eye (Eye of Providence), the Divine Eye, and the Udjat Eye, all ancient symbols of omnipresent vision and power. The Udjat Eye, or the Eye of Horus, a solar god in ancient Egypt, offers protection against evil; the Eyes of Transparency offer democracy similar protection. These slogans and logos explicitly and graphically link the idea of surveillance with democracy, democratic institutions, and human rights. Truth and understanding are thought to be produced through these acts of watching; however, we need to critically examine sight and its promises.

НЕ ЗАТВАРАЈТЕ ОЧИ!

Don't Close your Eyes!

Network "Eye"

Fig. 23. "Don't Close Your Eyes" was the slogan for the Center for Civic Initiatives election observation project. The logo for their "Eye Network" appears in the upper left.

Election Supervision and Transparency

An important component of transparency during the postwar elections in Bosnia-Herzegovina was international supervision. Each postwar election was supervised by between 700 and 3,500 short-term, international, Good Samaritan, democracy-watching volunteers. They served as the international community's "eyes and ears" (and sometimes hands) in its effort to conduct free and fair elections. Each international supervisor was assigned a polling station to watch and oversee on Election Day. The polling station committee members checked voter identification, handed out ballots, and the like. Supervisors watched over the committee members' efforts, the voters, and other observers. While polling station chairs were nominally in charge, supervisors also had substantial authority over and responsibility for the events in the polling stations. Polling station supervisors were not international aid workers already in Bosnia; rather, they were short-term volunteers promised to the election effort by OSCE member states. In 1998, for example, more than 2,600 polling station supervisors flew into Bosnia-Herzegovina from cities around Western and Eastern Europe (which were home to 46 percent and 37 percent of the total, respectively), the United States (16 percent), and Canada, Korea, and Japan (1 percent combined). For the most part, the supervisors were college-educated citizens interested in international politics, the Balkans, or humanitarian aid. They ranged in age from 22 to 82 and included retired army colonels, high school teachers, people trying to break into international aid circuits, and lawyers, democratization activists, and homemakers. Few had professional experience in electoral matters, although some had previously been involved either as volunteers or as professionals with elections in their home countries.

Election supervision is a form of election monitoring, a practice that has gained currency and strength in the past 25 years (see Carothers 1997b; Lean 2004). Widely promoted by foreign and regional ministries, the United Nations, the European Union, and NGOs such as the Carter Center and the National Democratic Institute, election monitoring has, according to Thomas Carothers, contributed to the dissemination and strengthening of basic standards of election administration and advanced competitive and regular elections as an international norm (1997b:20). For the most part, observers and monitors are watchdogs and reporters rather than responsible members of the polling station. Thus, their effectiveness primarily lies in detecting and deterring fraud and in encouraging wary citizens and politicians to participate. As Carothers notes, observers' ability to catch fraud is weak; rather, officials may abandon plans out of fear of being caught. As a monitoring strategy, then, supervision represents a hands-on effort to deter and detect fraud and to lend credibility to an otherwise unstable and untrusted event.

In Bosnia, the existence of international supervisors created a transparent electoral process. They were the subjects to whom election processes were to be transparent. However, supervisors also embodied transparency. They were both the mechanisms of transparency and its supposed guarantors, the subjects to whom electoral processes needed to be transparent as well as the objects that made it transparent. Or, more aptly, they were the transparency actant. Without their presence, there were no (authoritative) eyes and thus no mechanism for transparency to exist. Although some supervisors expressed discomfort with their oversight role, as a group they did not feel that the worst part of their tenure was the supervision, a finding that is not surprising given that the surveillance implicit in this role is cast as a positive and crucial component of liberal democracy: democratic processes are meant to be open to societal scrutiny and examination. In conjunction with self-discipline, this process suggests that democratic societies watch themselves rather than having governments do so.

The official or bureaucratic reason for the existence of supervisors in Bosnia-Herzegovina was to minimize errors. This goal is mentioned in almost all documentation given to international supervisors, including letters of recruitment, job descriptions, and training manuals:

> The current plan is for each Supervisor to be in charge of one or two polling stations, supervising the local staff, ensuring proper procedures are followed, and making corrections when things are amiss. (Recruitment letter)

> One safeguard against the perception of an inappropriate action is the presence of an International Polling Supervisor at the Polling Station. . . . The International Polling Supervisor monitors and presents independent confirmation that Polling and Counting procedures are followed in an impartial and appropriate manner. (*Polling and Counting Manual*)

Supervisors repeatedly received the same message: your role is to prevent and correct improper action. Importantly, the justifications and rationale for supervisors match the goals and presumed effects of transparency—promoting public confidence, eliminating the appearance of impropriety, and limiting the possibilities of fraud.

Acts of prevention could be presence based, as discussed in the chapter "Doing Nothing," or could rely on a proactive and roving eye to see errors, allowing supervisors to step in to correct the breach. *Irregularities*, the bureaucratic label subsuming all errors, included any improper electoral behavior on the part of either voters or election staff through incompetence, lack of knowledge, misunderstanding, apathy, disagreement, purposeful deception and manipulation, or disregard of the Rules and Regulations. Possible irregularities thus ranged from the seemingly trivial—not passing out the "how to vote" leaflets to voters waiting their turns or filling out forms in pencil instead of pen (or the wrong pen)—to the obvious, such as ballot stuffing, failing to check voters' identification, or invalidating ballots. Polling supervisors were not immune to the stigma of irregularity; they could, for example, also forget (or be apathetic about) the determined protocols and procedures. Did they sort ballots into stacks of twenty-five? Did they make sure the stacks were counted twice? Did they remember what to do next? Polling supervisors could also commit irregularities based on their unique identities as supervisors—for example, interfering in the electoral process without an important reason, overruling the chair for no valid reason, or giving statements to the press. Interestingly, supervisors were generally exempted from charges of fraud in the polling station—all their improper actions were categorized by international officials as involuntarily irregular, as stemming from their exuberance and power, or as resulting from incompetence. The construction of supervisors as expert and neutral left out even the possibility of fraudulent action. Bosnians did not necessarily share in this representation of neutral expertise—in 1997, for example, a political party accused international personnel of counting improperly. Bosnians, while urged to trust the system of transparency, were less blinded by claims of visibility and truth. It is important to note that the improper behavior of supervisors was not only "involuntarily irregular" but also sometimes voluntarily and explicitly so. It was just not labeled as an irregularity. My conversations and interviews with supervisors clearly demonstrated that supervisors often did not enforce all regulations, instead picking and choosing which rules would be rigidly enforced and which would be approached more leniently or flexibly. Bosnian polling station committee staff did not have this luxury; power mediates transparency.

To prevent irregularities, many electoral subjects and objects were watched: voters, polling station committees, and all items that could get into hands of voters and polling station committees, such as ballots or results forms. They were watched in three ways: via the eyes of internationals (mostly polling station supervisors), via the bureaucratic tracking devices set up to account for the movements of Bosnian people and democracy, and via the eyes and ears of Bosnian political party and civic observers. A majority of my electoral informants (but certainly not the organizational literature) viewed this latter watching mechanism— embodied by Bosnian political party and civic observers—as negligible or ineffective. This was patently not true, but it is true that some eyes were vested with more authority than other eyes. It is also true that the eyes of observers were limited and controlled—they were required to sit at a distance from the polling and counting, which effectively limited what they could see. However, they could hear. Ears were a mostly ignored element in fraud-prevention strategies. The watching performed by international eyes and internationally derived forms received a high-ranking place in the hierarchy of authority and effectiveness.

Electoral transparency in Bosnia-Herzegovina was organized around the body of international supervisors—what I have termed "embodied transparency." Supervisors performed the gaze that allowed the polling and counting processes to be declared transparent. This transparency or understanding was, as could be expected, rooted in vision and visibility. Its emphasis on vision, however, in an embodied state, allowed only a partial understanding. Knowledge, power, auditory signals, and human fallibility and inability to be omnipresent interacted with vision to produce political and partial rather than the neutral and complete transparency it called forth. Transparency cannot "see" the truth. Its gaze is not open to all, is not able to see everything, and does not know everything. However, it remains a powerful tool of government. A truth-creating practice, it acts through a representation of itself as open and truth bearing even while it has only a partial view and crucially depends on specialized knowledge.

Watching mechanisms were both repressive and productive. Some supervisors believed that local election staff wanted to perform their job duties "properly" (i.e., as defined by and to the standard expected by the supervisors). In such cases, supervisors looked on supervision as validating the Bosnian internalization of democratic procedures. That is, Bosnian staff were, at least in some polling stations, self-regulating. They were, according to supervisors' comments, eager to prove their professionalism and integrity. They did so, again according to supervisors, by asking questions when uncertain about what to do or by getting confirmation of the proper protocols.

> My staff was impartial and had integrity. I feel the support provided by OSCE gave them the confidence to administer a good registration.

> Without [the international supervisors], the local [voting registration center] staff will easily be exposed to threats or attempts to bribe them. My impression is that they want to secure free and fair elections, and our presence are [sic] helping them in doing their job in right way.

Their desire to be subjected to the gaze of transparency proved the absorption of democratic values into their beings. This, in itself, according to at least one supervisor with whom I spoke, was key to transparency—not obstructing it, nor simply submitting to it, but desiring and inviting it. His positive evaluation of the polling station committee reflected the good relations he thought he had with the staff and their overarching desire to be watched and validated by him. However, watching was also conceived in coercive terms. The explicit supervision was expected, at least at some level, to coerce the polling station staff, if needed, into following the rules and regulations. Many supervisors also mentioned this dimension.

Without my presence, many mistakes would have been made.

I felt like a policeman awaiting little mistakes.

If I had not been there, the staff would have accepted undocumented people. I was essential for a neutral registration.

[My] involvement meant that our Election Committee (heavily biased toward one side of the political spectrum) was unable to control the registration process or exclude certain sections of the population.

The source of this power lay in the supervisor's quasi-legal authority to shut down the polling station, thereby potentially nullifying any already cast ballots as well as disenfranchising any voters not yet arrived. Transparency thus can be thought of as a disciplinary technique. The watching can be desired and self-internalized; however, it also incorporates judgment and the possibility of punishment.

Supervisors and other internationals increasingly became subject to surveillance as the elections became more technical and disembodied. That is, as the elections incorporated more (and emphasized) disembodied forms of transparency and control, all electoral actants—including supervisors—became subject to the gaze of tracking devices (see the chapter "Transparent Forms and Bureaucratic Mechanisms of Watching"). However, during the earlier elections, supervisors retained much autonomy. Although Bosnian observers watched supervisors, the observers' role in a regime of transparency was directed toward the election, and supervisors were largely considered separate from the election. Although supervisors clearly were deeply embedded in the conduct of the election, they were also outsiders. Thus, although the gazes could have been bidirectional, more than anything else, a constructed outsider looked *in* at the election. It is a tricky sidestep that constructs an integral node as outside of a process, such as the electoral supervisor's role in the election; in many years, polling could not occur without the presence of a polling supervisor. This sidestep can occur because supervisors were considered neutral and without an interest in the outcome. Therefore, they did not need to be subjected to a formal and explicit gaze.

Training Supervisors: Producing Knowledgeable Eyes

In contrast to the representation of transparency as open and inclusive, supervisors became capable of successfully fulfilling their role only through intensive training. While the power of Presence comes in part from an implied knowledge, the potential power of transparency depends on actual knowledge. The validity of an election hinges on watching and knowledgeable eyes. In training classes, both at centralized training sites and at their field locations, supervisors were told that the "election depended upon them knowing the procedures better than the polling station committee staff." Specific and superior knowledge was considered necessary; without it, supervisors could not see or correct irregularities, let alone report or track them. Transparency requires specialized and particular knowledge. Eyes need to know how to interpret and judge the processes they see.

It is useful to distinguish between watching and legitimized watching because knowing how and what to watch is a key element of regimes of transparency. Supervisors could watch—look at—clearly defined, well-performed, and highly visible polling procedures, but if they did not know whether the procedures were being enacted correctly or incorrectly, transparency was not being served. A wide knowledge gulf distinguishes looking from watching—or watching from legitimized watching. In Bosnia-Herzegovina, voters and observers watched electoral procedures in addition to the supervisors but had only limited places in the regime of transparency. The procedures were theoretically clear and visible to them, but this knowledge was not given to or made available to everyone in the same depth. The Rules and Regulations were public documents, but they did not cover the specific technical polling and counting procedures whose knowledge enabled someone to move from looking to watching. This information was detailed in the polling and counting manuals given to supervisors and polling station committee staff. The transparency of the election depended on recognized experts with specific knowledge that gave them the authority and tools to properly understand and judge the correctness of the purportedly visible procedures.

However, even the "experts'" knowledge was fragmented, variable, and extremely superficial. Supervisors were taught the electoral procedures, but retention was often another matter entirely. Some supervisors took their lessons to heart, studying on their own in the evenings and cramming the night before the election. Others did not. For example, in a desperate attempt to blacklist a fellow supervisor, some Bulgarian supervisors forged a letter to their foreign ministry from the supervision office saying that he was not welcome back due to his misconduct and ineptitude. The supervision office learned of this attempt when the foreign ministry asked for verification of the letter. Officials could not verify the letter because they had not written it, but the supervisor's election officer had in fact considered the supervisor incompetent and a menace. Similarly, a subset of supervisors complained loudly among themselves about (other) supervisors they believed were in Bosnia-Herzegovina "just for the money" or for "adventure tourism." Most supervisors, however, appeared to take their charge seriously, attempting to learn as much as possible in the short time available despite jet lag, long bus rides, and daylong, fast-paced lessons delivered in English that most supervisors had to concentrate hard to understand. These people became experts with as little as twelve hours of training, often performed by trainers newly introduced to or confused by the procedures. In an evaluation questionnaire given to registration supervisors at the end of their tenure in 1998, many respondents commented that they felt that they had been inadequately prepared for their jobs. As one remarked, "The training was basically of no help at all. I learned the process by reading the manual myself." Election supervision may have relied less on technical knowledge and more on the skills assumed to be within the international supervisor. If so, however, this phenomenon would negate the effort put in by the trainers, who spent their professional days brainstorming pedagogy and effective presentation strategies. Presence and knowledge worked not in opposition to each other but in combination. Technical knowledge was considered crucial to the effective deployment of transparency. However, lapses in knowledge could be partially counteracted by the effects of a supervisor's body on the conduct of the election.

Training, even when a pedagogical marvel, which was not always the case, cannot make experts in such a short time and within these substantial structural limitations. Although some supervisors had electoral experience in other countries, short and long term, volunteer and career, many were newcomers. This was true across all six postwar elections. Of the 28 polling station supervisors I trained in November 2000 (the sixth and final internationally implemented election), 57 percent were on their first or second electoral missions. A survey of polling station supervisors conducted in April 2000 resulted in similar numbers: 30 percent were first-timers, despite the fact that four prior elections had taken place, and 56 percent were on their first or second missions. Twenty-eight percent had participated in at least four of the five postwar elections. Structural tensions between experience, training, and mass logistics deemphasized any expertise by supervisors and highlighted the specific knowledge relevant to a particular election. Prior expert knowledge was little appreciated, since all election supervisors became "experts" through the training process. While individual election officers attempted to take advantage of the built-up expertise of supervisors with experience (placing them, for example, in contentious or large polling stations), evaluation of expertise, if there was any, was for the most part based almost entirely on short interviews, personal connections, or assumptions of ability based on gender, age, or nationality (and English aptitude).

While some knowledges were unacknowledged or unappreciated, other forms of knowledge were consciously rejected or dangerous. Supervisors were taught almost nothing about the political situation in Bosnia-Herzegovina, despite their desire for such information. Some electoral staff believed that such knowledge (both of the political situation in Bosnia-Herzegovina and of the politics behind electoral administration) threatened supervisors' ability to see clearly. Like juries told to disregard information and knowledge learned outside the courtroom, supervisors with independent knowledge were suspected of having clouded vision. Many long-term international electoral officials espoused a "need to know" mentality and commented that too much political knowledge threatened supervisors' neutrality as well as their representation as neutral. Their job, an official told me, was to supervise technical procedures, not to engage in politics or political discussions. Effectively watching the polling and counting procedures, these officials believed, did not depend on knowing the political situation in Bosnia-Herzegovina—in the worst case, such knowledge might have limited a supervisor's effectiveness. Of course, not only are technical procedures political, but the Bosnian polling staff performing the procedures were openly interested and engaged in politics—they were, for the most part, recruited from political party membership rolls.

Rather than political perspectives, supervisors were taught technical electoral polling and counting procedures. Details were emphasized, as was the necessity of following the exact order of the procedures.[2] This step-by-step philosophy constituted part of an effort to maintain control and order, thus allowing the process to be effectively watched and understood as well as likely producing more accurate results. It is hard to watch and understand a chaotic process, as there is no discernible pattern to mentally fix and judge. It was thus important for the electoral bureaucracy to designate the electoral polling and counting processes in such a way that they could be watched transparently. The training modules created for and given to supervisors emphasized exact learning of procedures (and subsequently exact enactment and enforcement of them). The substance lay in the details.

However, details are problematic. Supervisors—fallible—could not watch, let alone remember, all of the details. For example, the very specific lists of acceptable identification documents (discussed in the chapter "Election Day" and listed in table 1 in that chapter) were fairly difficult to remember and changed in almost every election, and individual identity documents were hard to see or verify unless the supervisor was personally holding them. During training sessions, supervisors expressed concern about the difficulty of verifying the acceptability of documents as well as whether the person proffering the identification matched the photograph on the identification. After looking at photocopies of all the documents, supervisors told me that it would be nearly impossible to supervise this process if they were also expected to supervise other activities. How, they asked, could they watch the identification verification process as well as at least three other electoral processes—the issuing of ballots, the spraying of ink, and the casting of ballots? The emphasis on details was needed to follow the established rules and regulations, but transparency effectively was only possible with a high degree of specialized knowledge, and even then the supervisors declared that they did not think that it could be achieved. The process could be looked at and partially (but not totally) watched and understood. Transparency did not and could not exist.

Training modules covering counting procedures were also detail oriented. And similarly, the procedures were also problematic vis-à-vis transparency in that they could be watched but not well understood. Furthermore, equally problematically, practices were not necessarily trackable or traceable. For example, the electoral system used in 2000 to select parliamentarians allowed voters to select as many individual candidates within one political party list as they desired. Because of the open-ended nature of the voting system, limiting fraud was technically difficult (at either the counting or tallying point) because the only built-in checks and balances mechanism was that an individual candidate could not receive more votes than his or her party had received. To combat the high risk of fraud, procedures were developed to limit both purposeful and involuntary errors during the counting process. As described in the chapter "Electoral Actants," one person served as a reader, another served as a reader-checker, and two people tallied the votes individually, independently recording the reader's verbal listing of marked candidates. At the end of each set of 25 ballots, the two tally sheet totals were compared, and if any discrepancy existed, all 25 ballots had to be recounted (in a new column on the tally sheet). In addition, pens and pencils were banned from the counting table during the sorting and reading processes to limit the possibility of stray marks finding their way onto ballots and thereby resulting in the selection of additional candidates or invalidating the entire ballot. During training exercises, supervisors expressed concern about potential collusion between tally pairs as well as between readers and reader-checkers. Concerns also arose about the high potential for mistakes, especially given that the counting was to be done after twelve hours of polling. As one supervisor complained, "Last time we counted by candlelight. Wouldn't it be more accurate and efficient to sleep first and count in the morning?" "Frankly," said another group of supervisors, "counting is a very complex procedure." Breaking the procedures down into concrete steps was a means to maintain control and order over the process (e.g., the counting steps shown in table 3 in the chapter "Electoral Actants").

Only by breaking the process into detailed and specific steps could counting be watched with understanding and open to the verification gaze of a supervisor. Breaking up a process into smaller and smaller details helped to further mask the political agenda underlying procedures. The importance placed on details exemplifies the specialized knowledge that underpins transparency despite its representation as a public accountability mechanism open to all gazes. But the emphasis on details shifts explicit attention away from the workings of transparency. The attention to detail erroneously presumes transparency's control over and ability to watch all things, even when doing so may not be feasible or possible in reality.

What about Ears?

My research found a definitive emphasis on vision and visibility. Supervisors were told that they were the eyes *and* ears of the international community. But what about those ears? Hearing and other auditory stimuli were not substantially incorporated into electoral supervision and processes of transparency, to the detriment of more thorough (i.e., more controlling) understandings of polling and counting activities. The vast majority of supervisors had minimal skills in Serbo-Croatian or any of its successor languages. Supervisors relied on interpreters provided by their local election offices, but interpreters did not receive training in polling and counting procedures.[3] They were meant to act only as a communications conduit for the supervisors, and few interpreters consequently were knowledgeable enough to proactively know if procedures performed by polling station committee members or voters were questionable. Interpreters were used primarily in direct conversations with the polling station committee or electoral observers. Interpreters asked polling station staff questions on behalf of the supervisors and vice versa and then transmitted the answers. The vast majority of the interpreters were not skilled enough to provide simultaneous interpretation services, let alone translate for all persons conversing at any given time in a polling station. They rarely had the ability to interpret the general, ambient conversations in the polling station—conversations among voters waiting in line, among electoral staff, or between voters and staff members. Furthermore, not even professional interpreters work for twelve hours at a stretch. Supervisors told me that they had to make a point of asking interpreters to translate when they wished to understand conversations. More often than not, such requests resulted in summaries of conversations rather than translations, a process that glossed over many potentially disruptive conversations or clues signaling that something should be supervised more closely. Instead, supervisors relied on their (expert) eyes and on their interpreters' (unknowledgeable and sometimes apathetic) ears. With a poor interpreter and a hostile staff, a supervisor could have great difficulty doing his or her job. The emphasis on visibility also minimized the contribution national observers could make through their ability to hear conversations between polling station committee staff or among voters. Were staff intimidating or rude to some voters? Were they more demanding of some than others (e.g., requiring particular identification documents from some but allowing any identification from others)? Were voters campaigning while waiting in line?

The overdetermined reliance on vision further points to the partiality of transparency despite its representation as all knowing and all seeing. The intrinsic partiality suggests a need to expand the concept—if we are to keep it at all—to include other sources of sensory input. Like national hiring, interpretation and translation remained issues of consequence throughout the international administration of Bosnia-Herzegovina's postwar elections. However, even while recognizing the limitations placed on all staff, including international supervisors, by inadequate language skills and reliance on potentially unreliable interpretation, no efforts to offer rudimentary language lessons occurred, and the truth claims of transparency were never questioned. Such is the dominance of vision.

Over the course of the elections in Bosnia-Herzegovina, embodied transparency became less important and a bureaucratic-technical transparency began to dominate electoral practices. These systems coexisted during each election, but one was always emphasized over the other. In 2000, a shift occurred: a substantial reduction in supervisors placed a larger burden onto forms than had previously been given. The shift occurred in conjunction with increasing concerns over the continued international implementation of Bosnia-Herzegovina's elections, a decrease in the election budget, and a belief that Bosnian electoral workers and voters were more trustworthy than had previously been the case. This subtle movement from embodied transparency to bureaucratic-technical transparency characterized the country's democratization through attempts to naturalize and incorporate structural forms of surveillance and governance. In the following chapter, I turn to the disembodied gazes emanating from seemingly innocuous textual forms.

TRANSPARENT FORMS AND
BUREAUCRATIC MECHANISMS
OF WATCHING

Although supervisors formed a large portion of the transparency regime, they were supplemented by a variety of bureaucratic mechanisms that also monitored the election and provided another gaze to be read and interpreted by officials. These bureaucratic mechanisms consisted largely of forms—boring, mundane forms. These forms tracked the progress of the election and the movement of electoral objects, such as voters, ballots, tabulations, supervisors, ballot boxes, voting screens, and polling stations. Like supervisors, bureaucratic forms constituted a mechanism of transparency and government. An election ultimately rests on forms. It does not matter if the polling and counting are perfectly done if forms are not then filled out correctly. Without forms that accurately document or track Election Day activities, the results are ruined and suspect. Many of the internationals involved in Bosnia-Herzegovina's postwar elections applauded this argument. As part of the electoral training for the trainers, I was assigned to give an overview of the seemingly endless number of electoral forms. I struggled with a way to tie all the disparate forms into a single pedagogical unit, finally deciding to emphasize their shared status and intrinsic importance as forms. This strategy seemed a more interesting strategy as a lesson plan than simply reviewing how to fill in all the forms. At the time, I was not yet convinced of my argument, but I thought it would make a strong impact (and perhaps stave off naps). The other trainers seized on my impromptu argument as innovative and true, and my lesson plan was later incorporated into the official training for supervisors. Apparently, forms really are crucial.

Electoral staff also expressed a great deal of confidence and faith in the forms. At least prior to Election Day, some trainers believed that the forms could not possibly be filled out incorrectly. One trainer from a country in Eastern Europe told the supervisors he trained, "It has been made foolproof; you can't go wrong. The ballot counting and packing process has been thought out and tested." However, the 20 percent of results forms with mathematical errors and the 8 percent of polling station ballots that needed to be recounted in November 2000 as well as the mountainous pile of registration forms in 1997 that needed to be rebubbled and debubbled prove that forms are not foolproof.

In this chapter, I explore the world of transparency through a variety of accounting forms, results forms, and monitoring forms. While arguing that these forms constituted part of a transparency regime, I analyze how they acted on the ground in Bosnia-Herzegovina. Like the embodied transparency discussed in the previous chapter, the visibility and understandability of bureaucratic transparency are partial. Forms cannot completely re-create the election; they provide only partial and particular glimpses. They depend on the agents who fill them out. Nor is transparency available and open to all. Bosnians were asked implicitly to trust a system of transparency to which they had little access. What was open to view was limited and controlled. Items and processes always remain opaque or hidden. Finally, transparency supposedly provides clarity and truth. However, transparency is not at all self-evident. The forms cannot accurately re-create what they track. When forms are separated from their scribes, likes voters from the ballot, knowledge is flattened and intent is unrecoverable. Transparency, while increasingly a form of authority and governance, clearly is constructed and produced in very specific ways. Technicality did little to improve the dreams or intent of transparency. Rather, the promises and authority of transparency appeared more secure through the displacement of humans from the visible scene.

Tracking Election Day

Election Day in Bosnia-Herzegovina relied on two main forms: an accounting form (fig. 24) and a results form (or several results forms) (fig. 25). Accounting and results forms track the movements and behaviors of ballots, voters, and other electoral objects. Tracking is a device of transparency in that it attempts to make visible a particular process and understand it through the gaze provided by a form. The accounting

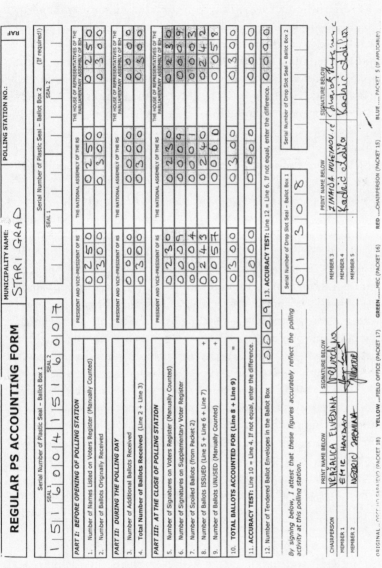

Fig. 24. Accounting form, 2000. This sample accounting form condenses three races into one form. When compared to the 1997 accounting form (fig. 9), it is possible to track spatial realignments, changes in wording, changes meant to clarify the form and reduce errors, and the shift from polling station supervisor and chair responsibility to the polling station committee as a whole. The supervisor disappears from the form, except as the carrier of the yellow copy of the form (which went back to the OSCE field office). *(Courtesy of the Organization for Security and Co-Operation in Europe, Mission to Bosnia and Herzegovina.)*

forms claimed to know the number of votes cast and forecast the location of ballots by accounting for voters' signatures and ballots. The forms did so by providing spaces to record the number of ballots unused, the number of voters who had signed the voter register, and the number of spoiled ballots. These three numbers—if everything occurred correctly—would add up to the total number of ballots received. For example, if a polling station received 1,000 ballots, at the end of polling but before opening the ballot box—because this is an exercise in forecasting—the polling station committee should count signatures on the voter register, the number of unused ballots, and the pile of spoiled ballots. If they count 690 signatures, 8 spoiled ballots, and 302 unused ballots, then all the ballots are accounted for. Similarly, if the voter register contained 800 names, then the committee members know that they had an 86 percent turnout rate.

The forms locate, label, and quantify ballots. For example, the number on line 7 of figure 24 determines how many spoiled ballots envelope 2 should contain. Likewise, the signatures on the supplemental voter register (line 6) predetermine the number of tendered ballots that should appear in special envelopes in the ballot box when it is opened. The committee should find a predetermined number of regular ballots in the ballot box—the number of regular ballots should equal the number of signatures on the voter register (line 5). Used ballots should equal the number of final voter register signatures, supplemental voter register signatures, and spoiled ballots (line 8). Results forms also traced voters and ballots, although the emphasis was on the ballots found in the ballot box rather than on the expected number. On results forms (fig. 25), signatures (which reflect the expected number of ballots) are matched to the number of counted ballots in the ballot box. During the sorting process, ballots were also separated into valid and invalid votes, including blank ballots, and mismarked ("other") ballots. In elections prior to 2000, blank ballots were not distinguished from other mismarked ballots. However, my informants surmised that senior officials had decided they wanted to know about potential protest votes (e.g., blank ballots). Multiple accuracy checks sought to ensure and create accurate knowledge. Through technical counting and mathematical steps, the checks presumed to clearly record polling day actions in the polling stations.

Accuracy checks attempted to use accountability mechanisms to limit fraud. Mathematical comparisons and checks for equal results (i.e., signatures versus ballots) were thought to have some efficacy at holding

THE NATIONAL ASSEMBLY OF THE REPUBLIKA SRPSKA CONSTITUENCY 6

MUNICIPALITY NAME: **306** POLLING STATION NO.: SUMMARY OF RESULTS FORM (OPEN LIST) SM2

SUMMARY OF VOTES

		Valid Votes
A)	Invalid (Blank) Ballots	
B)	Invalid (Other) Ballots	
C)	Total Invalid Ballots (Line A + Line B)	
D)	Total Valid Votes	
E)	Total All Ballots (Line C + Line D)	
F)	Accuracy Test (Line E = Line 2.) If not equal, enter the Difference.	

1. Total number of signature on the Voters Register (Line 5. of the Accounting Form)

2. Number of Ballots in the Ballot Box

3. Accuracy Test (Line 1. = Line 2.) If not equal, enter the difference.

Serial Number of Plastic Seal for TEB with Unused Ballots (WHITE)

Serial Number of Plastic Seal for TEB with Tendered Ballots (RED 7) (if applicable)

Serial Number of Plastic Seal for TEB with Open List Ballots (BLUE)

Serial Number of Plastic Seal for Clear Plastic bag with Voter register

Votes for: **СТРАНКА НОВОГ ПОЧЕТКА**

NO	Candidate Name	Valid Votes Received
1	НУРДИН ЧЕНГИЋ	
2	САМИР ХАНУША	
3	ЈАСНА СИПОВИЋ	
4	САБИНА РЕСУЛБЕГОВИЋ	
5	ДОБРИНА КУСМУК	
6	ФАХРУДИН ЧУСТО	
7	МИТХАД БЕГИРСПАХИЋ	
8	АДИС ПАШОВИЋ	
9	ЗОРАН МИТРОВИЋ	

Votes for: **ГОРАН БИЈЕДИЋ**

NO	Candidate Name	Valid Votes Received

	PRINT NAME BELOW	SIGNATURE BELOW
CHAIRPERSON		
MEMBER 1		
MEMBER 2		

	PRINT NAME BELOW	SIGNATURE BELOW
MEMBER 3		
MEMBER 4		
MEMBER 5		

Fig. 25. Summary of results form 1, 2000. Many of the forms pictured here are from training exercises. Fictional political parties were used on the preprinted forms. Examples on this form include the Old Film Party, the World Party, and the Pensioner's Party. Besides these mythical parties however, the preprinted forms mimic the actual political parties' names. (*Courtesy of the Organization for Security and Co-Operation in Europe, Mission to Bosnia and Herzegovina.*)

staff accountable. When the numbers are off, suspicion is heightened and motives questioned, as in this excerpt from an audit report.

> The audit team re-counted this Polling Station as in Electoral Races 207 and 409 the number of ballots in the box exceeded the total votes.

Electoral Race	Signatures	Recorded # ballots	Actual # ballots
207	189	237	201
409	189	211	205
512	189	208	not recounted

> The data for this Polling Station has been entered. There is a consistent number of ballots greater than the actual signatures, this station has no record of issuing tendered ballots. In my opinion the irregularities show that a degree of fraud has taken place and the results should be removed from the data bank.

The lack of accuracy, known through the transparency mechanism of the accounting and results forms, signaled irregularities and triggered administrative corrective action. However, demonstrating that despite its attempts, transparency does not necessarily control conduct or enforce standards, the audit reported that 7.4 percent of polling stations had ballots that needed to be recounted and offered a summary of the election.

> It appears to be a widely accepted practice with local election officials of all grades and posts that the signatures of voters are not counted correctly, the number of ballots in the box exceeds the number of voters' signatures, total votes exceeds the number of ballots. The results sheets are submitted to audit in this condition which is unacceptable.

Transparency cannot reveal the full truth for which it calls. These error-filled forms show that mistakes were made. It was rarely possible to determine with certainty whether the error was an inadvertent mistake, resulted from misunderstanding or confusion, or was the product of willful deception. Transparency is not able to see or read intent.

C-2 Forms: The New Role for Polling Supervisors

Along with bureaucratic forms, supervisors made the practices of electoral polling and ballot counting visible and understandable, although, as I have argued, this visibility and understanding was partial and particular. Over four years and five elections, supervisors also increasingly served as the reporting mechanisms of transparency. In early elections, supervisors were directed to use poll books to comment on polling and counting irregularities, disputes, or fraud. However, in the earlier elections, supervisors also were charged with preventing and/or correcting the flaws they reported: that was why the supervisors were there. In later elections—specifically, the two conducted in 2000—election administrators showed increasing concern for getting and recording (i.e., knowing) the supervisor's knowledge on Election Day itself rather than post facto through reviews of poll books. The concern rose in direct proportion to a decline in supervisors' active participation, authority, and full-time presence in polling stations. Polling supervisors had less authority and were tasked with less proactive participation in the polling and counting procedures, and they neither assisted in computing nor signed off on the results. Significantly, there were also many fewer polling supervisors. Supervision in 2000 was "partial" rather than "full." Instead of staying at one polling station during the entire day (and night) for the entirety of the polling and counting, supervisors traveled between an average of five or six polling stations. They spent their day spot-checking polling stations, visiting each for 20–40 minutes. During the counting process, they fully observed one station, leaving the others without supervision.[1]

As they became less intrusive, supervisors became subject to reporting mechanisms that attempted to transfer supervisory knowledge of polling and counting activities to the election administration and high-level international officials. Because the process was no longer fully transparent in an embodied manner—the polling station was not under constant surveillance—other strategies were necessary. A subtle shift occurred as the supervisor's role changed from being the primary gaze and mechanism of transparency to being just one of a series of tracking devices that together produced a transparent process. A preponderance of reports and forms began to grow in importance, and the process began to be watched in a bureaucratic, standardized, regulative, and disembodied way. Whereas supervisors had previously acted as eyes, now their eyes were harnessed as reporting devices.

During the two 2000 elections, supervisors reported their observations of polling and counting activities directly to electoral administrators rather than recording observations in poll books. Under this change in procedures, supervisors lost much of their autonomy; transparency was increasingly regulated. The frequency and timing of reports as well as the topics to be reported were specifically prescribed for supervisors. The reporting structure was encapsulated in a booklet of instructions that each supervisor received.[2] For months prior to the election, the instructions were debated during administrative electoral meetings. For example, was it technically feasible to receive 800 reports three times a day? Could the phone network handle the volume of traffic? What information was needed in real time? Significant discussion also concerned whether these actions should be considered instructions or directions. "Instructions" held greater bureaucratic weight as binding actions, while "directions" were less enforceable guidelines. The reporting ultimately received the status of instruction—that is, not a request but a requirement.

The instructions demanded that supervisors submit verbal reports three times during polling activities (via phone or radio), between nine and eleven o'clock in the morning, between one and three o'clock in the afternoon, and between five and seven o'clock in the evening. Their report was expected to include specific information—nothing more, nothing less.

A. Polling station under report

B. Visit time (from/to)

C. Number of signatures on the voter register

D. Number of signatures on the supplemental voter register

E. Efficiency of the voting process (Answers: good, bad, or # of minutes of line)

F. Are only acceptable ID documents used and correctly checked? (Answers: yes, no)

G. Has any voter received more than one ballot? (Answers: yes, no)

H. Are the procedures for blind, illiterate, and bodily incapacitated voters strictly followed? (Answers: yes, no)

I. Is the secrecy and freedom of the vote guaranteed (in and out of the polling station)? (Answers: yes, no)

J. Any other irregularities spotted or reported from the NGO observers? (Answers: yes, no; if yes, please record name of observer)

K. Any other irregularities in the polling procedure?

When reporting, polling station supervisors were told to report only answers to the questions; if further explanations were desired, the supervisors would be asked: they were not to supply explanations or commentary without prompting. Thus, the radio reports consisted of rapid-fire communication using the military-style phonetic alphabet to indicate which question was being answered:

ALPHA 001B211, BRAVO 0900 to 1000, CHARLIE 267, DELTA 9, ECHO GOOD, FOXTROT YES, GOLF NO, HOTEL NO, INDIA YES, JULIET NO, KILO NO, OUT.

Logisticians hoped that brevity would increase the likelihood that 2,400 reports could be transmitted each day via radio and telephone.[3] Similar strict reporting guides covered the surveillance of the counting process, with reports transmitted twice during the evening—once when the first count (the tabulation of votes cast for political parties and coalitions) was completed, and once when the second count (the tabulation of votes for candidates within the political parties) was completed. Each supervisor was also asked to submit a written report at the end of his or her day, no longer than three handwritten pages, with information on all of the supervisor's observed polling stations. In addition, each supervisor had to fill out a polling supervisor form for polling activities (C-2) form at each polling station visited. All of these forms had to be handed in when the supervisor was debriefed.

Although the reporting mechanisms attempted to standardize watching and to create a new disembodied and centralized mechanism of transparency, it is unclear whether that result was achieved. An analysis of reporting forms highlights an enormous amount of variation both in the manner of reporting and in the supervisors' activities and observations. The practices of transparency changed: a new mechanism was created, but it provided neither standardized visions nor full understandings of polling station activities to those attempting to harness or actualize transparency. The forms attempted to collect various information and to transform it into knowledge. The C-2 form—submitted by supervisors to their electoral offices the day after the election—tracked the polling station visited (and time of visit), the number of signatures on the voter register, the status of the voter queue and wait times, and a number of practices open to error and fraud, such as checking voter identification, issuing or having more than one ballot, and intimidation. The questions are consistent, but the responses vary.

The creator of the form intended it to be filled out for each visit to each polling station. That is, each form should have documented one visit to one polling station by a polling supervisor. At the end of their Election Day tasks, supervisors should have had approximately 15 filled-out forms. However, some supervisors used the same form to document all their visits to a particular polling station. In these cases, they manipulated the form structure to include documentation of their multiple visits. The space for entering "Visit Time (from/to)" was always filled out, but never consistently. For example, the proper information (to be turned into knowledge) for a visit lasting from 10:45 A.M. to 11:30 A.M. would have looked like this:

Visit time (from/to): 1045/1130.

Instead, supervisors recorded information such as multiple visits, only their arrival times, and their overall number of visits to a polling station in the same space (fig. 26). While in a few cases, the form appeared to have been misunderstood, in many other cases, supervisors modified the form to have it fill more functions than the one for which it was created. Some supervisors labeled each of their visits (e.g., I, II, III, IV, V) and noted their multiple answers by these labels (e.g., I—0 voters, II—171 voters, III—364 voters, IV—410 voters, V—642 voters). As supervisors tried to make clear their experience, the form was pressed into action for more than its intended use. Other supervisors, while retaining multiple visits, noted just one number for "number of signatures." The form did not adequately provide space to record or capture their experiences.

Some polling station supervisors reacted negatively to the form's inability to translate their experience. For example, the supervisor who filled out the C-2 form in figure 27 appears to mock the questions. She reports that the number of signatures on the voter register was "different each time" she visited the polling station. Similarly, she disputes her ability to answer the questions in the authoritative manner asked of her. For example, in question 3b, she notes that during her visits, identification was thoroughly checked, but she explicitly denies making a statement on what happened when she was not present. An educated and critical American, she makes a political statement on her "partial supervision" and any knowledge that might be garnered from it.

The supervisor who filled out the C-2 form in figure 28 leaves the information harvester without clear knowledge. Although the polling station was visited three times during the day, only one figure is reported for number of signatures. Is it from the end of the day? What about the other times? Was the turnout evenly distributed throughout the day or

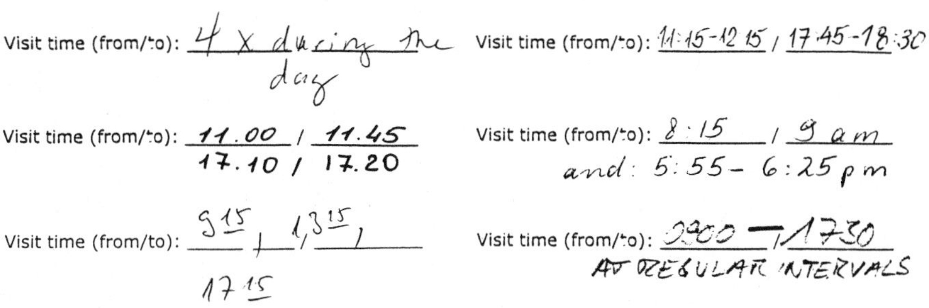

Visit time (from/to): _4 x during the day_   Visit time (from/to): _14:15-12 15 / 17.45-18:30_

Visit time (from/to): _11.00 / 11.45_   Visit time (from/to): _8:15 / 9 am_
_17.10 / 17.20_   _and: 5:55- 6:25 pm_

Visit time (from/to): _9 15 / 13 15 /_   Visit time (from/to): _0900 — 1730_
_17 15_   _AT REGULAR INTERVALS_

Fig. 26. Six samples of variance in polling station visitations extracted from supervisors' C-2 forms, 2000. *(Courtesy of the Organization for Security and Co-Operation in Europe, Mission to Bosnia and Herzegovina.)*

heavier during the morning or afternoon? Can the information harvester feel confidence in the other information reported, especially as it appears to have been filled out after the counting procedures were complete (as shown by the answer to question 2C, which references sorting ballots)?

Responses to other questions on the C-2 reporting form continue to demonstrate variance in supervisors' experiences, in what they looked for, in what they thought were problems, in their proactivity, and in their confidence in seeing and reacting to errors and fraud. The majority of C-2 forms had one-word answers—yes or no—given without comment or explanation. The wide range of responses problematizes the visibility and understanding that transparency evokes. These forms, as objects of knowledge and transparency, fail to provide the consistent and clear knowledge that they are thought to provide as part of a transparency regime. It is not possible to consistently know what happened in the polling stations post facto via these forms; it is not even possible to know what supervisors saw during their visits.

The form in figure 29 has several peculiarities from the perspective of attempting to gather knowledge from its information. First, the polling station supervisor visited the station six times during the polling period (0600–1900), but the form does not indicate when. The form asks for time frames but does not receive the information, as 0600–1900 was the designated time for polling (including an hour to set up the station prior to the arrival of voters). Near the end of the day, the supervisor reports that 687 people voted (i.e., signed the voter register) but records no numbers for the first five visits. It becomes unclear when the (rest of the)

POLLING SUPERVISOR FORM
FOR POLLING ACTIVITIES

This form is to be used while supervising activities in polling stations and should be handed-in to the election officer during the de-briefing at the field office. For verbal reporting during polling day, polling supervisors should use the Reporting Form (Annex C-3).

Reporting to Field Office: _Banja Luka Annex_ Visit time (from/to): _3x during day_

Polling Station number: _034_

1. Number of signatures on Voter Register: _different each time_
2. a) Number of signatures on Tendered Ballots Supplementary Voter Registers*: _N/A_
b) Is the Voter Register thoroughly checked before issuing a Tendered Ballot? _yes_
c) Is the Tendered Ballot procedure followed properly? If not, give details.
3. a) Is the ID officer thoroughly checking names against the Voter Register? _yes_
b) Are only acceptable ID documents used? If not, what documents were accepted instead? _during my visits, yes_
c) Were people without acceptable ID allowed to vote? _as far as I saw, no_
d) Action taken:

Fig. 27. Mocking the C-2 form? This supervisor has filled out the form with attitude, specifically noting its incompatibility with her experience. The polling station number has been modified to protect anonymity. (*Courtesy of the Organization for Security and Co-Operation in Europe, Mission to Bosnia and Herzegovina.*)

POLLING SUPERVISOR FORM
FOR POLLING ACTIVITIES

This form is to be used while supervising activities in polling stations and should be handed-in to the election officer during the de-briefing at the field office. For verbal reporting during polling day, polling supervisors should use the **Reporting Form (Annex C-3).**

Reporting to Field Office: _Banja Luka_

Polling Station number: _034_

Visit time (from/to):
```
0840    0845
1555    1615
1840  / 0230
        (close)
```

---

1. Number of signatures on Voter Register: _582_

2. a) Number of signatures on Tendered Ballots Supplementary Voter Registers*: _10_

   b) Is the Voter Register thoroughly checked before issuing a Tendered Ballot? _yes_

   c) Is the Tendered Ballot procedure followed properly? If not, give details. _yes - except for 1_ _one voter did not put ballots in tendered envelope. "+" was written on the ballots_ _and they were identified & placed in the envelope when we sorted ballots._

3. a) Is the ID officer thoroughly checking names against the Voter Register? _yes_

   b) Are only acceptable ID documents used? If not, what documents were accepted instead? _yes_

   c) Were people without acceptable ID allowed to vote? _no_

   d) Action taken: _____

Fig. 28. Ambiguity marks this C-2 form. (*Courtesy of the Organization for Security and Co-Operation in Europe, Mission to Bosnia and Herzegovina.*)

POLLING SUPERVISOR FORM
FOR POLLING ACTIVITIES

This form is to be used while supervising activities in polling stations and should be handed-in to the election officer during the de-briefing at the field office. For verbal reporting during polling day, polling supervisors should use the Reporting Form (Annex C-3).

6 times visited

Reporting to Field Office: *Banjo Luko*   Visit time (from/to): *6:00 / 19:00*

Polling Station number: _____

---

1. Number of signatures on Voter Register: _____ *687* _____ (*of 18-15*)

2. a) Number of signatures on Tendered Ballots Supplementary Voter Registers*: _____

   b) Is the Voter Register thoroughly checked before issuing a Tendered Ballot? _____

   c) Is the Tendered Ballot procedure followed properly? If not, give details. _____
   Problems with REGISTRATION — 10% were
   sent away   People don't want tendered ballots

3. a) Is the ID officer thoroughly checking names against the Voter Register? _____ *yes*

   b) Are only acceptable ID documents used? If not, what documents were accepted instead? _____ *yes*

   c) Were people without acceptable ID allowed to vote? _____

   d) Action taken: _____

4. a) Has any voter received more than one ballot? _____ *no*

   b) If yes, how many? Give details. _____

   c) Action taken? _____

5. a) Are voting procedures for blind, illiterate and bodily incapacitated voters strictly followed? _____

   b) If not, what kind of violation have you seen? How many times? _____

   c) Have you seen the same person assist voters more than once? _____ *yes   members of Com*

   d) Action taken? _____ *yes !*

OSCE Mission to Bosnia and Herzegovina

6. Efficiency of the voting process

a) Approximate # of voters queuing: _5 - 50_

b) Approximate waiting time: _10 - 70 Min._

c) Approximate time spent in the booths:
3 - 5 Min.

☐) Any corrective action necessary? _____
_no_

d) Are there shortages of resources in the polling stations? _/. no_

e) If yes, what kind and how was the problem addressed? _____
_/._
_____
_____

7. Secrecy and freedom of vote

a) Is the secrecy and freedom of the vote guaranteed?
yes
_____
_____

b) Any instances of intimidation? Perpetrated by whom?
_/_
_____
_____

c) Were there more than one voter behind the screen? _____
yes
family - voting

d) Were people bussed in? If yes, give details. _____
_____
_____
_____

e) Action taken: _____
yes   did
_____

8. a) Any other irregularities spotted or reported by NGO observers (if yes, record the name):
_____
_____
_____
_____

b) Give details of what you have seen. _____
_____
_____
_____

c) Action taken: _____
_____
_____

* Note: To avoid confusion, be aware that there are three types of Supplementary Voter Registers (SVR) apart from the main one: 1) SVR for Tendered Ballots 2) SVR for Homebound and Institutionalised Voters 3) Other SVR for special circumstances.

OSCE Mission to Bosnia and Herzegovina
November 2000 General Elections

Fig. 29. An exemplar of unclarity, C-2 form, 2000. *(Courtesy of the Organization for Security and Co-Operation in Europe, Mission to Bosnia and Herzegovina.)*

information was recorded on the form or if any of it relates to any specific time. When, for example, was the line 5 people long, and when was it 50 people long (question 6a)? Second, the supervisor noted irregularities in both the processing of blind, illiterate, and bodily incapacitated voters and the secrecy and freedom of the ballot. Both times, as shown in questions 5d and 7e, the supervisor "took action!" However, the information harvester lacks information about what sort of action. The question's implication (Action Taken?) is one of asking what action was taken, not whether action was taken. The form is ambiguously written, but given that it provides four blank lines for the desired response, presumably a semi-detailed answer is desired if not expected. Third, the supervisor reports different information than that requested. Question 2c asks whether particular processes are being followed. He or she responded by commenting on the poor registration process and noting that 10 percent of people are being sent away and that voters do not want tendered ballots. The second comment is troublesome vis-à-vis democracy—why are they being sent away? But, in the context of the first and third comments, it is likely that the voters were not found on the voter register and refused to vote via tendered ballot. Thus, they were sent away. The proper procedure might have been followed, but because of mistakes made during the registration process and a distrust of the validity of tendered ballots (which were often seen—correctly—as a mechanism for pacifying voters not found on the voter register), voters were effectively denied franchise. Alternatively, of course, these people were not registered voters, were not eligible to vote, and thus should have been sent away.

Comparing forms against each other demonstrates the variance of experience and interpretation among supervisors and the form's inability to effectively capture the diversity of how they spent and thought about their day. One supervisor filled out his or her form thoroughly and (given the form's intent), accurately; the supervisor visited twice, and both sets of arrival and departure times are documented (fig. 30). During the 60 minutes she observed the polling activities, she noticed and attempted to rectify the problems with accepting unacceptable identification documents, giving multiple ballots to one person, and not following the proper procedures for assisting needy voters. Another supervisor provides fairly thorough information, but the responses make it clear that whether or not procedures are followed is not a crisply black-and-white matter (fig. 31). People at times gathered behind the voter booth—is it always a problem? Does it really suggest a less democratic

POLLING SUPERVISOR FORM
FOR POLLING ACTIVITIES

This form is to be used while supervising activities in polling stations and should be handed-in to the election officer during the de-briefing at the field office. For verbal reporting during polling day, polling supervisors should
use the Reporting Form (Annex C-3).

Reporting to Field Office: _RC Banja Luka Annex_   Visit time (from/to): _10 $\frac{00}{17 \underline{40}}$_ / _10 $\frac{45}{17 \underline{55}}$_
Polling Station number: _034_

---

1. Number of signatures on Voter Register: _17 (10 $\underline{00}$), 101 (17 $\underline{40}$)_

2. a) Number of signatures on Tendered Ballots Supplementary Voter Registers*: _———_

   b) Is the Voter Register thoroughly checked before issuing a Tendered Ballot? _____

   c) Is the Tendered Ballot procedure followed properly? If not, give details. _____

   _____

   _____

---

3. a) Is the ID officer thoroughly checking names against the Voter Register? _no_

   b) Are only acceptable ID documents used? If not, what documents were accepted instead? _not_
   "notifications" of PSC that person is on the Voter Register

   c) Were people without acceptable ID allowed to vote? _yes_

   d) Action taken: _warning to the chairperson of the PS (ap-_
   parently, respected only my stay there)

---

4. a) Has any voter received more than one ballot? _yes_

   b) If yes, how many? Give details. _3 kit of ballots were provided to 1 old_
   lady ~~that~~ who claimed to vote for disabled persons (relatives).

   c) Action taken? _I asked CP to take back ballots for other 2 persons_
   and to follow Manual (part "possible exceptions to the regular
   voting process" - persons live next door).

---

5. a) Are voting procedures for blind, illiterate and bodily incapacitated voters strictly followed? _no_

   b) If not, what kind of violation have you seen? How many times? _case mentioned below,_
   3-4 people to help illiterate. % of illiterate voters – 80% (!)

   c) Have you seen the same person assist voters more than once? _yes_

   d) Action taken? _———_

Fig. 30. Thorough completion of the C-2 form, 2000. *(Courtesy of the Organization for Security
and Co-Operation in Europe, Mission to Bosnia and Herzegovina.)*

6. **Efficiency of the voting process**

a) Approximate # of voters queuing: _3-4_

b) Approximate waiting time: _3-4_

c) Approximate time spent in the booths:

_4-5_

:) Any corrective action necessary? _Only to_ _keep time further away from_ _voters_

d) Are there shortages of resources in the polling stations? _tendered envelopes_

e) If yes, what kind and how was the problem addressed? _MEC solved it after_ _some phone calls_

7. Secrecy and freedom of vote

a) Is the secrecy and freedom of the vote guaranteed?

more or less, but _many people congregated_ _around the screens_

b) Any instances of intimidation? Perpetrated by whom?

not that I saw

c) Were there more than one voter behind the screen? _Sometimes_

d) Were people bussed in? If yes, give details. _not to my_ _knowledge_

e) Action taken: _The chairperson told them again + again_ _to leave space around the screens, but people_ _will be social_

8. a) Any other irregularities spotted or reported by NGO observers (if yes, record the name):

not to me

b) Give details of what you have seen. _____

c) Action taken: _____

* Note: To avoid confusion, be aware that there are three types of Supplementary Voter Registers (SVR) apart from the main one: 1) SVR for Tendered Ballots 2) SVR for Homebound and Institutionalised Voters 3) Other SVR for special circumstances.

OSCE Mission to Bosnia and Herzegovina
November 2000 General Elections

Fig. 31. Zones of gray fill this C-2 form, 2000. *(Courtesy of the Organization for Security and Co-Operation in Europe, Mission to Bosnia and Herzegovina.)*

process? Sometimes yes, sometimes no. How does one distinguish between sociability and coercive behavior? Can sociability also be coercive?

What is left out or off of these forms? Most forms provided little information besides yes or no, leaving open to question the accuracy or fullness of the response. Of the 97 forms I collected, the most grievous incident reported dealt with an attempt to stuff the ballot box. It was reported in the space for question 8, the last section on the C-2 form, which asks if the national observers have reported any other irregularities.

> 8 a) At 1900 hours the Chairperson asked me to allow him and the whole board (including national observers) to fill up the ballot box with an additional 100–150 ballot sets. According to him, to cover up the poor turnout. The behavior of the whole board after my immediate and strong refusal to let them do so gave the impression that indeed they intended to do so. Therefore the whole counting and packing procedure was carried out under my personal guidance with effectively taking over control of the board. Because of this no further fraud attempts were possible. All names of those probably linked to this incident can be found in the pollbook at closing time.

The polling station supervisor reported the incident despite the lack of reserved space for a problem of this category. As before, the form was called on to do more than the purpose for which it had been designed. These forms narrowed the possibilities for watching. Supervisors received particular directions, which potentially left unexamined alternative gazes, views, and observations, including, for example, verbal harassment or coercion. When transparency is explicitly detailed, it is even more likely that processes and practices will fall out of the transparent gaze. These behaviors are less subject to a gaze. They cannot be categorized as nontransparent or opaque; they are simply not considered. While some supervisors used the form beyond its designed purposes, we must be careful about disembodied mechanisms of transparency, because their knowledge and the way they gather it are problematic.

Finally, like the poll books mentioned earlier in this chapter, what was subsequently done with these forms remains unknown. For example, during one election, I collected the forms on behalf of my election officer and left them on her desk. She likely glanced through them (much as I did before making copies and collecting them as data) before putting them in a file. She probably was asked to provide a summarized report of the supervisor's observations, but even this report, made days or weeks after the election, would not have affected the results. The transparency and knowledge produced by the forms had little immediate effect. Thus, although the forms acted as a surveillance mechanism, their postelection value was inconclusive. Although beyond the scope of this research, it is worthwhile to ask about the value of knowledge that transparency provides, in what contexts it provides that value, and for whom.

The Politics of Transparency: Subjectivity and Trust

In response to internal and external criticism that transparency was a one-way process, the international electoral bureaucracy began to publicize and open up some of its practices and decision-making processes (cf. Divjak 2001). In the name of transparency, the bureaucrats submitted themselves to view. However, because they held the dominant position of authority, they could determine what was watched and how it could be watched. For example, although observers had access to all ballot-counting areas, some areas were more accessible and visible than others. Because of the large number of absentee, out-of-country, and tendered ballots cast, the counting process lasted several weeks. This non-polling-station ballot counting took place at counting centers, which employed 550 counters, sorters, and other staff in November 2000.[4] Based on the number of nonregular ballots cast in prior elections, counting was expected to run the equivalent of 10,000 person days, or at least 18 full days. The budget for the counting center was 414,141 Euro (809,989 deutschmarks), 4 percent of the entire election budget. This was a huge operation, with international supervisors as well as Bosnian observers. Observers were allowed in all areas, although (as in the polling station), they were not allowed to touch anything. Simultaneously, the audit center reviewed counting results from polling stations. I was a member of the audit team. During two weeks of verifying forms, opening ballot bags, and recounting races, we never had an observer or supervisor look in on us. We presumed that our center was open to viewing, but we wondered why no one was interested in our work, whether we would have had better facilities if someone had been watching us, or if our counting practices would have been more by the book under an external gaze. We agreed among ourselves that if someone asked to watch, he or she would have probably been allowed to do so, but the existence of the audit center was not common knowledge. It did not appear on television news broadcasts each night, as did the counting center. It was off the knowledge and visible horizon and hence fell outside of any regime of transparency.

It might be argued that we watched ourselves, which was somewhat true through a discourse of professionalism, but in many ways supervision was perceived as not being needed because the international community believed its members incapable of fraudulent behavior. Mechanisms existed that made the audit process orderly and perhaps able to be watched—counting in teams of four, for example (mimicking the counting in the polling station, as per the Rules and Regulations). However, efficiency frequently was as important as transparency and accuracy. Furthermore, our counting shortcuts were problematic because we had no direct vested interest in the result. We did not care which candidates won. We were never watched except structurally (i.e., in teams) and internally (i.e., the self-discipline of professionals); as a consequence, the demands of transparency bore down more heavily on some subjects than on others.

In Bosnia-Herzegovina, voters were asked to trust the electoral process through an explicit regime of transparency. In a speech to Bosnian election officials, a high-ranking international official responsible for both political and technical aspects of the elections repeatedly remarked that the major remaining challenge was to build confidence in the elections. Her remarks ultimately rooted confidence in transparency. Confidence (of the Bosnian electorate and the international community alike), the official claimed, currently was based on the existence of safeguards and other structural limitations or constraints. We had so much security, she said, because we wanted voters to have confidence in the free and fair administration of the election machinery—to believe that safeguards existed everywhere. For example, ballots were delivered to municipal electoral commissions under armed escort, voters' fingers were sprayed with ink to prevent them from voting more than once, and supervisors watched over the process to prevent fraud. But confidence, she declared, should be based more on accuracy and transparency; voters should believe that elections would be conducted properly.

A lot of emphasis is placed on the voter register—it needs to be as accurate and as transparent as possible. Voters need to have confidence in it. . . . We also need to transfer election administration to the municipal election commissions. Most [of you and your colleagues] are professional, but the unscrupulous actions of a few affect the confidence of the whole country. . . . OSCE is ending their financial commitment to the municipal election commissions, but I know that most of you will continue to work professionally because of your commitment to democracy.

Later, when asked how to achieve this confidence, the official said,

Well, it depends a lot on time and education—you can try things like municipal election commissions having public meetings. In most places, people know that if they are invited [to meetings], then it is probably okay. It's when meetings are private that worries begin. If you hold yourself accountable, [trust and confidence will grow].

Transparency was functionally seen as a confidence-building technique. The willingness to open meetings and practices to others would prove that there was nothing to hide. This international call for Bosnians to act more transparently again brings up the question of who is subject to a gaze and who is not. Why could the practices of internationals be opaque yet still trustworthy? Internationals, of course, were not unanimously trusted, as seen by accusations of miscounting and of purposely losing ballots. Rather, internationals thought they should be trusted regardless of the opacity of their practices.

Further Shifts in Transparency: Nationalization

The November 2000 parliamentary elections were the last ones organized and implemented by the OSCE. That such would be the case was known much earlier in 2000; it was not a surprise. The handover of responsibility was framed as something that needed to happen for Bosnia (taking ownership of the process) as well as for the international community (unable indefinitely to sustain the investment). Thus, with the August 2001 passage of an election law, a Bosnian election commission and secretariat took over responsibility for organizing and implementing elections. The handover of responsibility should not be thought of as an event but rather as a process. International consultants remained heavily involved in the first official non-OSCE election in

2002, including many people who had been or remained OSCE staff. Similarly, many national staff at the secretariat had been OSCE employees. The second election, in 2004, was primarily a Bosnian affair, but international involvement in the upper administrative echelon continued: for example, three of the seven members of the election commission were international staff from the OSCE or OHR, and lawyers from the organizations regularly attended or commented on the election commission's meetings.

In the context of a massive withdrawal of international personnel and resources, what can be said about the practices of election implementation in Bosnia-Herzegovina? Did an "international legacy" endure? What changes, if any, did the nationalization (or deinternationalization) of election administration bring? With regard to transparency, a few changes were readily apparent. First, watching the election appeared to be less a concern than in previous years. There would be no international supervisors, although ODIHR sent a 23-person observation mission for a total of six weeks (ODIHR 2005). As mentioned earlier, observers have no authority to prevent or control irregularities that they see, although scholars feel that observers may have an indirect preventative role. Rather, observers are tools for external assessment and evaluation. No Bosnian NGOs planned to observe the polling or counting. Unlike previous elections, when the Center for Civic Initiatives organized more than 10,000 civil observers to scrutinize polling stations around the clock on Election Day and championed the role of these observers in the development of civil society and in ensuring transparent elections, in 2004 the center planned to field only a small contingent of mobile observers who would visit municipal election boards rather than polling stations to verify (or not) the adequate collection and compilation of result tabulations, ballot storage and transportation, and political party communications. The priorities of the Center for Civic Initiatives now emphasized voter education, "get out the vote" programs, and the broader accountability of municipalities to citizens and voters (e.g., resolving voter registration problems, spearheading a movement for handicapped-accessible polling stations). They wanted elections to be more voter friendly. Some of this shift was pragmatic, resulting from the realities of financing—the huge network of observers needed huge financial support, and the center was not in a position to fund its Eye Network without the aid of the international donors (who had, for the most part, pulled out or drastically reduced their funding commitments as well as their donor agendas). These shifts of civic involvement into other electoral sites and democracy locations involves an important recognition that democracy is more than Election Day (see Schmitter and Karl 1991) but leaves polling stations in the dark. The discourse of transparency simply had less salience for the Center for Civic Initiatives as other issues became more pressing and more feasible. According to the center, it needed to motivate people to fulfill their democratic responsibilities. Officials of the center believed that the apathy they saw among Bosnians evidenced a loss of faith not in the process but in the politicians. At the same time, transparency's promise to limit the possibilities of fraud was transferred from outside, nonpartisan eyes (either national or international) to partisan political parties. Accuracy and faithful reflection of voters' wills were thought to be possible through the active participation of multiple political parties (which had been championed by the last international director of elections, who presided over the handover). The multiplicity of interested bodies (which included but did not emphasize eyes) was thought to be a mechanism that would act as a check on fraud.

The main concern of the electoral administration in the summer of 2004 was financial. How would the election be funded? In light of issues raised by informants, a key question is how much transparency costs. For example, election officials expressed concerns about the presence of experienced polling station staff (or any staff) given that it was not clear if municipalities could afford to pay, let alone train, people. Training was substantially cut and, according to some electoral personnel, was essentially disregarded at the national level. Within a decentralization of electoral administration, the municipal election commissions now had responsibility for deciding whether to train their polling station staff. Some commissions budgeted for training, but others did not or could not. Unlike earlier elections, no centrally published polling and counting manual existed; rather, a local electoral NGO was asked to write and publish this document. In an interview, the head of the NGO worried, "They said if I didn't do it, there just wouldn't be any training or manual." He hoped to be able to find funding. Similarly, municipal election commissions worried about paying for the procedures being dictated and demanded of them. One member asked in a nationwide meeting how transportation could be provided for staffers at distant polling stations if no funding was available and those staffers lacked their own transportation. At the level of national electoral administration, concerns about transparency had not completely disappeared but, like the NGOs and municipal election commissions, were now linked more

explicitly to pragmatic worries such as making deadlines and procedu-
ralism and the effect on their tenuous legitimacy if they failed to do so.

I am arguing neither that transparency exists nor that our practices must
improve to more perfectly achieve transparency. The main issue is not a
disjunction between transparency as an ideal and transparency in practice. Rather, the dissection of transparency in this and the preceding
chapter demonstrates transparency's ideological premises and shows
how the model interacts with on-the-ground practices and relationships.
The practices and relationships demonstrate transparency's contingent
nature and contextual meanings as well as the power relationships neatly
obscured through its mantra on visibility.

CIRCUITS OF POWER

Jet-Setters, Foreign Policy, and Democratic Works

Over drinks in the evenings, talk normally turned away from work and toward the hilarious and stupid. One night after I arrived home from dinner with a group of regular international dinner companions, I wrote down a joke that a friend had recounted for our amusement. He had heard it from a Bosnian colleague.

> A ship sinks and the passengers scramble for the lifeboats, each trying to save himself and as many of his prized possessions as possible. One lifeboat holds a Russian, an Irishman, and a Bosnian, but the lifeboat is overloaded and is in danger of sinking. After much hand-wringing and discussion, they decide that each passenger will sacrifice one valuable with the hope that then the lifeboat will no longer be in danger. The Russian goes first, singing a lament to Russian poetry as he flings a copy of Pushkin overboard. The Irishman is next; he looks forlorn as he musters up the courage to heave a case of Guinness into the ocean. The Bosnian, knowing he is next, looks up and down the boat, sighs deeply, turns to the American aid worker sitting next to him and says, "Okay, jump out!"

Jokes are good to think with. Full of simultaneous enjoyment and threat, jokes play on social anxiety and perhaps ambivalence (Nelson 1999, 2001). In the process, they can affirm social values articulated by the transgression, the double entendre, or the uncomfortable intimacy of

234

getting the joke (Nelson 2001; Seizer 1997). Here, the local version of the well-trodden shipwreck genre speaks to the stereotypes of national cultures and goods—Pushkin and Guinness. It could just as easily be Swiss watches, Belgian chocolate, or Mexican mariachis. And, thus, uneasily, perhaps with an accompanying groan, we accept or acknowledge the obvious national transgression of stereotypes as well as the punch line: the anxiety and uncomfortable potentiality of the American aid worker as one of Bosnia's prized national goods. The joke would of course play differently to different audiences. To the international listeners who heard it with me, the joke should have reminded them of Bosnian ambivalence toward their presence as well as the gratitude and necessity that they likely also read into the shipwreck narrative and the fate that they personified the sacrificed character in the story.

The joke, only slightly reworked, would resonate around any of the globe's "trouble spots." In 2004, post-tsunami Sri Lanka was inundated with relief organizations. Anthropologists who had been working in Sri Lanka for decades suddenly were talking about the "white jeep syndrome," the chaos of matching donors with receivers, and the local ambivalence toward aid workers (see Goldman 2005; Harris 2005). In postconflict sites, the ambivalence often interacts with politics as well. In El Salvador during the 1990s, elites often saw internationals as little different than the guerrillas, while some on the left resented internationals' salaries, mainstream politics, or imperialist overtones (Ellen Moodie, personal communication, February 2006).

Humanitarian aid is not a particularly new phenomenon. What is new about its current incarnation, in addition to its recent capture of the anthropological imagination, is its rapid blossoming and shifts in rationale. The web of relief agencies has vastly increased in scope and quantity in the past twenty-five years (Duffield 2002; Mosse and Lewis 2005). Organizations no longer respond to humanitarian crises as lone or autonomous entities, nor are they only intent on saving lives and alleviating suffering. The world has moved beyond the image of Florence Nightingale or the nurses of the Red Cross. First, the distinctions among governmental, nongovernmental, and multilateral (or multinational) organizations no longer hold weight. Second, humanitarian aid agencies are no longer interested merely in making life possible or bearable but increasingly have become involved in governance, state services, and social reconstruction/transformation (Duffield 2002; Ferguson and Gupta 2002).

The boundaries between NGOs, IGOs, and states are increasingly blurred in relief and development arenas; NGOs are not necessarily grassroots, alternative, civic, voluntary, or private groups. They now offer their services to states and IGOs as policy partners and implementers and submit project proposals to foreign ministries in hopes of winning a piece of the funding pie. As an NGO seeks to support and maintain itself, it may find itself purposively or accidentally reaching outside of its original scope toward donors' funding priorities. Not only do IGOs and NGOs depend on each other financially and outsource their projects to each other, but they also share personnel, and their employees spend time together. Personnel and personal networks overlap among agencies, volunteers, and employees. For example, Red Cross employees in Bosnia moved in the same circles as other internationals, living, eating, drinking, and socializing at the same houses, restaurants, and bars. When their contracts ended, they often stayed in-country seeking new employment, and almost always found positions with other agencies such as the OSCE.

More and more often, foreign militaries and UN peacekeeping forces are also involved in humanitarian aid activities. Military forces include humanitarian efforts within their armed operations, and humanitarian organizations have found military liaisons useful for reaching their goals and agendas. However, Mark R. Duffield argues that these newfound sharing arrangements only constitute part of the reorganization: "Non-state organizations are not only learning to work with military establishments in new ways, aid practice itself has been redefined as a strategic tool of conflict resolution and social reconstruction" (2002:1062). Sometimes these military-civilian relations are relatively harmonious, as in Bosnia-Herzegovina (see the chapters "Hyper-Bosnia" and "Doing Nothing"). In other areas (e.g., Guatemala after the 1996 peace treaty or Iraq and Afghanistan post-9/11), civilian agencies have tried to distance themselves from military and military-humanitarian endeavors. Médecins sans Frontières, for example, found itself identified with the U.S. presence in Afghanistan after the fall of the Taliban and decided to withdraw from Iraq shortly after setting up a mission as a consequence of perceptions of complicity with the U.S. military occupation (Redfield 2005:354).[1] Humanitarian aid has become an industrial complex. Analyzing the social and political practice of what Alex de Waal (1997) identifies as the "humanitarian mode of power" showcases relations and disjunctions and gives voice and import to everyday bureaucrats (the role played by rank-and-file internationals in Bosnia-Herzegovina).

This book has documented and analyzed the work of a small section of this industrial complex in one small part of the world—that is, the cultural and political work of producing democracy in postwar Bosnia-Herzegovina. To that end, some of the volume's main strands appear in its emphases on the human and nonhuman practices of intent and intentionality, privilege and authority, and epistemological legitimacy and naturalization. The thick description of internationals, their practices, and their interpretations of those practices showed authoritative actants (internationals as well as the nonhuman material items they handle) at work, the experience of everyday privilege and eliteness, and the complicated industry of morality and virtue within which internationals worked. Analysis of the articulation and deployment of electoral actants demonstrated the work put into, for example, transparency, ballots, presence, and polling supervisors. The rest of this concluding chapter weaves this work into the larger contexts of the codification of knowledge and the practice of foreign policy. At the junction of the humanitarian industrial complex and electoral actants lies the practice of global governance and foreign policy. Seen through that lens, Bosnia-Herzegovina emerges as an early node in the professionalization and standardization of democratic techne and democratic knowledge as tools of foreign policy aims—that is, the liberal and neoliberal transformation of regimes in the name of peace and security.

Democratic Peace

In 2003, I was asked if I was interested in being a part of a small contingent that the United States was sending to Serbia as part of ODIHR's election observation mission. Of course I was. I had wrapped up the bulk of my research, and the international election effort in Bosnia was substantively over. I was eager to see how elections were being handled in other areas, but doing so required a place in the humanitarian networks. I had managed to obtain a short assignment as a polling supervisor in Kosovo in 2001 but had declined an eight-month offer for electoral work in Cambodia. I worried that I had fallen off the list of worthy candidates.

Unlike my forays into election work during the previous six years, the 2003 appointment required that I pass a four-module test developed by the U.S. Institute for Peace, whose staff includes academic fellows in political science, anthropology, history, and international relations, among other disciplines. The modules included information about the OSCE's history and aims; the work of OSCE missions in the field; the history and politics of Southeastern Europe; and the practices and strategies of conflict management, prevention, and transformation. All potential volunteers and employees from the United States were now required to pass the tests before being deployed on OSCE missions. The study guide for the tests places special focus on the relationship between peace and democracy, mentioning the diplomatic agreement on which the OSCE was founded as premised on the democratic peace hypothesis: the belief that democratic states seldom or never engage in violent conflict with other democratic states. However, OSCE's philosophy broadened the hypothesis to incorporate democracy as an antidote to violence and the best long-term foundation for peace.

> The underlying philosophy behind the Helsinki Final Act of 1975 and the Copenhagen Document of 1990 is that the best antidote to violence is:
>
> 1. the creation of democratic societies, governed by the consistent rule of law;
> 2. showing respect for the rights of persons belonging to minority groups and for individual members of that society;
> 3. experiencing broad-based economic development and a healthy environment.
>
> The "democratic peace hypothesis" has been widely accepted by OSCE participating states, namely the belief that democratic states seldom or never engage in violent conflict with other democratic states. Consistent with this belief has been the assertion by leading OSCE states that the long-term foundations for peace may be best constructed through encouraging the widespread development of democratic regimes throughout the OSCE region. (U.S. Institute of Peace 2001:5)

Although the study guide discusses the hypothesis as a belief, scholars talk about it as the one truth of international relations: democratic states do not wage war against other states (Dixon 1996; Gowa 1999; Ray 1997; Russett 1993). While some commentators argue that the idea surfaced with Immanuel Kant's 1795 essay, *Perpetual Peace,* others find it burgeoning in public policy as a result of Woodrow Wilson's utopian visions. Meanwhile, analyses as to why democracy has pacifying effects cite political culture, the costs to trade disruption, and the limitations or checks on leaders in democratic states as possible reasons for the apparent peace that democracy brings. The theory also has popular forms.

Thomas Friedman's "Golden Arches theory"—that two countries that have McDonald's restaurants have never been at war with each other—seems to be the democratic peace hypothesis in a neoliberal guise:

> Armed with this data, I offered up the "Golden Arches Theory of Conflict Prevention," which stipulated that when a country reached the level of economic development where it had a middle class big enough to support a McDonald's network, it became a McDonald's country. And people in McDonald's countries didn't like to fight wars anymore, they preferred to wait in line for burgers. (2000:249)

I once heard an international summarize the Golden Arches theory and suggest that the expansion of McDonald's into Sarajevo might improve relations between Bosnia and Serbia. (McDonald's has been in Belgrade since 1988.)[2]

Some well-documented criticisms have been lodged against the democratic peace hypothesis, including, for example, that it ignores the evidence that democratizing states are particularly unstable and prone to violence and that democratic states go to war with nondemocratic states. Furthermore, the hypothesis rests on a definition of *war* as more than 1,000 battle deaths (Ray 1997). "Minor conflicts" are ignored. So, with caveats, the most perhaps that can be said about the democratic peace hypothesis is that democratic regimes do not kill masses of soldiers from other democratic countries. Of course, we should examine carefully what counts as peace and as democracy as well as examine why people content to vote and to wait in line for burgers are willing to accept and sometimes condone high levels of violence within their country (see e.g., Caldeira 2000; Farmer 2003 on structural violence; Holston and Caldeira 1998 on extreme violence and brutality within democratic regimes; "Peacetime Crimes" in Scheper-Hughes and Bourgois 2004).

The democratic peace theory must be taken seriously, even when we find it flawed, because it underpins contemporary global foreign policy. The rationale for sending hundreds of observers and thousands of supervisors around the world ultimately rests on the transformative promises of democracy. However, as Nicolas Guilhot points out, "promoting democratization or defending human rights are privileged channels for the exportation of political technologies, economic recipes, or juridical models" (2005:8). Democracy no longer places limitations on politics or critiques power but has become a tool and language of power.

Guilhot's argument about the appropriation of democracy by the powerful, the professionalization of activism, and the colonialization of social movements by these forces specifically concerns academics, policymakers, and members of the institutional elite. In his words, "the individuals involved in these initiatives not only had the impression they were remaining somehow loyal to their principles but also managed to read progressive purposes into these hegemonic projects" (2005:10). His argument resonates for rank-and-file democratizers as well: many of my colleagues from Bosnia self-identified, at least partially, as activists. However, the frames in which they work have changed in character, tone, and meaning. Democracy promotion by the humanitarian industrial complex less often features the popular struggle for democracy and more often touts the transition to well-defined practices of good governance and institutional efficacy.

Professionalization and Codification

The U.S. Institute for Peace tests I took are just one example of worldwide attempts to standardize knowledge, democratic assumptions, and base skills for democracy promoters. Other mechanisms of standardization include courses and training, handbook and guideline publications, and the expansion of electoral NGOs and consultancies. The European Union, for example, has moved decisively into election observation and standardization work. Its 2002 *Handbook for European Union Election Observation Missions* outlines, among other things, a common "European" approach for the methods used by European Union teams and justifies observation along the lines discussed in previous chapters: neutrality, transparency, the deterring influence of international presence, and the democratic peace hypothesis (Swedish International Development Cooperation Agency 2002:1). The European Union's committed move into election observation resulted from the passage of a 1999 regulation that provided a legal basis for considering democratization a cornerstone of European Union foreign policy and development cooperation (Commission of the European Communities 2000:3). Prior to 2000, the European Union was also involved in elections, but its commitments were not particularly visible because they were generally smaller, were of a financial nature, or occurred via partners such as the OSCE, UN, or Organization of American States (Commission of the European Communities 2000). The 1999 regulation and 2002 handbook represented strategic moves away from the ad hoc character of prior involvements.

An observation mission can serve as a conflict prevention mecha-nism, providing an impartial assessment of the elections, defusing tension and by its very presence deterring fraud. To meet these ambitious objectives, the E[uropean] U[nion] has given itself additional tools and resources. . . . Indeed, the European Parlia-ment, the Council and the Commission now share a common approach to election observation and have clarified the role of each institution in this field. Focal contact points have been set up in the European Parliament and in the Commission, and observers from all E[uropean] U[nion] Member States have been trained on the common European approach to election observa-tion. This has enabled E[uropean] U[nion] Election Observation Missions to develop in recent years into a much more credible, responsible and visible activity. (Swedish International Develop-ment Cooperation Agency 2002:1)

This approach, according to the European Union's literature, "reflects the collective experience of the international election community at large, as it relates to the best method of arriving at a consistent, compre-hensive and authoritative statement on an election process" (Swedish International Development Cooperation Agency 2002:3). Since 2000, the European Union has fielded between five and eight missions a year with personnel on the ground for about 8–12 weeks (as well as short-term observers on the ground for 1–4 weeks). These missions have spanned the globe from Venezuela to Cambodia (Swedish International Development Cooperation Agency 2002). All of these efforts follow the same methodological, structural, and technical framework.

Over the years, I have seen colleagues struggle to stay in the humani-tarian aid/election circuit and to make doing so feasible. Some trans-formed relatively little experience into short-term, advanced, and per-manent positions in elections. Others tried to improve their lot through credentialization: master's degrees in journalism, political science, or democratization studies or certificates in election administration. Bosnia, too, served as a training ground, given its early location on democratization as foreign policy agendas. For example, of the ten core staff members on the European Union's election observation mission to Indonesia in 2004, eight had experience (primarily electoral) in Bosnia. I know of colleagues who left Bosnia and went on to work in Kosovo, Ser-bia, Croatia, Macedonia, Uganda, East Timor, Kazakhstan, Palestine, the Ivory Coast, Haiti, Afghanistan, Iraq, Peru, Indonesia, and Fiji. This election personnel circuit that my friends struggled to get and remain on is professionalizing and codifying. As personnel and knowledge mesh, new democracies look increasingly similar.

The groan I uttered at the shipwreck joke resembled my reaction to reading about "Instant Democracy: Pneumatic Parliament®" in Bruno Latour and Peter Weibel's *Making Things Public: Atmospheres of Democracy* (2005):

> The Pneumatic Parliament is a parliament building that is quick to install, transparent, and inflatable; it can be dropped in any grounds and then unfolds itself. In a mere one and a half hours, a protective shell for parliamentary meetings is ready, and within the space of twenty-four hours, the interior ambience for these proceedings can be made as comfortable as an agora. The Pneumatic Parliament seats 160 parliamentarians and fits into a 20-foot-long container for easy transport. Thus, in only twenty-four hours plus flying time, the architectonic prerequisites for the democratic process can take shape. (Sloterdijk and von der Haegen 2005:952)

According to Latour and Weibel, the lesson of the fantastical Pneumatic Parliament is that to imagine a parliament without its material set of complex instruments is ludicrous (2005:18). In my view, however, though, the unspoken punch line was not the lighting, air conditioning, and energy supply—although I have argued along similar lines in this volume—but the reality of the idea's theater of the absurd. If we tweak the Pneumatic Parliament just a little bit, then Instant Democracy is already happening. The democratic techne I documented in postwar Bosnia-Herzegovina is now being repeated each year around the globe. The truth is but a sliver away from the farcical.

In 2001, two months after the destruction of the World Trade Center in New York City, I was asked to be a polling supervisor in Kosovo. The 10-day election trip was like a return to Bosnia-Herzegovina. Although the site was different, many of my friends and colleagues were there, and while the political situation in Kosovo was very distinct from that in Bosnia-Herzegovina, the technical electoral structure was nearly identical. My fieldnotes for this trip begin with a jolt:

I'm in a time warp. Starting in Frankfurt Airport, the recognizable face count began. It moved onto real colleagues and friends upon arrival at the airport, but it was only at the hotel while moving through the "in-processing" that I realized that we were repeating 1998 but in a new location.

Life as an international polling station supervisor was so similar to that of a polling station supervisor in Bosnia-Herzegovina that supervisors with Bosnia experience were oddly taken aback by the few changes that had taken place. Furthermore, many former supervisors in Bosnia-Herzegovina were surprised by what they saw as the predominantly Muslim Kosovar Albanians' lack of comradeship or feelings of shared victimhood toward Bosnian Muslims. This phenomenon speaks to the distinctions between international and ex-Yugoslav experiential and interpretive frameworks for the Yugoslav wars but also suggests the extent to which the mimicry of electoral matters bled into other arenas, heightened, in this case, by the historical and political proximity of Bosnia, Serbia, and Kosovo. Subtle differences existed in electoral techne and bureaucratic administration, but the democratic message was the same. As in Bosnia, details were important, were ordered, and served as mechanisms for control. It mattered less to freedom and fairness, transparency, or the standardization of democratic knowledge that the ballots had heat-sensitive spots as an antifraud device, that the voter register included registrants' photos, or that the designated counting steps were "suggestions" rather than procedures. The similarities lay in the deployment of actants and the work of elections. Supervisors, for example, remained in charge of "sensitive material" (and there was still "sensitive material"), remained ultimately responsible even while the polling station chair was in charge, and remained in a position of everyday privilege, authority, and hyper-state existence. "Clear intent" remained an ordering principle despite its definition in very particular ways, despite the fact that voters had to be taught how to express clearly their intent, and despite the fact that polling staff needed guidelines for recognizing "clear intent." Residents of Kosovo were still urged to take up the mantle of democracy in the name of participation and control over their political destiny, still taught how to vote properly, and still subject to the antipolitics of electoral techne.

In some cases, a sense of improvement over Bosnian election administration existed—a feeling that the lessons of Bosnia had been learned or at least that the problems had been pondered. For example, the interpreters for the supervisors in Kosovo also received election training, making them assistant/interpreters rather than just interpreters. Consequently, they could be more proactive and inform supervisors if they saw or heard infractions or irregularities. This well-meaning fix had unintended effects, however. At one polling station, a supervisor and his assistant/interpreter clashed at the hands-on assistance that the assistant was able and eager to give to the polling station committee staff: "I needed a Velcro strap on mine. He was either elsewhere or too involved." The assistant was seeking to be helpful and useful, but the supervisor was worried about his authority as well as maintaining an aura of neutrality, which the assistant did not embody. To the supervisor, the assistant was as suspect as the staff. The supervisor did not want to have to watch the assistant or act diplomatically if the staff began to think the supervisor was acting in a partisan manner. A second improvement, according to supervisors, was the incorporation of political briefings on the political parties, the state of affairs in Kosovo, and the particular politics in specific towns and villages. As in Bosnia, however, this openness toward political information as useful knowledge was somewhat negated by the fact that trainers and managers urged the supervisors not to discuss politics, show their political or religious affiliation, or ask the members of the polling station committee about political party affiliations. As my trainer, Ella, said, "If you don't know their political party, you can work more objectively." The details were wrapped in the same packaging, over and over again. It was not just that many of the people were (or could have been) the same but that the structure, rhetoric, and techne were, too.

Elections are of course sites of political struggle. However, elections, the choices they deliver, and the truths they articulate are also effects of the politics of techne. Elections cannot necessarily deliver the change or the better life that are often promised; they offer only the limited choices produced through the implementation of particular forms of knowledge. Democracy, contingent on Election Day and its claims of choice and participation, provides an avenue for further retrenchment of a liberal style of government, which works through these claims as articulated through material items. Election Day, considered a purely technical enterprise, is legitimated through seemingly apolitical practices and knowledge formations. However, as choice and participation have been shown to be political and constructed in particular configurations, so too are the seemingly acultural and apolitical articulations that make up Election Day and democracy. Technical forms and practices are not simply functional or instrumental—a way to get things done. The consideration of democracy as a cultural and technical practice demonstrates the fine, mundane, and quotidian—and hence often hidden—epistemological and legitimation work put into elections through its actants, including handbooks, international supervisors, ballots, songs, propagandistic beer mats and shopping bags, and audit reports. As tools of elections and democracy, these items naturalize and depoliticize the constructed and contested ideas of representation, participation, and trust.

NOTES

Prologue

1. In 1886, in the United States, only the state of Wyoming allowed women to vote. Kansas had rejected both "Negro" and woman suffrage in 1867, and an 1878 federal amendment that would have given women the right to vote had been resoundingly defeated.

2. All documentary translations were obtained during fieldwork through research assistants or through the in-house translation services of the particular international agency.

3. Democracy and democratization may be double bind situations, where individuals are confronted with equally valued but incongruent obligations or messages of logical types. The double bind is not simply an awkward situation or a binarism, but rather an incompatability of alternatives. Writing about the contradictions of democratic practice presents the double bind—there are different logical types in one experential field. On double bind situations, see Kim Fortun (2001) *Advocacy after Bhopal,* and Carlos Sluzki and Donald Ransom, eds. (1976) *Double-bind.*

Introduction

1. For example, Dahl (1997) argues that a robust "democratic culture" carries a country through its tough times. Putnam (1993), using a similar formulation of "culture," finds that the northern regions of Italy had more effective government than the southern regions because of their long historical traditions of civic community.

2. In 2003, eight years after the signing of the peace treaty and its concomitant placement of international power in Bosnian affairs, a vociferous debate was unleashed occurred on the paradoxical nature of "democracy by international fiat" by the unaccountable "Bosnian Raj" (hearkening back to the colonial British administrators in India). The article by Knaus and Martin (2003) engendered numerous published and electronic responses (see Belloni 2003; Bieber 2003; Brown 2003; Perry 2003). Although the paradox of imposing democracy also frames this book, I am concerned with the normalization and naturalization

of particular democratic forms, aesthetics, and modes of governance rather than with the unaccountability of international governance.

3. For works analyzing the dynamics of power within the international interventions in the Balkans and Eastern Europe more generally, see Bougarel, Duijzings, and Helms 2006; Campbell 1998; Chandler 1999a, 1999b; Cowan 2003; Gilbert 2004, 2005, 2006; Hayden 1999a, 1999b, 2002; Helms 2003a, 2003b; Pandolfi 2002, 2003; Verdery 2003; Wedel 1998.

4. These fears and pessimism were materially realized through growing lists for emigration visas at foreign consulates and a substantial brain drain. Internationals worried that Bosnians were not taking "ownership" of their country. Rather they were seeking a better life by leaving rather than by agitating for change. See UN Development Programme 1998 for more detail on brain drain statistics and effect forecasting.

5. In 2000, the voter information department was almost entirely staffed by Bosnians, including its director and second in command. This was not the case in earlier years, when, for example, international election consultants headed the office. Marketing slogans and graphics were in-house creations, by-products of creative brainstorming by both internationals and nationals.

6. International law stipulates that a refugee is a person who has crossed an international border. Thus, a Bosnian who fled his or her home and crossed into Croatia (and then perhaps onto Germany or Austria) is a refugee, while a Bosnian who fled to another area within the sovereign Bosnia-Herzegovina territory is considered a displaced person.

7. Fascinating ethnographic work is being done in this broad area, including scholarship on the experiences of refugees (as well as those who stayed), memory, and state-building via the lens of refugee aid policy (see, e.g., among a much larger multidisciplinary literature, Bringa and Loizos 2001; Dahlman and Tuathail 2005; Gilbert 2004, 2005; Huseby-Daruas 1995; Jansen 1998, 2002).

8. Many international positions did not require particularly specialized skills; however, the information technology consultants were skilled computer programmers. I had previous professional experience in the computer industry and had minored in computer software as an undergraduate student.

9. Cain, Postlewait, and Thomson 2004 recounts similar hastiness in international bureaucracies in Cambodia, Somalia, Haiti, Rwanda, and Liberia as well as the arbitrariness of international personnel assignments.

10. When I received the chief of administration job, I asked myself if I had the skills for it. My anxieties were immediately made manifest when, on the first day of work, I was asked by one of my staff which filing system I thought would be the most efficient, alphabetical by country and then last name or simply by last name. After an awkward pause in which I tried to assess filing system efficiency, I answered that since she was going to be the person rummaging through those files, she should choose the system she thought best. Delegation can be a skill or a strategy.

11. The official language of Yugoslavia was Serbo-Croatian. As Yugoslavia broke apart into territories based on national distinctions, a concurrent move toward linguistic differentiation took place. Serbo-Croatian split into three new languages, Serbian, Bosnian, and Croatian. Since the war, each language has dif-

ferentiated and codified itself with the publication of dictionaries, textbooks, and the creation of new words.

Blueprints and Builders

1. Smillie (2001) estimates than in 1996, one year after the signing of Dayton, between 156 and 240 international NGOs were resident in Bosnia-Herzegovina. Two years later, the International Council on Voluntary Agencies (1998) recorded 185 INGOs, and the UN Development Programme (1998:26) counted between 500 and 1,600 local NGOs. Many local NGOs were formed as conversions of projects established by international NGOs (Smillie 2001).

2. Projects were implemented with varying degrees of Bosnian leadership and administrative, technical, and manual labor. Bosnian participation in the upper and middle echelons of organizations increased between 1997 and 2000 but remained low. Some internationals saw this as a problem, while others remarked that international employees were in fact the key component of international organizations.

3. The now substantial scholarship on international institutions more generally begins with Keohane 1984; Krasner 1983. The constructivist school within international relations has established international organizations as influential actors in the world arena—shaping norms and state interests, for example. Thus, counter to the assumptions of the dominant realist school, states are not the only actors on the global stage, and self-interests are neither static nor solely based on maximization of power.

4. The term *expats* was not in currency in Bosnia-Herzegovina. Although some internationals may have qualified as expats (particularly, for example, diplomats or UN employees), I believe the short time horizon for many positions conjoined with the lack of families (for many years, the major agencies categorized Bosnia-Herzegovina as a nonfamily mission; thus, those who wanted to be with their families did so on the sly and at their own expense) made international life less definable this way. International life in Bosnia-Herzegovina clearly resonates with aspects of other expat experiences though; see, for example, Fechter 2006; Kurotani 2005; Willis, Fakhri, and Yeoh 2002.

5. The members of the Peace Implementation Council steering board were Canada, France, Germany, Italy, Japan, Russia, the United Kingdom, the United States, the presidency of the European Union, the European Commission, and the Organisation of the Islamic Conference, represented by Turkey. The UN Security Council is composed of representatives of fifteen states: five permanent members (the United States, Russia, France, China, and the United Kingdom) and ten countries selected on a rotating two-year basis.

6. The non-NATO forces included Albania, Austria, Argentina, Bulgaria, Estonia, Finland, Ireland, Latvia, Lithuania, Morocco, Romania, Russia, Slovakia, Slovenia, and Sweden.

7. I documented a shift starting in 1998 of the categorization of Bosnians from *local* to *national*. Carlane (2000) argues that contact between local interveners (normally spontaneously started) and international actors frequently

resulted in local actors taking on the behaviors, form, and eventually nature of the international intervention—bureaucratic, donor driven, and project centered—as a consequence of the donor-driven process of international aid. Gagnon 2002; Helms 2003a,b; Smillie 2001 also critically and crucially analyze local-international interactions and tensions at the level of NGO project and civil society development.

8. The history of Bosnia-Herzegovina is highly contested in reference to what early scholars of Yugoslavia called the "national question." One view holds that the different ethnic groups have had a tension-filled and uneasy cohabitation. The other view offers a more sanguine perspective, arguing that the Balkan people lived relatively peacefully, incorporating multiple traditions, and that ethnicity as a primary identity became politically salient only relatively recently. To contextualize this debate, I briefly sketch out some historical details (relying heavily on Malcolm 1994). Bosnian history generally begins with the Slav invasions in the sixth and seventh centuries. From the arrival of the Croats and the Serbs (both Slavic tribes) around 620 to the emergence of an independent Bosnian state in 1180s, rule and alliances shifted and varied in different arenas (e.g., religious and political). For example, Malcolm (1994) notes that early medieval Bosnia was Roman Catholic, but that it also often came under Orthodox Serb rule. During the 400-year period of Ottoman rule (1400s to 1800s), a great number of conversions to Islam occurred, although exactly who converted and why is debated, as is the possibility of multidirectional religious conversions (e.g., to and from Islam or from one church to another) (Bringa 1995; Donia 1981; Donia and Fine 1994; Lockwood 1979). Scholars suggest that the Bosnian church was poorly organized at that time and may have had heretical and/or fluid doctrinal interpretations. Conversions to Islam were likely pragmatic strategies to improve status and economic well-being (Lockwood 1979). Croatian and Serbian nationalism started to take hold at the end of the nineteenth century (Denich 1994; Donia and Fine 1994; Malcolm 1994) as ideas about the primordial unity of people and nations, the legitimacy of self-determination, and the necessary relationship between people and territory became prominent (see Eley and Suny 1996). The rise of Bosnian Muslim ethnopolitical consciousness also began at the end of the nineteenth century, in part as a consequence of a general rise in nationalist ideology among the south Slavs and of the Christian Austrian-Hapsburg occupation (from 1878 to 1918, after their defeat of the Ottoman Empire). Bosnian Muslims became set apart through political developments, ideological distinctiveness, and increased cultural differentiation (Lockwood 1979). Donia (1981) adds that the political "awakening" of Bosnian Muslims was gradual, erratic, and mired in local factional struggles during the period of Austrian rule. Bosnian nationalism's success culminated in the 1960s with the Tito regime's official recognition of Bosnian Muslims as a *narod*, or nationality. Bosnian Muslims had previously been considered a religious rather than ethnic minority (Lockwood 1979). Although Titoism claimed to be a unifying regime, it actively prohibited discussion of ethnic matters and religion and repressed unofficial organizations and opposition, most of which were organized along ethnic lines (Denich 1994). As a result, argues Denich (1994), opposition became even more focused on the "forbidden fruit." For more detailed discus-

sion of the area's history and historiography, see Allcock 2000; Bougarel 1999; Bringa 1995; Donia and Fine 1994.

9. Merry (2000) discusses the difficulties of ceding control and the anxiety it provoked within the context of U.S. colonials in Hawaii. How could they be sure that the church, the office, or whatever institution would continue to be run "properly"? What was to prevent the "natives" from falling back into their old ways?

10. Scholars of the former Yugoslavia have worked to debunk the "ancient ethnic hatreds" view from a variety of angles; see, for example, Donia and Fine 1994; Gagnon 2004; Hayden 1996; Woodward 1995a; Živković 2001.

11. But see Gilbert 2005 on the humanitarization of politics.

12. Stari Most, thought to be the largest single-span arch bridge in the world at the time it was built (1567), is now listed as a UN World Heritage Site. It was reconstructed with UNESCO assistance and reopened with great fanfare in the summer of 2004.

13. Ten years after the peace treaty, tourism sites explicitly de-emphasized the war in Bosnia. Bosnia tourism's official web site, for example, mentions the beautiful and touching memorial centre at Srebrenica—the site of the war's largest massacre (of 8000 Muslim men and boys)—but emphasizes the beautiful dense forests, the plethora of bears and wolves, and natural thermal springs of the Srebrenica area (Tourism Association of Bosnia and Herzegovina 2006).

14. Property has been a focal point for liberal reforms of postsocialist areas; see esp. Verdery 1998.

15. The politics and logistics of property and returning refugees and displaced persons were immense and difficult. Many Bosnian municipalities actively hampered efforts to return property to its original residents. Even without obstruction from municipalities, the process at times was also difficult and time-consuming because for one family to return, another family had to leave, and they did not always have the means or desire to do so. Some homes had been destroyed, while in other cases reacquiring property would have required the eviction of yet another family. Often one property return actually involved three or four properties. For this process, see Bringa and Loizos 2001.

16. For an established literature on justice, war prosecutions, crimes against humanity, and international courts, see, for example, Borneman 1997; Hagan 2003; Hagan, Levi, and Ferrales 2006; Stiglmayer 1994.

Hyper-Bosnia

1. The large international organizations in Bosnia-Herzegovina—most importantly, the UN and the UN's International Police Task Force—included a number of non-European members. Unfortunately, some Bosnians adopted European-style prejudices toward non-Europeans or non-European-looking internationals. Engaging in Othering processes, Bosnians would question the ability of a Nigerian or Pakistani policeman to teach about the rule of law or stopping police brutality. A few non-European Islamic NGOs also worked in Bosnia-Herzegovina.

2. Both Verdery (1991, 1996) and Wedel (1998) point out the grave mis-perceptions (and political consequences) "foreigners" have when dealing with postsocialist "transitional" Eastern European countries. Verdery argues that the idea of transition is problematic because it suggests a known end point (i.e., neoliberal capitalism). Instead, transformation more clearly describes the changes occurring in Eastern Europe. Furthermore, using *transformation* rather than *transition* effectively removes the suggestion that it is being done incorrectly.

3. The degree to which internationals opted out of Bosnian regulation changed over time. For example, by 2000, many international vehicles (mostly NGO but also IGO) were registered with Bosnian license plates rather than the previously more prevalent diplomatic plates, UN plates, other special plates, or foreign plates. Furthermore, some organizations began to tell their employees that they would be subject to Bosnian traffic fines for actions such as illegal park-ing and excessive speeding, a sharp contrast from previous years, when many organizations had advised their internationals not to stop when ordered to pull over by Bosnian policemen.

4. The Central Bank of Bosnia-Herzegovina, run by a foreign governor until January 2005 (when a Bosniac filled the position), uses a currency board exchange rate regime that includes the fixed exchange rate, full foreign exchange backing, and full convertibility. Kamhi and Dehejia (2005) argue that the currency board regime is a major factor in postwar Bosnia's macroeconomic and financial stability.

5. It was illegal for banks to charge commission on KM-deutschmark con-versions, but conversion charges arose for transactions out of deutschmark into other currencies.

6. Religion, a central problematic in Bosnia-Herzegovina, was not a major site of difference between internationals and Bosnians. Othering was more pro-nounced along secular-religious than, for example, Christian-Muslim or Protes-tant-Orthodox dichotomies. Internationals with whom I spoke about religion expressed discomfort with "fundamental" Muslims—such as women wearing chadors or believers praying at each of the calls to prayer. They had no discom-fort with less politicized public signs of Islam, such as mosques or the call to prayer itself. Few internationals saw the specifically Christian tenor of humani-tarian aid and development work (see Bornstein 1999, 2001).

7. The Council of Europe is a 43-member IGO dedicated to protecting human rights, pluralist democracy, and the rule of law and to promoting legisla-tive and constitutional standards and reform. Membership is open to any Euro-pean state that accepts the principle of the rule of law and guarantees human rights and fundamental freedoms (Council of Europe 2005).

8. Whether they could learn, acquire, achieve, or adopt the "proper atti-tude" constituted a mostly unspoken debate among internationals. Most inter-nationals believed that Bosnians could change through teaching, learning by example, and by having things demonstrated for them. The dominant mode of international intervention was pedagogical, implicit as well as explicit. This does not mean that statements verging on biological determinism were not heard. Some observers offered such comments as, "Well, there have been some success

stories," while others said, "I don't care if it's not proper to say: They just don't change. Nothing ever changes."

9. Many committee members also had electoral experience under Tito or during the post-Tito era.

10. Many nationals still wished for 100 percent supervision, telling me that fraud remained rampant and that it was important to have an international supervisor present to stop or at least minimize fraud attempts and coercion. However, according to some more senior election officials, the election also faced financial pressure from international donors as being overly expensive. Thus, full supervision was no longer considered financially feasible. The decrease in supervisor numbers and duration from 2,600 to 800 and from 12 days to 11 days saved over US$2 million in per diem costs alone (i.e., not including supervision support, insurance, transportation, and so forth).

Doing Nothing

1. Any analysis of the successes and failures of the international effort is problematic as it presumes a particular and unified definition of success and failure. Such a definition does not exist and clearly depends on the perspective taken by internationals as well as their local, nonlocal, intellectual, or policy-oriented interlocutors. Conversely, the international presence had many easily identifiable material effects, ranging from increased salaries for Bosnians working for international agencies to increased prostitution near foreign military barracks.

2. Barnett and Finnemore (1999) label international organizations the "new missionaries" and contend that part of their mission is to spread, inculcate, and enforce norms of "good" state behavior. Their argument, arising out of the constructivist school of International Relations, is made at the level of state interests, practices, and behavior. I would expand their argument beyond the state to include the international organizations' spreading new norms that define acceptable and legitimate subject or citizen behavior.

3. UNPROFOR also monitored cease-fires, ensured demilitarization, delivered humanitarian relief, ensured the functioning of the Sarajevo airport, and protected convoys (UN 1996).

4. Even the military presence shifted much of its rationale to providing a secure environment conducive to civil and political reconstruction and to supporting organizations involved with the civilian aspects of the peace (UN 1996).

5. SFOR military evacuation plans incorporated civilian internationals, including a provision allowing them onto SFOR bases in emergency situations provided they had an international organization identification card or their passport.

6. Before the war, the population was 4.4 million (UN Development Programme 1998).

7. NATO/IFOR personnel numbered approximately 64,000 before the signing of Dayton. SFOR initially had 32,000 troops, but that number fell to 20,000 with a restructuring in early 2000.

8. In 2001, there were 2,000 UN International Police Task Force police-men, 340 other UN international employees, 220 OHR internationals (secon-dees, consultants, interns), and 180 OSCE internationally seconded members.

9. Estimates based on data from the International Council of Voluntary Agencies.

10. People occasionally expressed concerns about what could be termed negative social visibility. For example, international visibility could also act as a reminder of economic inequality, given the economic gaps in Bosnian society between Bosnians who worked for international organizations and those who did not or those who did not work at all.

11. This salad menu was taken from a 2002 Google search. While writing an early draft of this chapter, I berated myself for not having collected a menu from Fantasia. I consoled myself that it was probably on the Internet given that NGOs need to publicize and report on their projects; these reports are almost always available on the Internet. The menu was indeed there, even some fifteen months after my last meal at the restaurant. During a 2006 search, however, I could not find the menu, and the Web link is inactive. The NGO that helped set up Fanta-sia has moved on to other projects.

12. Logistics personnel commented that it was not always easy to find accom-modations in towns without hotels and with housing shortages as a result of destruction or refugee influxes.

13. Job titles have been changed to protect the anonymity of the individuals concerned. I have attempted to maintain parallel job responsibilities and sta-tuses in the changed positions.

14. At my request, several MEC supervisors kept ethnographic journals dur-ing their six-week tenures. I explained that I was interested in the everyday expe-riences of people engaged in the building of democracy and asked for volunteers to keep diaries of their activities and thoughts, writing between a paragraph and a page on a regular basis (e.g., daily, weekly).

15. This is not to pass over the comments of a certain minority who responded that the best part of the job was "handing in equipment on the last day of registration" or that "it was not something gratifying."

16. Indeed, they did carry an authority—specifically, the authority to close a polling station given enough evidence of voting or administrative irregularities. To my knowledge, in five elections with a total of 12,960 polling stations, polling supervisors initiated no permanent closures.

17. Whether they were demonstrating professional and democratic behavior is another question altogether. Some internationals certainly did not exhibit professional or democratic behavior (assuming agreement on what that entails). Furthermore, Bosnians were not silent; they criticized errors and problems as well as international policies.

Election Day

1. More recently, ritual analysis has been applied to Western state political arenas (e.g., Abélès 1988; Kertzer 1996; McLeod 1999; see also Bellah 1985).

2. Rituals may reflect myth and order but also help produce and reconfigure them (see Apter 1992; Comaroff and Comaroff 1993; Moore and Myerhoff 1977). Instead of simply or only expressing authority, ritual acts construct relationships of authority and submission (Bell 1997:82). Analyzing ritual as practice allows an interpretation of elections as action that through citizen participation legitimates state governance and symbolically authorizes elected candidates to govern citizens. An election also fits well into many of the characteristics and categories of ritual and ritual-like action: formalism, traditionalism, disciplined invariance and repetition, rule governance, sacral symbolism, and performance (Bell 1997). Elections are, for example, held regularly, highly regulated, structured, and repetitive both within and between electoral occurrences. They are often emotionally charged through the creation and manipulation of political symbols. Election Day, as a ritual and viewed as signifying practice, might be thought to symbolize the (changing) values of democracy. Mass participation and incorporation into the decision-making and governance structure give meaning to democracy. Through mass participation, elections are important rituals of legitimation, even if there is no effect on the power structure or on public policies (Kertzer 1988). Boycotts are dangerous for exactly this reason: they threaten both the legitimacy of the current government and governance more generally. Elections also reflect democratic values through their promotion as the expression of free, informed choices (Kertzer 1988). Elections, then, serve to bolster societal solidarity and feelings of community inclusiveness, give political authority to elected leaders, and signify values commonly associated with democracy such as tolerance, equality, and self-governance.

3. This sentiment and the problems it produced were also visible in the November 2000 U.S. presidential election counts in Florida. The media channels were chastised for their preresult announcements, yet there was general clamoring for immediate results. There was little recognition that tabulation and verification are tedious, exacting, and lengthy processes. Electoral reform in the U.S. since 2000 has tinkered with how results (and exit polls) are publicized, but little has been done to slow down the speed with which results are expected.

4. This brings up issues of personhood, bodies, and identification as they relate to democracy and the state. Bodily marks on persons might be an acceptable way of marking voters and ensuring anonymity, but they do not ensure that voters are citizens and adults.

5. Box 4a was for additional ballots received during polling, something I never witnessed.

6. Only many years later did I learn about a 0.5 percent acceptable error rate. Given the small number of voters, we needed perfect counts; however, most polling stations could afford to be off by a few. Supervisors were never told about this error rate.

Electoral Actants

1. The European Union has moved away from *free* and *fair* and toward *genuine* as the adjective of choice, with the hope that this word captures a wider set of criteria.

2. I follow Latour's (1999) analytical conceptualization of *actant* as a human or nonhuman actor, defined by what it does. This allows a focus on what it is required for an actant to come into existence rather than assuming its stable placement as a component of a system.

3. Suffrage and the extension of citizenship have a long and storied history. Broadly, suffrage was slowly extended to nonpropertied men, women, and minorities over the course of the 18th, 19th, and 20th centuries. At present, most countries allow citizens to vote unless they have been convicted of specific crimes or are judged mentally incompetent. There are often age and residency requirements.

4. Other races in 2000 included cantonal races (200s), National Assembly of Republika Srpska (300s), House of Representatives for the Federation of Bosnia-Herzegovina (400s), and the president and vice president of Republika Srpska (600).

5. In many elections, officials rotate positions on the ballot so that no party or candidate garners better spatial positions (i.e., at the top of the ballot, at the beginning of the list). For example, in the 2002 California recall special election, some ballots were printed starting with the letter *B*, others with the letter *L*, others with the letter *S*, etc.

6. In some cases, where counting occurred was also noteworthy. In 1998, Serb authorities expressed concern about counting ballots cast in Serb-controlled areas in Sarajevo. In response to their protests and political threats, the OSCE set up a second counting center in Serb-held territory to tabulate absentee and tendered ballots from Serb territories. Location and authority are neither necessarily distinct nor apolitical. Similarly, some counting sites are subject to more oversight than others; political parties and the media avidly watched the counting center in 2000, but the audit center was generally ignored.

7. The number of ballots counted at the counting centers was electorally significant. In November 2000, for example, 14.6 percent of ballots (235,721) were counted at the counting center.

8. Critiques of the international community, of the Dayton Peace Accords, or of their goals were minimized in political party platforms through electoral regulations specifying limitations, prohibitions, and requirements for political parties and candidates. For example, for the April 2000 elections, candidates could not have been charged with obstructing Dayton or have been illegally occupying property owned by a refugee or displaced party. Political party platforms had to be reviewed and certified by the OSCE for language and content (e.g., they could not contain inflammatory language and had to cover all of the required issues, which included return of refugees and displaced persons, economy, minority rights, reconstruction and development, education, and social services).

9. A quota system also is commonly used to articulate proportion. In quota systems, vote shares are subtracted from totals.

Embodied Transparency

1. Transparency is now often evoked as a necessity for states, businesses, corporations, and governments even though it is vaguely defined in most public

documentation (Power 1994; Strathern 2000). Transparency has become a key feature of good governance practices required by international lending organizations and other neoliberal institutions before, for example, they offer loans to states although many observers have remarked on the lack of transparency and accountability in those international institutions (e.g., Lodge 1994; Woods and Narlikar 2001).

2. What and what does not count as a detail is itself an interesting question.

3. Interpreters for the Kosovo 2001 election received electoral training and were categorized as assistants. Supervisors were repeatedly reminded that assistants were not just interpreters.

Transparent Forms and Bureaucratic Mechanisms of Watching

1. These nonsupervised stations probably had national observers present—political party observers, civic observers, or both. However, national observers were credited with little ability to prevent irregularities or affect polling station committee behavior.

2. Although this description is from data collected during the fall 2000 election period, similar protocols governed the activities of supervisors in both the spring 2000 municipal and fall 2000 general elections.

3. Both Bosnia-Herzegovina and the international community in Bosnia-Herzegovina were heavily militarized; most of the OSCE's logistics and security operations were handled by military staff on loan to the OSCE or by persons with military backgrounds. Part of the concern with reporting facts over public airwaves was that other parties might capture the information too, especially if they knew the questions.

4. This estimate was one of the few I ever came across that did not distinguish between international and national staff.

Circuits of Power

1. Médecins sans Frontières is a bit of an anomaly given its degree of financial independence and hence its relative ability to exercise projects outside of donor dictates (Redfield 2005).

2. In response to criticism about the 1999 U.S.-led NATO bombing of Belgrade, Friedman countered that NATO did not have a McDonald's franchise, that the NATO intervention was not a war but an intervention into a civil war, and that people were misunderstanding his metaphor of McDonald's about the impact of globalization on geopolitics. He did, however, rephrase his statement in light of the bombing and the subsequent ouster of Slobodan Milosevic in October 2000: "People in McDonald's countries don't like to fight wars anymore, they prefer to wait in line for burgers—and those leaders or countries which ignore that fact will pay a much, much higher price than they think" (Friedman 2000:253).

REFERENCES

Abélès, Marc. 1988. Modern political ritual: Ethnography of an inauguration and a pilgrimage by President Mitterrand. *Current Anthropology* 29 (3): 391–99.

Alexander, Stella. 1979. *Church and state in Yugoslavia since 1945.* Cambridge: Cambridge University Press.

Allcock, John B. 2000. *Explaining Yugoslavia.* New York: Columbia University Press.

Anderson, Benedict. 1983. *Imagined communities: Reflections on the origin and spread of nationalism.* London: Verso.

Apter, Andrew H. 1992. *Black critics and kings: The hermeneutics of power in Yoruba society.* Chicago: University of Chicago Press.

Bachrach, Peter, and Morton S. Baratz. 1970. *Power and poverty: Theory and practice.* New York: Oxford University Press.

Bakic-Hayden, Milica. 1995. Nesting orientalisms: The case of former Yugoslavia. *Slavic Review* 54 (4): 917–31.

Bakic-Hayden, Milica, and Robert M. Hayden. 1992. Orientalist variations on the theme "Balkans": Symbolic geography in recent Yugoslav cultural politics. *Slavic Review* 51 (1):1–15.

Banac, Ivo. 1984. *The national question in Yugoslavia: Origins, history, politics.* Ithaca: Cornell University Press.

Barnett, Michael, and Martha Finnemore. 1999. The politics, power, and pathologies of international organizations. *International Organization* 53 (4): 699–732.

Barry, Andrew. 2002. The anti-political economy. *Economy and Society* 31 (2): 268–84.

Barry, Andrew, Thomas Osborne, and Nikolas S. Rose, eds. 1996. *Foucault and political reason: Liberalism, neo-liberalism, and rationalities of government.* Chicago: University of Chicago Press.

Barry, Andrew, and Don Slater. 2002a. Introduction: The technological economy. *Economy and Society* 31 (2): 175–93.

Barry, Andrew and Dan Slater. 2002b. Technology, politics, and the market: An interview with Michel Callon. *Economy and Society* 31 (2): 285–306.

Baudrillard, Jean. 1994 [1981]. *Simulacra and simulation.* Ann Arbor: University of Michigan Press.

Bax, Mart. 2000. Warlords, priests, and the politics of ethnic cleansing: A case-study from rural Bosnia-Hercegovina. *Ethnic and Racial Studies* 23 (1): 16–36.

Bell, Catherine M. 1997. *Ritual: Perspectives and dimensions.* New York: Oxford University Press.

Bellah, Robert N. 1985. *Habits of the heart: Individualism and commitment in American life.* Berkeley: University of California Press.

Belloni, Roberto. 2003. Dubious democracy by fiat. *Transitions Online,* 20 August. http://balkanreport.tol.cz.

Bennett, Brian C. 2000. Hope, Arkansas to Hope, Albania: Naivete and idealism to reality and tragedy. *Collegium Antropologicum* 24 (1): 27–34.

Bertsch, Gary K. 1976. *Values and community in multi-national Yugoslavia.* Boulder: East European Quarterly. Distributed by Columbia University Press.

Bieber, Florian 2003. Far from Raj. *Transitions Online,* 31 July. http://balkanreport.tol.cz.

Blodgett, James H. 1889. Suffrage and its mechanism in Great Britain and the United States. *American Anthropologist* 2 (1): 63–74.

Borneman, John. 1997. *Settling accounts: Violence, justice, and accountability in post-socialist Europe.* Princeton: Princeton University Press.

Bornstein, Erica. 1999. On faith and development: Christian NGOs, religious ideas, and "doing good" in Zimbabwe. Paper presented at the American Anthropological Association Conference, November, Chicago.

Bornstein, Erica. 2001. Child sponsorship, evangelism, and belonging in the work of World Vision Zimbabwe. *American Ethnologist* 28 (3): 595–622.

Bornstein, Erica. 2005. *The spirit of development: Protestant NGOs, morality, and economics in Zimbabwe.* Palo Alto, Calif.: Stanford University Press.

Bougarel, Xavier. 1999. Yugoslav wars: The "revenge of the countryside" between sociological reality and nationalist myth. *East European Quarterly* 33 (2): 157–75.

Bougarel, Xavier, Elissa Helms, and Ger Dürjzings, eds. 2006. *The New Bosnian Mosaic: Identities, memories, and moral claims in post-war society.* Burlington, VT: Ashgate.

Bowen, John R. 1996. The myth of global ethnic conflict. *Journal of Democracy* 7 (4): 3–14.

Brent, Peter. 2006. The Australian ballot: Not the secret ballot. *Australian Journal of Political Science* 41 (1): 39–50.

Bringa, Tone. 1995. *Being Muslim the Bosnian way: Identity and community in a central Bosnian village.* Princeton: Princeton University Press.

Bringa, Tone, and Peter Loizos. 2001. *Returning home* [documentary film]. Sarajevo: Saga Film and Video Productions.

Brown, Keith. 2003. Global newsstand: Unraveling Europe's Raj. *Foreign Policy* 139 (November–December): 84–85.

Burke, Timothy. 1996. *Lifebuoy men, lux women: Commodification, consumption, and cleanliness in modern Zimbabwe.* Durham, N.C.: Duke University Press.

Cain, Kenneth, Heidi Postlewait, and Andrew Thomson. 2004. *Emergency sex and other desperate measures: A true story from hell on earth.* New York: Hyperion.

Caldeira, Teresa P. R. 2000. *City of walls: Crime, segregation, and citizenship in São Paulo.* Berkeley: University of California Press.

Caldeira, Teresa P. R., and James Holston. 1999. Democracy and violence in Brazil. *Comparative Studies in Society and History* 41 (4): 691–729.

Call, Charles T., and Susan E. Cook. 2003. On democratization and peacebuilding. *Global Governance* 9 (2): 233–46.

Callon, Michel. 1998. *The laws of the markets.* Oxford: Blackwell/Sociological Review.

Callon, Michel, Arie Rip, and John Law. 1986. *Mapping the dynamics of science and technology: Sociology of science in the real world.* Basingstoke: Macmillan.

Campbell, David. 1998. *National deconstruction: Violence, identity, and justice in Bosnia.* Minneapolis: University of Minnesota Press.

Campbell, David. 1999. Apartheid cartography: The political anthropology and spatial effects of international diplomacy in Bosnia. *Political Geography* 18 (4): 395–435.

Carlane, John. 2000. The "international" and the "local": Globalisation, capitalism, and the bureaucratisation of post-conflict regeneration of war-torn societies. Paper presented at the Critical Citizenship: NGOs, Civil Society, and Citizenship Conference hosted by the University of California, San Diego, May.

Carothers, Thomas. 1997a. Democracy without illusions. *Foreign Affairs* 76 (1): 85–99.

Carothers, Thomas. 1997b. The observers observed. *Journal of Democracy* 8 (3): 17–31.

Ceh, Nick, and Jeff Harder, eds. 1996. *The golden apple: War and democracy in Croatia and Bosnia.* Boulder, Colo.: East European Monographs. Distributed by Columbia University Press.

Center for Civic Initiatives. 2000a. *Final report: BiH municipal elections, April 2000.* Sarajevo: Center for Civic Initiatives.

Center for Civic Initiatives. 2000b. *Final report: Domestic election monitoring, general election, November 11, 2000.* Sarajevo: Center for Civic Initiatives.

Chandler, David. 1999a. *Bosnia: Faking democracy after Dayton.* London: Pluto.

Chandler, David. 1999b. The Bosnian protectorate and the implications for Kosovo. *New Left Review* 235 (May–June): 124–34.

Chatterjee, Partha. 1986. *Nationalist thought and the colonial world: A derivative discourse?* London: Zed.

Chu, Julie Y. 2005. Document (n)ation: Some notes and queries about the "work" in paperwork. Paper presented at University of California Santa Cruz.

Clifford, James, and George E. Marcus. 1986. *Writing culture: The poetics and politics of ethnography.* Berkeley: University of California Press.

Cohn, Bernard S. 1996. *Colonialism and its forms of knowledge: The British in India.* Princeton: Princeton University Press.

Collier, David, and Steven Levitsky. 1996. *Democracy "with adjectives": Conceptual innovation in comparative research.* South Bend, Ind.: University of Notre Dame, Kellogg Institute for International Studies.

Comaroff, Jean, and John L. Comaroff. 1991. *Of revelation and revolution: Christianity, colonialism, and consciousness in South Africa.* Chicago: University of Chicago Press.

Comaroff, Jean, and John L. Comaroff, eds. 1993. *Modernity and its malcontents: Ritual and power in postcolonial Africa.* Chicago: University of Chicago Press.

Comaroff, Jean. 1997. *Of revelation and revolution: The dialectics of modernity on a South African frontier.* Chicago: University of Chicago Press.

Commission of the European Communities. 2000. *Communication from the Commission on EU election assistance and observation.* Brussels: Commission of the European Communities.

Cooper, Frederick, and Ann Laura Stoler, eds. 1997. *Tensions of empire: Colonial cultures in a bourgeois world.* Berkeley: University of California Press.

Corwin, Phillip. 1999. *Dubious mandate: A memoir of the UN in Bosnia, summer 1995.* Durham, N.C.: Duke University Press.

Council of Europe. 2005. About the Council of Europe. http://www.coe.int/T/e/Com/about_coe/.

Cowan, Jane. 2003. The supervised state. Paper presented at the American Anthropological Association Conference, November, Chicago.

Cushman, Thomas. 1997. *Critical theory and the war in Croatia and Bosnia.* Seattle: Henry M. Jackson School of International Studies, University of Washington.

Cushman, Thomas, and Stjepan G. Mestrovic. 1996. *This time we knew: Western responses to genocide in Bosnia.* New York: New York University Press.

Dahl, Robert A. 1961. *Who governs? Democracy and power in an American city.* New Haven: Yale University Press.

Dahl, Robert A. 1971. *Polyarchy: Participation and opposition.* New Haven: Yale University Press.

Dahl, Robert A. 1997. Development and democratic culture. In *Consolidating the third wave democracies,* edited by L. Diamond, M. F. Plattner, Y.-h. Chu, and H.-m. Tien. Baltimore: Johns Hopkins University Press.

Dahlman, Carl, and Gearóid Ó. Tuathail. 2005. The legacy of ethnic cleansing: The international community and the returns process in post-Dayton Bosnia-Herzegovina. *Political Geography* 24 (5): 569–99.

Danielsen, Dan, and Karen Engle, eds. 1995. *After identity: A reader in law and culture.* New York: Routledge.

Das, Veena. 1995. *Critical events: An anthropological perspective on contemporary India.* Delhi: Oxford University Press.

Dean, Jodi, ed. 2000. *Cultural studies and political theory.* Ithaca: Cornell University Press.

Dean, Mitchell. 1999. *Governmentality: Power and rule in modern society.* London: Sage.

Denich, Bette. 1994. Dismembering Yugoslavia: Nationalist ideologies and the symbolic revival of genocide. *American Ethnologist* 21 (2): 367–90.

de Waal, Alex. 1997. *Famine crises: Politics and the disaster relief industry in Africa.* Oxford: Currey.

Diamond, Larry. 1996. Is the third wave over? *Journal of Democracy* 7 (3): 20–37.

Divjak, Boris. 2001. *The international community is not immune to the corruption plague either.* Banja Luka: Transparency International Bosnia and Herzegovina.

Dixon, William J. 1996. Review of *Democracy and international conflict: An evalua-*

tion of the democratic peace proposition, by James L. Ray. *American Political Science Review* 90 (3): 703–4.

Donia, Robert J. 1981. *Islam under the double eagle: The Muslims of Bosnia and Hercegovina, 1878–1914*. Boulder, Colo.: East European Quarterly.

Donia, Robert J., and John V. A. Fine. 1994. *Bosnia and Hercegovina: A tradition betrayed*. London: Hurst.

Duffield, Mark R. 2001. *Global governance and the new wars: The merging of development and security*. London: Zed.

Duffield, Mark R. 2002. Social reconstruction and the radicalization of development: Aid as a relation of global liberal governance. *Development and Change* 33 (5): 1049–71.

Eley, Geoff, and Ronald G. Suny, eds. 1996. *Becoming national*. New York: Oxford University Press.

Elklit, Jørgen, and Palle Svensson. 1997. What makes elections free and fair? *Journal of Democracy* 8 (3): 32–61.

Escobar, Arturo. 1997. Anthropology and development. *International Social Science Journal* 49 (4): 497–516.

Farmer, Paul. 2003. *Pathologies of power: Health, human rights, and the new war on the poor*. Berkeley: University of California Press.

Fechter, Anne-Meike. 2006. Living in a bubble: Expatriates' transnational spaces. In *Going first class? New approaches to privileged travel and movement*, edited by V. Amit. Oxford: Berghahn.

Ferguson, James. 1994. *The anti-politics machine: "Development," depoliticization, and bureaucratic power in Lesotho*. Minneapolis: University of Minnesota Press.

Ferguson, James. 1995. From African socialism to scientific capitalism: Reflections on the legitimation crisis in IMF-ruled Africa. In *Debating development discourse: Institutional and popular perspectives*, edited by D. B. Moore and G. J. Schmitz. New York: St. Martin's.

Ferguson, James. 1999. *Expectations of modernity: Myths and meanings of urban life on the Zambian copperbelt*. Berkeley: University of California Press.

Ferguson, James, and Akhil Gupta. 2002. Spatializing states: Towards an ethnography of neoliberal governmentality. *American Ethnologist* 29 (4): 981–1002.

Fortun, Kim. 2001. *Advocacy after Bhopal: Environmentalism, disaster, new global orders*. Chicago: University of Chicago Press.

Foucault, Michel. 1977. *Discipline and punish: The birth of the prison*. New York: Vintage.

Foucault, Michel. 1991. Governmentality. In *The Foucault effect: Studies in governmentality*, edited by G. Burchell, C. Gordon, and P. Miller. Chicago: University of Chicago Press.

Friedman, Thomas L. 2000. *The Lexus and the olive tree*. London: HarperCollins.

Fukuyama, Francis. 1992. *The end of history and the last man*. London: Penguin.

Gagnon, V. P. 2002. International NGOs in Bosnia and Herzegovina: Attempting to build civil society. In *The power and limits of NGOs: A critical look at building democracy in Eastern Europe and Eurasia*, edited by S. Mendelson and J. K. Glenn. New York: Columbia University Press.

Gagnon, V. P. 2004. *The myth of ethnic war: Serbia and Croatia in the 1990s.* Ithaca: Cornell University Press.

Gilbert, Andrew. 2004. States of uncertainty and uncertain states: The problems of personhood in Bosnia-Herzegovina. Paper presented at the European Association of Social Anthropologists Conference, September, Vienna.

Gilbert, Andrew. 2005. Humanitarianization and politika in the refugee return process in Bosnia-Herzegovina. Paper presented at the Politics and Society 10 Years after Dayton Conference, November, Sarajevo.

Gilbert, Andrew. 2006. The past in parenthesis: (Non)post-socialism in post-war Bosnia-Herzegovina. *Anthropology Today* 22 (4): 14–18.

Goddard, Victoria A., Josep R. Llobera, and Cris Shore. 1994. *The anthropology of Europe: Identity and boundaries in conflict.* Oxford: Berg.

Goldman, Paula. 2005. Assisting "innocent" victims: The second tsunami in Sri Lanka. Paper presented at the American Anthropological Association Conference, December, Washington, D.C.

Gordon, Colin. 1991. Government rationality: An introduction. In *The Foucault effect: Studies in governmentality,* edited by G. Burchell, C. Gordon, and P. Miller. Chicago: University of Chicago Press.

Gowa, Joanne S. 1999. *Ballots and bullets: The elusive democratic peace.* Princeton: Princeton University Press.

Green, Linda. 1999. *Fear as a way of life: Mayan widows in rural Guatemala.* New York: Columbia University Press.

Greenhouse, Carol J., Elizabeth Mertz, and Kay B. Warren. 2002. *Ethnography in unstable places: Everyday lives in contexts of dramatic political change.* Durham, N.C.: Duke University Press.

Guilhot, Nicolas. 2005. *The democracy makers: Human rights and international order.* New York: Columbia University Press.

Gupta, Akhil. 1995. Blurred boundaries: The discourse of corruption, the culture of politics, and the imagined state. *American Ethnologist* 22 (2): 375–402.

Hagan, John. 2003. *Justice in the Balkans: Prosecuting war crimes in the Hague Tribunal.* Chicago: University of Chicago Press.

Hagan, John, Ron Levi, and Gabrielle Ferrales. 2006. Swaying the hand of justice: The internal and external dynamics of regime change at the International Criminal Tribunal for the former Yugoslavia. *Law and Social Inquiry* 31 (3): 585–616.

Hannerz, Ulf. 1987. The world in creolization. *Africa* 57 (4): 546–59.

Haraway, Donna J. 1991. Situated knowledges: The science question in feminism and the privilege of partial perspective. In *Simians, cyborgs, and women: The reinvention of nature.* New York: Routledge.

Harris, Simon. 2005. Livelihoods in post-tsunami Sri Lanka. *Forced Migration Review* (special issue): 34–35.

Hayden, Robert. 1996. Imagined communities and real victims: Self-determination and ethnic cleansing in Yugoslavia. *American Ethnologist* 23 (4): 783–801.

Hayden, Robert. 1998. Bosnia: The contradictions of "democracy" without consent. *East European Constitutional Review* 7 (2): 47–51.

Hayden, Robert. 1999a. *Blueprints for a house divided: The constitutional logic of the Yugoslav conflicts.* Ann Arbor: University of Michigan Press.

Hayden, Robert. 1999b. Humanitarian hypocrisy. *Eastern European Constitutional Review* 8 (2): 91–96.

Hayden, Robert. 2002. Dictatorships of virtue? States, NGOs, and the imposition of democratic values. *Harvard International Review* 24 (2): 56–61.

Helleiner, Eric. 1999. Historicizing territorial currencies: Monetary space and the nation-state in North America. *Political Geography* 18 (3):309–39.

Helleiner, Eric. 2003. *The making of national money: Territorial currencies in historical perspective.* Ithaca: Cornell University Press.

Helms, Elissa. 2003a. The "nation-ing" of gender? Donor policies, Islam, and women's NGOS in post-war Bosnia-Herzegovina. *Anthropology of East Europe Review* 21 (2): 85–93.

Helms, Elissa. 2003b. Women as agents of ethnic reconciliation? Women's NGOs and international intervention in post-war Bosnia-Herzegovina. *Women's Studies International Forum* 26 (1): 15–33.

Hobsbawm, Eric, and Terence Ranger, eds. 1983. *The invention of tradition.* Cambridge: Cambridge University Press.

Hockenos, Paul. 2003. *Homeland calling: Exile patriotism and the Balkan wars.* Ithaca: Cornell University Press.

Hodge, Carole. 1995. Slimy limeys: The Brits vs. the Bosnians (Hapless United Nations Protection Forces (UNPROFOR) in Bosnia-Herzegovina). *New Republic,* January 9, 21–23.

Holmes, Douglas R., George Marcus, and David A. Westbrook. 2006. Intellectual Vocations in the City of Gold. *PoLAR: Political and Legal Anthropology Review* 29 (1): 154–79.

Holston, James, and Teresa P. R. Caldeira. 1998. Democracy, law, and violence: Disjunctions of Brazilian citizenship. In *Fault lines of democracy in post-transition Latin America,* edited by F. Agüero and J. Stark. Boulder, Colo.: Rienner.

Hooker, Robert. 1996. European enlightenment, absolute monarchy, and enlightened absolutism. http://www.wsu.edu/~dee/ENLIGHT.

Huber, Evelyne, Dietrich Rueschemeyer, and John D. Stephens. 1997. The paradoxes of contemporary democracy: Formal, participatory, and social dimensions. *Comparative Politics* 29 (3): 323–42.

Human Rights Watch. 1995. The fall of Srebrenica and the failure of U.N. peacekeeping. *Human Rights Watch* 7 (13).

Huntington, Samuel P. 1997. After twenty years: The future of the third wave. *Journal of Democracy* 8 (4): 3–12.

Huseby-Daruas, Eva, ed. 1995. Refugee women of the Balkans. Special issue of Anthropology of East Europe Review 13 (1).

Institute for Democracy and Electoral Assistance. 1997. *The international IDEA handbook of electoral system design.* Stockholm: Institute for Democracy and Electoral Assistance.

Institute for Democracy and Electoral Assistance. 2002. Voter turnout from 1945 to date. http://www.idea.int/vt/intro/intro3.cfm.

International Centre for Migration Policy Development. 1999. Repatriation Information Centre—Municipality Information Fact Sheets. http://www.icmpd-ric.org/main/mifs.asp.

International Committee of the Red Cross. 1997. *The silent menace: Landmines in Bosnia and Herzegovina*. Geneva: International Committee of the Red Cross.

International Council on Voluntary Agencies. 1998. *Directory of development and humanitarian agencies in Bosnia and Herzegovina*. Sarajevo: International Council on Voluntary Agencies.

International Crisis Group. 1996a. *Elections in Bosnia-Herzegovina*. Sarajevo: International Crisis Group.

International Crisis Group. 1996b. *Why the Bosnian elections must be postponed*. Sarajevo: International Crisis Group.

International Crisis Group. 1999. *Is Dayton failing? Bosnia four years after the peace agreement*. Sarajevo: International Crisis Group.

International Crisis Group. 2000a. *Bosnia's municipal elections 2000: Winners and losers*. Sarajevo: International Crisis Group.

International Crisis Group. 2000b. *Bosnia's November elections: Dayton stumbles*. Sarajevo: International Crisis Group.

International Foundation for Electoral Systems. 2002. *A guide to transparency in election administration*. Washington, D.C.: International Foundation for Electoral Systems.

Jain, Sarah. 2004. "Dangerous instrumentality": The bystander as subject in automobility. *Cultural Anthropology* 19 (1): 61–94.

Jansen, Stef. 1998. Homeless at home: Narrations of post-Yugoslav identities. In *Migrants of identity: Perceptions of "home" in a world of movement*, edited by N. Rapport and A. Dawson. Oxford: Berg.

Jansen, Stef. 2002. The violence of memories: Local narratives of the past after ethnic cleansing in Croatia. *Rethinking History* 6 (1): 77–93.

Kamhi, Nadja, and Vivek H. Dehejia. 2005. *An assessment of the currency board regime in Bosnia and Herzegovina*. Carleton Working Paper. Ottawa: Carleton University.

Kaplan, Robert D. 1993. *Balkan ghosts: A journey through history*. New York: St. Martin's Press.

Kaufmann, Georgia. 1997. Watching the developers: A partial ethnography. In *Discourses of Development: Anthropological Perspectives*, edited by R. D. Grillo and R. L. Stirrat. Oxford: Berg.

Karl, Terry Lynn. 1986. Imposing consent? Electoralism versus democratization in El Salvador. In *Elections and democratization in Latin America, 1980–1985*, edited by P. W. Drake and E. Silva. San Diego: Center for Iberian and Latin American Studies, University of California.

Keck, Margaret E., and Kathryn Sikkink. 1998. *Activists beyond borders: Advocacy networks in international politics*. Ithaca: Cornell University Press.

Keohane, Robert O. 1984. *After hegemony: Cooperation and discord in the world political economy*. Princeton: Princeton University Press.

Kertzer, David I. 1988. *Ritual, politics, and power*. New Haven: Yale University Press.

Kertzer, David I. 1996. *Politics and symbols: The Italian communist party and the fall of communism*. New Haven: Yale University Press.

Kipling, Rudyard. 1899. The white man's burden. *McClure's*, 12 (Feb.).

Klotz, Audie. 1995. Norms reconstituting interests: Global racial equality and U.S. sanctions against South Africa. *International Organization* 49 (3):451–78.

Knaus, Gerald, and Felix Martin. 2003. Travails of the European Raj. *Journal of Democracy* 14 (3): 60–74.

Krasner, Stephen D. 1983. *International regimes.* Ithaca: Cornell University Press.

Kurotani, Sawa. 2005. *Home away from home: Japanese corporate wives in the United States.* Durham, N.C.: Duke University Press.

Latour, Bruno. 1988. *The pasteurization of France.* Cambridge: Harvard University Press.

Latour, Bruno. 1999. *Pandora's hope: Essays on the reality of science studies.* Cambridge: Harvard University Press.

Latour, Bruno. 2005. From Realpolitik to dingpolitik; or, How to make things public. In *Making things public: Atmospheres of democracy,* edited by B. Latour and P. Weibel. Cambridge, Mass.: MIT Press.

Latour, Bruno, and Peter Weibel, eds. 2005. *Making things public: Atmospheres of democracy.* Cambridge, Mass.: MIT Press.

Latour, Bruno, and Steve Woolgar. 1979 [1986]. *Laboratory life: The construction of scientific facts.* Princeton: Princeton University Press.

Law, John, and John Hassard. 1999. *Actor network theory and after.* Oxford: Blackwell/Sociological Review.

Lazarus-Black, Mindie, and Susan F. Hirsch, eds. 1994. *Contested states: Law, hegemony, and resistance.* New York: Routledge.

Lean, Sharon. 2004. The transnational politics of democracy promotion: Election monitoring in Latin America. Ph.D. diss., University of California, Irvine.

Lewis, Martin W., and Kèaren Wigen. 1997. *The myth of continents: A critique of metageography.* Berkeley: University of California Press.

Lijphart, Arend. 1977. *Democracy in plural societies: A comparative exploration.* New Haven: Yale University Press.

Lijphart, Arend. 1984. *Democracies: Patterns of majoritarian and consensus government in twenty-one countries.* New Haven: Yale University Press.

Lijphart, Arend. 1999. *Patterns of democracy: Government forms and performance in thirty-six countries.* New Haven: Yale University Press.

Lijphart, Arend, and Don Aitkin. 1994. *Electoral systems and party systems: A study of twenty-seven democracies, 1945–1990.* Oxford: Oxford University Press.

Lockwood, William G. 1975. *European Moslems: Economy and ethnicity in western Bosnia.* New York: Academic Press.

Lockwood, William G. 1979. Living legacy of the Ottoman Empire: The Serbo-Croatian speaking Moslems of Bosnia-Hercegovina. In *The Mutual Effects of the Islamic and Judeo-Christian Worlds: the East European Pattern,* edited by A. Ascher, T. Halasi-Kun and B. K. Kiraly. Brooklyn, New York: Brooklyn College Press. Distributed by Columbia University Press.

Lodge, Juliet. 1994. Transparency and democratic legitimacy. *Journal of Common Market Studies* 32 (3): 343–69.

Lynch, Michael, Stephen Hilgartner, and Carin Berkowitz. 2005. Voting machinery, counting, and public proofs in the 2000 US Presidential election. In *Making things public: Atmospheres of democracy,* edited by B. Latour and P. Weibel. Cambridge: MIT Press.

Maass, Peter. 1996. *Love thy neighbor: A story of war.* New York: Knopf.

Malcolm, Noel. 1993. Balkan ghosts. (Response to article by Robert Kaplan in this issue, p. 109–110). *National Interest* (33): 110–11.

Malcolm, Noel. 1994. *Bosnia: A short history.* New York: New York University Press.

Malkki, Liisa H. 1994. Citizens of humanity: Internationalism and the imagined community of nations. *Diaspora* 3 (1): 41–68.

Malkki, Liisa H. 1995. *Purity and exile: Violence, memory, and national cosmology among Hutu refugees in Tanzania.* Chicago: University of Chicago Press.

Malkki, Liisa H. 1998. Things to come: Internationalism and global solidarities in the late 1990s. *Public Culture* 10 (2): 431–42.

Manning, Carrie. 2004. Elections and political change in post-war Bosnia and Herzegovina. *Democratization* 11 (2): 60–86.

Manning, Carrie, and Miljenko Antić. 2003. The limits of electoral engineering. *Journal of Democracy* 14 (3): 45–59.

Marcus, George E. 2000. *Para-sites: A casebook against cynical reason.* Chicago: University of Chicago Press.

Markoff, John. 1999. Where and when was democracy invented? *Comparative Studies in Society and History* 41 (4): 660–90.

Maurer, Bill. 2001. Visions of fact: Languages of evidence: History, memory, and the trauma of legal research. *Law and Social Inquiry* 26 (4): 893–910.

McLeod, James R. 1999. The sociodrama of presidential politics: Rhetoric, ritual, and power in the era of teledemocracy. *American Anthropologist* 101 (2): 359–73.

Merry, Sally E. 1991. Law and colonialism. *Law and Society Review* 25 (4): 889–922.

Merry, Sally E. 2000. *Colonizing Hawai'i: The cultural power of law.* Princeton: Princeton University Press.

Mitchell, Timothy. 1989. The world as exhibition. *Comparative Studies in Society and History* 31 (2): 217–36.

Mitchell, Timothy. 2002. *Rule of experts: Egypt, techno-politics, modernity.* Berkeley: University of California Press.

Moore, Patrick. 2002. Bosnia's brave new order. http://w3.tyenet.com/kozlich/taletale.htm.

Moore, Sally F., and Barbara G. Myerhoff, eds. 1977. *Secular ritual.* Assen: Van Gorcum.

Mosse, David, and David Lewis, eds. 2005. *The aid effect: Giving and governing in international development.* London: Pluto.

Mozaffar, Shaheen, and Andreas Schedler. 2002. The comparative study of electoral governance—Introduction. *International Political Science Review* 23 (1): 5–27.

Nader, Laura. 1972. Up the anthropologist: Perspectives gained from studying up. In *Reinventing anthropology,* edited by D. H. Hymes. New York: Pantheon.

Nelson, Diane M. 1999. *A finger in the wound: Body politics in quincentennial Guatemala.* Berkeley: University of California Press.

Nelson, Diane M. 2001. Indian giver or Nobel savage? Duping, assumptions of identity, and other double entendres in Rigoberta Menchú Turn's stoll/en past. *American Ethnologist* 28 (2): 303–31.

Netherlands Institute for War Documentation. 2002. *Srebrenica—A "safe" area:*

Reconstruction, background, consequences, and analyses of the fall of a safe area. Amsterdam: Netherlands Institute for War Documentation.

The new ballot law. 1892. *Los Angeles Times,* August 21, 9.

Newburg, Paula R., and Thomas Carothers. 1996. Aiding—and defining—democracy: Democracy assistance in Central Europe. *World Policy Journal* 13 (1): 97–108.

Nordstrom, Carolyn. 1997. *A different kind of war story.* Philadelphia: University of Pennsylvania Press.

O'Donnell, Guillermo. 1993. On the State, democratization, and some conceptual problems: A Latin American view with glances at post-communist countries. *World Development* 21 (8): 1355–69.

Office of Democratic Institutions and Human Rights. 1997. *Final report on the municipal elections in Bosnia and Herzegovina, 13–14 September 1997.* Warsaw: Office for Democratic Institutions and Human Rights.

Office of Democratic Institutions and Human Rights. 1999. The *ODHIR election observation handbook.* 4th ed. Warsaw: Office for Democratic Institutions and Human Rights.

Office of Democratic Institutions and Human Rights. 2005. *Final report on the municipal elections in Bosnia and Herzegovina, 2 October 2004.* Warsaw: Office of Democratic Institutions and Human Rights.

Office of the High Representative. 2000a. The High Representative and the BiH Presidency Discuss the Development of the Public Broadcsting Service, July 14, 2000 http://www.ohr.int/ohr-dept/presso/pressr/default.asp?content_id=3978.

Office of the High Representative. 2000b. Property rights/Right to return. May. http://www.ohr.int/ohr-dept/hr-rol/thedept/pr-rights-rr/background/default.asp?content_id=5230.

Office of the High Representative. 2002a. Office of the High Representative in Bosnia and Herzegovina. http://www.ohr.int.

Office of the High Representative. 2002b. OHR BiH media round-up. November 9. http://www.ohr.int/ohr-dept/presso/bh-media-rep/round-ups/default.asp?content_id=27892.

Ong, Aihwa. 1999. *Flexible citizenship: The cultural logics of transnationality.* Durham, N.C.: Duke University Press.

Organization for Security and Co-operation in Europe. 1997. *Annual report 1996 on OSCE activities.* Vienna: Organization for Security and Co-operation in Europe.

Ottaway, Marina. 2002. The post-war "democratic reconstruction model": Why it can't work. Paper presented at Building democracy after war? "State-of-the-art" thinking about governance and peacebuilding conference, April 3–4. Providence, R.I.

Paley, Julia. 2001. *Making democracy: Power and social movements in post-dictatorship Chile.* Berkeley: University of California Press.

Paley, Julia. 2002. Toward an anthropology of democracy. *Annual Review of Anthropology* 31:469–96.

Pandolfi, Mariella. 2002. "Security and/or pleasure: De-politicizing, de-totalizing, re-naturalizing biopower." Paper presented at the American Anthropological Association Conference, November, New Orleans.

Pandolfi, Mariella. 2003. Contract of mutual (in)difference: Governance and humanitarian apparatus in Albania and Kosovo. *Indiana Journal of Global Legal Studies* 10 (1): 369–81.

Papić, Žarko, ed. 2001. *International support policies to SEE countries—Lessons (not) learned in Bosnia-Herzegovina.* Sarajevo: Open Society Fund Bosnia-Herzegovina.

Pastor, Robert A. 1998. Mediating elections. *Journal of Democracy* 9 (1): 154–63.

Pels, Peter, Jean-Louis Briquet, and Romain Bertrand, eds. 2007. *Cultures of Voting: The hidden history of the secret ballot.* London: C. Hurst.

Perry, Valery. 2003. Bosnia: An intellectual Raj. *Transitions Online.* 24 July. http://balkanreport.tol.cz.

Post, Tom, Theodore Stanger, Karen Breslau, and Charles S. Lee. 1994. Blues for the blue helmets: Bosnia: U.N. forces have been humiliated and harassed. It's partly their own fault. *Newsweek,* February 7, 22–24.

Power, Michael. 1994. *The audit explosion.* London: Demos.

Power, Michael. 1997. *The audit society: Rituals of verification.* Oxford: Oxford University Press.

Putnam, Robert D. 1993. *Making democracy work: Civic traditions in modern Italy.* Princeton: Princeton University Press.

Rabinow, Paul. 1999. *French DNA: Trouble in purgatory.* Chicago: University of Chicago Press.

Ramet, Pedro. 1985. *Yugoslavia in the 1980s.* Boulder, Colo.: Westview.

Rapp, Rayna. 1999. *Testing women, testing the fetus: The social impact of amniocentesis in America.* New York: Routledge.

Ray, James L. 1997. The democratic path to peace. *Journal of Democracy* 8 (2): 49–64.

Redfield, Peter. 2005. Doctors, borders, and life in crisis. *Cultural Anthropology* 20 (3): 328–61.

Renan, Ernest. 1996 [1882]. What is a nation? In *Becoming national: A reader,* edited by G. Eley and R. G. Suny. New York: Oxford University Press.

Rew, Alan. 1997. The donor's discourse: Official social development knowledge in the 1980s. In *Discourses of Development: Anthropological Perspectives,* edited by R. D. Grillo and R. L. Stirrat. Oxford: Berg.

Rieff, David. 1995. *Slaughterhouse: Bosnia and the failure of the West.* New York: Simon and Schuster.

Rieff, David. 1999. A new age of liberal imperialism? *World Policy Journal* 16 (2): 1–10.

Riles, Annelise. 1998. Infinity within the brackets. *American Ethnologist* 25 (3): 378–98.

Riles, Annelise. 2000. *The network inside out.* Ann Arbor: University of Michigan Press.

Riles, Annelise. 2002. User friendly: Informality and expertise. *Law and Social Inquiry* 27 (3): 613–20.

Riles, Annelise, ed. 2006. *Documents: Artifacts of modern knowledge.* Ann Arbor: University of Michigan Press.

Rose, Nikolas S. 1993. Government, authority and expertise in advanced liberalism. *Economy and Society* 22 (3):283–99.

Rose, Nikolas S. 1996. Psychiatry as a political science: Advanced liberalism and the administration of risk. *History of the Human Sciences* 9 (2): 1–23.

Rose, Nikolas S. 1999. *Powers of freedom: Reframing political thought.* Cambridge: Cambridge University Press.

Rosga, Ann Janette. 2005. The Traffic in Children. *PoLAR: Political and Legal Anthropology Review* 28 (2): 258–81.

Rubin, Ben. 2005. Dark source. Public trust and the secret at the heart of the new voting machines. In *Making things public: Atmospheres of democracy*, edited by B. Latour and P. Weibel. Cambridge: MIT Press.

Russett, Bruce. 1993. *Grasping the democratic peace: Principles for a post–cold war world.* Princeton: Princeton University Press.

Said, Edward W. 1978. *Orientalism.* New York: Pantheon.

Scarry, Elaine. 1985. *The body in pain: The making and unmaking of the world.* New York: Oxford University Press.

Scheper-Hughes, Nancy, and Philippe I. Bourgois. 2004. *Violence in war and peace.* Malden, Mass.: Blackwell.

Schirmer, Jennifer G. 1998. *The Guatemalan military project: A violence called democracy.* Philadelphia: University of Pennsylvania Press.

Schmitter, Philippe C. , and Terry Lynn Karl. 1991. What democracy is . . . and is not. *Journal of Democracy* 2 (3): 75–88.

Schumpeter, Joseph A. 1947. *Capitalism, socialism, and democracy.* 2nd ed. New York: Harper.

Schwenkel, Christina. 2006. Recombinant history: Transnational practices of memory and knowledge production in contemporary Vietnam. *Cultural Anthropology* 21 (1): 3–30.

Scott, James C. 1998. *Seeing like a state: How certain schemes to improve the human condition have failed.* New Haven: Yale University Press.

Seizer, Susan. 1997. Jokes, gender, and discursive distance on the Tamil popular stage. *American Ethnologist* 24 (1): 62–90.

Shapiro, Ian, and Casiano Hacker-Cordón. 1999. *Democracy's value: Contemporary political theory.* New York: Cambridge University Press.

Shore, Cris. 2000. *Building Europe: The cultural politics of European integration.* London: Routledge.

Silber, Laura, and Allan Little. 1995. *The death of Yugoslavia.* London: Penguin/BBC Books.

Sloterdijk, Peter, and Gesa Mueller von der Haegen. 2005. Instant democracy: The pneumatic parliament. In *Making things public: Atmospheres of democracy*, edited by B. Latour and P. Weibel. Cambridge, Mass.: MIT Press.

Sluzki, Carlos, and Donald Ransom, eds. 1976. *Double-bind: The foundation of the communicational approach to the family.* New York: Grune & Stratton.

Smillie, Ian, ed. 2001. *Patronage or partnership: Local capacity building in humanitarian crises.* Bloomfield, Conn.: Kumarian.

Squires, Judith. 2002. Democracy as flawed hegemon. *Economy and Society* 31 (1): 132–51.

Stiglmayer, Alexandra, ed. 1994. *Mass rape: The war against women in Bosnia-Herzegovina.* Lincoln: University of Nebraska Press.

Strathern, Marilyn. 2000. *Audit cultures: Anthropological studies in accountability, ethics, and the academy.* London: Routledge.

Sugar, Peter F. 1963. *Industrialization of Bosnia-Hercegovina, 1878–1914.* Seattle: University of Washington Press.

Swedish International Development Cooperation Agency. 2002. *Handbook for European Union election observation missions.* Stockholm: Swedish International Development Cooperation Agency.

Taagepera, Rein. 1999. The tailor of Marrakesh: Western electoral system advice to emerging democracies. In *Electoral systems for emerging democracies: Experience and suggestions,* edited by J. Elklit. Copenhagen: Danida.

Taagepera, Rein, and Matthew S. Shugart. 1989. *Seats and votes: The effects and determinants of electoral systems.* New Haven: Yale University Press.

Thorold, Alan, ed. 1995. *Miracle in Natal: Revolution by ballot-box.* Cambridge: Prickly Pear Press.

Todorova, Maria N. 1997. *Imagining the Balkans.* New York: Oxford University Press.

Tourism Association of Bosnia and Herzegovina. 2006. Tourism-Srebrenica, http://www.bhtourism.ba/eng/srebrenica.wbsp.

Traweek, Sharon. 1988. *Beamtimes and lifetimes: The world of high energy physicists.* Cambridge: Harvard University Press.

Tsoukas, Haridimos. 1997. The tyranny of light: The temptations and paradoxes of the information society. *Futures* 29 (9): 827–43.

Turner, Victor W. 1970. *The forest of symbols: Aspects of Ndembu ritual.* Ithaca: Cornell University Press.

United Nations. 1996. *United Nations protection force profile.* http://www.un.org/Depts/DPKO/Missions/unprof_p.htm.

United Nations Development Programme. 1998. *Human development report, Bosnia and Herzegovina, 1998.* Sarajevo: United Nations Development Programme.

U.S. Institute of Peace. 2001. *U.S. online Training Course for OSCE, including REACT. Module 2. OSCE Mission Structures and Functions.* http://react.usip.org/Main.html.

Verdery, Katherine. 1991. Theorizing socialism—A prologue to the transition. *American Ethnologist* 18 (3): 419–39.

Verdery, Katherine. 1996. *What was socialism, and what comes next?* Princeton: Princeton University Press.

Verdery, Katherine. 1998. Transnationalism, nationalism, citizenship, and property: Eastern Europe since 1989. *American Ethnologist* 25 (2): 291–306.

Verdery, Katherine. 2003. *The vanishing hectare: Property and value in postsocialist Transylvania.* Ithaca: Cornell University Press.

Wagner, Sarah. 2006. Return of identity: Technology, memory, and the recognition of Srebrenica's missing. Ph.D. diss., Harvard University.

Weber, Max. 1918. *Politics as a vocation.*

Wedel, Janine R. 1998. *Collision and collusion: The strange case of Western aid to Eastern Europe, 1989–1998.* New York: St. Martin's.

Willis, Katie, S. M. A. K. Fakhri, and Brenda Yeoh. 2002. Introduction: Transnational Elites. *Geoforum* 33 (4): 505–7.

Woods, Ngaire, and Amrita Narlikar. 2001. Governance and the limits of accountability: The WTO, the IMF, and World Bank. *International Social Science Journal* 53 (170): 569–83.

Woodward, Susan L. 1995a. *Balkan tragedy: Chaos and dissolution after the cold war*. Washington, D.C.: Brookings Institution.

Woodward, Susan L. 1995b. *Socialist unemployment: The political economy of Yugoslavia, 1945–1990*. Princeton: Princeton University Press.

Woodward, Susan L. 1997. Role of outsiders in Balkan violence. In *Violence and subjectivity*, edited by V. Das, A. Kleinmann, M. Ramphele, and P. Reynolds. Berkeley: University of California Press.

World Bank. 1996. *Bosnia and Herzegovina: Towards economic recovery*. Washington, D.C.: World Bank.

World Bank. 2005. Afghanistan Reconstruction Trust Fund. http://www.world bank.org/artf.

Yablon, Charles M. 1992. Forms. In *Deconstruction and the possibility of justice*, edited by D. Cornell, M. Rosenfeld, and D. G. Carlson. New York: Routledge.

Živkovic, Marko. 2001. Serbian stories of identity and destiny in the 1980s and 1990s. Ph.D. diss., University of Chicago.

INDEX

Note: Page numbers in *italics* indicate figures and tables.

EOs and, 81–82, 100, 105

European Union, and role in observation mission of, 196–97, 240–41

expertise evaluations of, 204

four-module test for observers in
Serbia, 237–38

fraud, and role of, 89, 98, 106, 145,
197, 198, 207, 215

free and fair elections, and role of,
89, 194, 196, 200

full supervision and, 82, 89, 215,
253n10

humanitarian aid and, 237

improper actions of, 199

information requested for verbal
reports and, 216–17, 257n2

intent issues, and information on
forms, 210, 218–19, *219*

interpreters and, 207, 244, 257n3

irregularities and, 198–99

knowledge and, 198, 200, 202, 203,
204, 237, 244

Kosovo and, 242–43

language skills of, 207, 208

national polling staff and, 131, 204,
207, 244, 257n1, 257n3

nationals' distrust of, 111, 199, 230

neutrality and, 199, 201

OSCE and, 129, 196

oversight and, 98

partial supervision and, 82, 89, 215

poll books and, 133, 135, 147, 215

Polling and Counting Manual, 120,
130, 202

polling supervisor form for polling
activities (C-2) and, 217–27

Presence, and role of, 89, 108, 197,
198

Presence and, 109, 203

problems with scheme of, 89

reconciliation issues, and role of,
105

redundancy and, 98

reporting mechanisms of transparency and, 215, 216, 219

role of, 89, 197, 198

short-term volunteers and, 196

statistics on experience of, 203–4

statistics on recruits, 196–97

technical practices and, 129

transfer of responsibilities to
nationals and, 215, 230

transition from internationals to
nations and, 131

transparency, and role of, 192, 196,
197, 198, 205, 210, 215, 219, 227,
230

U.S. volunteers, and role as, 197

verbal reports and, 216–17, 257n2,
257n3

watching/observation role of, 110,
130, 196, 199, 201–2, 215

written reports and, 217

See also watching/observation concept

internationals

airplane flights to Bosnia for, 60

attitudes about national workers
and, 80–84

authority issues and, 29, 80, 237

binationals, 106–7

capabilities of nationals, and judgments by, 66, 81, 82, 200

careers in international employment and, 34, 42

character issues and, 31, 42, 43–44,
237

concepts and perceptions about
violence by, 36, 39

congeniality, and role of, 104–5

control of institutions, and role of,
43

counting center workers and, 228,
257n4

definition and parameters of
Europe and, 75

differentiation issues and, 65–66

displacement of state governance
and, 71, 72

education of, 43

election personnel circuit and,
241–42

El Salvador, and attitudes about,
235

state governance (*continued*)
  political structure of Bosnia and, 183, *184*
  Presence, and role in, 86, 88, 89, 112
  state-building issues and, 13, 69, 78, *79,* 84
Stephens, John D., 17
Stiglmayer, Alexandra, 251n16
Stoler, Ann Laura, 14
Strathern, Marilyn, 193, 256n
suffrage issues, 1, 2, 155, 247n1, 256n3
Sugar, Peter F., 72, 73
Suny, Ronald G., 44, 250n8
supervisors, election. *See* international polling supervisors
surveillance issues, 193, 201
Svensson, Palle, 121, 155, 157
Swedish International Development Cooperation Agency, 240, 241

Taagepera, Rein, 182, 187
technical practices
  antipolitics and, 151, 243
  bureaucratic practices as, 15
  democracy and, 10, 15, 122, 123, 124, 126, 153, 245
  depoliticization, and role of, 245
  elections and, 16, 122, 123, 124, 127, 151, 243, 244, 245
  free and fair elections and, 152
  Kosovo elections and, 243
  results of elections and, 189–90
  society/social sphere and, 15, 125–26, 153, 255n2
  trust and, 151
tendered ballots
  accounting forms and, 212
  ballot boxes, and notation on, 144
  counting of, 127, 129, 145, 173, 174, *174,* 182, 256n6
  definition of, 23
  distrust of, 145–46, 224
  fraud and, *141,* 144, 145, 214
  history of, 144, 149, 164–65
  as pacification mechanism, 145

polling stations and, 144, 165
procedures and, 143
refugees and, 144
text on envelopes for, *143,* 144
verification and, 146
Thomson, Andrew, 248n9
Thorold, Alan, 8
Todorova, Maria N., 73
tourism, 48, 50, 60, 203, 251nn
Tourism Association of Bosnia and Herzegovina, 251n13
transformation
  Dayton and goals of, 36–37
  democracy, and mission of, 21–22
  elections and concept of, 16, 21
  and global governance, mission of, 12, 112
  international community, and mission of, 12, 31, 86–87
  Presence, and role in, 86, 88, 89, 98, 108
  results of elections and, 189–90
  side effects and unintended outcomes of, 87–88
  transition vs., 252n2
transparency
  accounting forms and, 210, 214
  actants/agents of elections and, 192, 196, 197, 198, 205, 213
  appropriate uses for, 191
  Bosnian access to system of, 210
  bureaucratic mechanisms of watching and, 192, 199, 209, 210, 227
  clear/open elections and, 192, 193
  confidence-building techniques and, 109, 151, 152, 191, 198, 229
  criteria for, 192, 193
  definition of, 191, 192
  democracy, and role of, 191
  disciplinary techniques and, 201
  embodied transparency, 192
  exclusionary nature of, 192
  free and fair elections, and role of, 191
  inclusiveness and, 192, 193
  influences on, 192
  intent issues and, 214